The Prehistory of Colorado

and Adjacent Areas

The Prehistory of Colorado and Adjacent Areas

Tammy Stone

THE UNIVERSITY OF UTAH PRESS
SALT LAKE CITY

Typography by WolfPack

Library of Congress Cataloging-in-Publication Data

Stone, Tammy, 1961–
    The prehistory of Colorado and adjacent areas / Tammy Stone.
        p.   cm.
    Includes bibliographical references and index.
    ISBN 0-87480-578-3 (alk. paper)
    1. Paleo-Indians—Colorado. 2. Paleo-Indians—Four Corners
Region. 3. Indians of North America—Colorado—Antiquities.
4. Indians of North America—Four Corners Region—Antiquities.
5. Colorado—Antiquities. 6. Four Corners Region—Antiquities.
I. Title.
E78.C6S76   1999
979.2'5901—dc21   98-31020

CONTENTS

LIST OF FIGURES

LIST OF TABLES

Preface

This book synthesizes our current understanding of human history in Colorado and its adjacent areas before the European influx. Archaeological research aimed at increasing our knowledge of prehistoric occupation has been conducted in the state since the late 1800s and continues. Yet despite our knowledge of Colorado prehistory, there is much to be discovered.

As a professional archaeologist, it is my belief that further knowledge will come from traditional, scientifically based approaches. At the same time, however, the multivocality offered by often differing perspectives from within the profession can be enhanced by listening to the perspectives of Native Americans, who may approach the data with a different outlook.

Our archaeological past is a cultural treasure from which we can all learn, but archaeological sites are nonrenewable resources. Despite legal protection at both the state and national levels, artifacts and sites are rapidly being destroyed by vandalism and urban expansion. Each of us has a responsibility to protect these treasures and support study of them before the clues they hold to our heritage are lost forever. Only in this way can we understand our cultural diversity and, therefore, ourselves.

In writing this book, I benefited greatly from discussions with numerous individuals and the written comments of others. Although these individuals are too numerous to name, I dedicate this book to the students and colleagues who inspired it and most of all to my husband, Carroll Reichen, for his support while it was being written.

x

Introduction

Colorado has been occupied for at least 12,000 years, but archaeological research in the state began only in the late nineteenth century. The fascinating history of this work and the lives of the men and women who conducted it has been written by a number of scholars (Cassells 1992; Matlock and Duke 1992; Smith 1992). Detailed accounts of specific sites that have been crucial to our understanding the prehistory of the state are numerous and widely available (Cassells 1983).

Rather than repeat the efforts of these previous works, I have tried to present a broader view of the scope of human history in the state. On occasion, findings from specific sites are discussed only as an example of a generalized model of behavior. I have tried to reconstruct past lifeways using current theory and explanations for behavior and changes in human culture. These reconstructions are supported with relevant data; however, the emphasis here is synthetic and concentrates on current archaeological theory regarding what prehistoric people did and why, and why they changed what they were doing at various times. As such, this book is similar to other regional syntheses (Bell 1984; Cordell 1984; Matson and Coupland 1995; Milanich and Fairbanks 1980; Muller 1986; Morse and Morse 1982; Snow 1980). Because the emphasis here is explanatory rather than descriptive, the bulk of the works cited are theoretical rather than descriptive, and this book is directed toward individuals with an archaeological interest but who are unfamiliar with the prehistory of the various regions of the state.

The prehistoric inhabitants of Colorado lived in a dynamic world and were affected by their environment and their relationships with the people in their own communities, as well as their neighbors. Therefore, a regional rather than a site-specific approach is taken. Also, because modern borders were not recognized in prehistory, information on events in neighboring states is presented to enrich our view and our understanding of the prehistory of Colorado.

An environmental baseline against which human activities occurred is presented in Chapter 1. Specific attention is paid to the climatic changes the ancient inhabitants endured and the effects these changes had on the available resources. The climate and distribution of plant, animal, and geological resources is outlined.

Chapter 2 deals with the initial peopling of Colorado and the earliest period of occupation—the Paleoindian. However, to understand this era in Colorado, an appreciation of the worldwide changes in population distribution is needed. Therefore, I present a discussion of the peopling of the New World in general.

Once in Colorado, prehistoric populations adapted to the social and ecological environments of their new home. In the southwestern (Chapter 4) and northwestern (Chapter 5) portions of the state these adaptations eventually led to settled village life and an economy dependent, to varying degrees, on corn horticulture. Conversely, on the Plains (Chapter 3) and in the mountains (Chapter 6), a highly resilient economic system based on hunting-and-gathering was maintained throughout prehistory. Despite the similarities in economy, however, peoples in the eastern half of the state were incredibly diverse in their ritual and social systems. They interacted with and manipulated ties to individuals in other regions, resulting in the state's organizational diversity.

Despite the variability in economy, mobility, religion, and social organization in the past, all of the state's prehistoric inhabitants were affected by periodic, and sometimes protracted droughts, which were compounded by various social and political factors. Between A.D. 1200 and 1450 most of the original inhabitants of the state left quickly to be replaced by new emigrants from the north and west. These new peoples are the groups encountered by Europeans and Americans as they entered the state. The emigrants' arrival and the historic period occupations are recounted in Chapter 7.

The history and prehistory of Colorado's indigenous peoples is fascinating. It is my goal here to illuminate the complex web of human interaction and to provide an appreciation of the state's cultural diversity to you, the reader.

CHAPTER I

The Natural Environment: Past and Present

Colorado's geography and climate have always been highly variable, an important factor in understanding the state's prehistoric and historic occupation. The distribution of natural resources, seasonal temperatures, and precipitation are the backdrops for the land-use strategies, resource exploitation, and human interaction that occurred in prehistory.

GEOLOGY AND GEOGRAPHY

Colorado's three major and two minor landforms dramatically affect weather patterns (Fig. 1.1). Approximately 40 percent of the state lies in the Great Plains, 35 percent is dominated by the Rocky Mountains, 20 percent is within the Colorado Plateau, and the remaining 5 percent is in the Green River basin and Uinta Mountains (Huber 1993). The Great Plains is the lowest region, with elevations ranging from 3300 feet on the Kansas border to 5000 feet where the Plains intersect the eastern foothills of the Rocky Mountains (Chronic 1980; Griffiths and Rubright 1982). The Colorado plains are characterized by semiarid, gently rolling grasslands dissected by rivers and streams.

The exposed geology is a thick alluvium dominated by sandy silts with gravel and pebble-sized inclusions that are occasionally consolidated by calcareous deposits. These deposits overlie poorly consolidated conglomerates of late Tertiary sands, gravels, and clays (Armstrong 1972; Greiser 1985; Griffiths and Rubright 1982). The underlying composites and exposed soils are the result of erosion on the eastern slope of the Rocky Mountains.

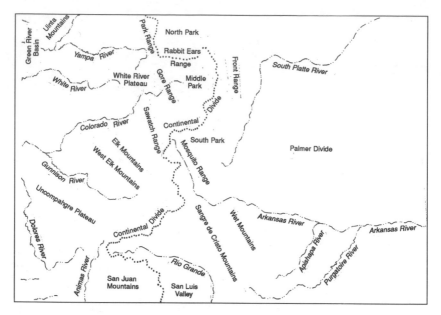

Figure 1.1 Major topographic features in Colorado.

Pierre shale, which underlies both, is a sedimentary stratum laid down during the Cretaceous period, when much of the central United States was covered by a shallow sea. These deposits can be as much as 700 feet below the surface (Chronic 1980).

The Denver basin is a shallow depression on the western edge of the Great Plains formed by stream erosion feeding into the South Platte River system. In this area, Tertiary alluvium has been stripped away, exposing older strata. As a result, the surface soils and loose gravels are relatively thin and overlie 12,000 feet of sedimentary rocks, including layers of oil-rich shale, limestone, and sandstone (Armstrong 1972). Many of these layers are exposed in uptilted hogbacks on the western edge of the basin (Chronic 1980; Taylor 1992).

In terms of prehistoric technology, two important geological resources are exposed on the surface in the Denver basin and in the Hogback region (Taylor 1992). On the plains are gravels of petrified wood, whereas in the Hogback, chert nodules are exposed.

A second basin, eroded by the Arkansas River drainage, is in the southern part of the state. The uplifted area between the South Platte and Arkansas Rivers is known alternatively as the Colorado piedmont, the

Arkansas divide, and the Palmer divide (Griffiths and Rubright 1982). The southern edge of the Arkansas drainage is located in the Raton area, where sandstone is exposed. This topography represents a transitional form from the Central High Plains to the eastern edge of the American Southwest and is dominated by mesas and plateaus, many of which are capped with volcanic material. The plateaus are dissected by deep canyons formed by stream erosion (Armstrong 1972).

The Rocky Mountains are a series of north–south-trending ranges with peaks exceeding 14000 feet in elevation, interspersed with high-elevation parklands and passes (see Fig. 1.1). The Rockies were formed during two major uplifts, one approximately 75 million and the other one 28 million years ago (Chronic 1980).

The San Juan Mountains, the West Elk Mountains, and the White River Plateau are of recent volcanic origin. Conversely, the Front Range and Wet Mountains consist of older uplifted igneous (predominantly granite) and metamorphic (gneiss and schist) rocks. The Front Range's fault lines often expose mineral-rich ores (Armstrong 1972; Chronic 1980). Ranges on the western slope feature exposed strata of sandstone, limestone, various conglomerates, and shales.

Meltwater from snowpack feeds four major river systems in the West. The Colorado River, with its major tributaries (the San Juan, Gunnison, White, and Yampa Rivers), drains the western slope. Three other rivers drain the eastern slope. The Rio Grande has its headwaters in the San Juan Mountains, the Arkansas River begins in the central mountains near Leadville, and the South Platte drains the Front Range (Chronic 1980; Huber 1993).

Between the high mountain peaks of the Rockies are a number of basins, valleys, and parklands. The four largest of these are North Park, Middle Park, South Park, and the San Luis Valley (see Fig. 1.1). North and Middle Park are 8000 feet above sea level, separated from each other by the volcanic formation of Rabbit Ears Range (Chronic 1980; Griffiths and Rubright 1982). Both are characterized by sediments eroded from the surrounding mountain ranges, but with very different topographies. North Park contains a slightly rolling landscape with occasional hills, whereas Middle Park has hills in the east and south and volcanic mesas and buttes in the south and west. The intervening floor is highly dissected by stream paths (Armstrong 1972).

South Park (9000 feet elevation) consists of an undissected, flat park floor (Armstrong 1972). The San Luis Valley lies at 7600 feet between the

Sangre de Cristo and San Juan Mountains (Armstrong 1972; Jodry and Stanford 1992). It has a relatively high water table and houses a number of lakes at the northern end in an otherwise desertlike environment.

To the west of the Rocky Mountains lies the Colorado Plateau, a large topographic feature covering much of northern Arizona, northwestern New Mexico, eastern Utah, and western Colorado. It is characterized by mesas and plateaus dissected by river drainages resulting in deep canyons that expose lower deposits (Armstrong 1972). Steep-sided canyons are narrower and more common in the southwestern part of Colorado, whereas the northwestern corner of the state has wider basins and rolling uplands (Chronic 1980).

The plateau regions of northwestern Colorado and southwestern Wyoming are connected to the Great Plains to the east through a low-lying topographic corridor known as the Wyoming basin (La Point 1987), which ranges from 6500 to 7500 feet in elevation. In prehistoric and historic times it was a major corridor for human traffic.

The southwestern edge of the Wyoming basin includes the Uinta Mountains and the Green River basin. The Uintas are an east–west-oriented range in northwestern Colorado and northeastern Utah. On the southeastern edge of the Uinta Mountains is the Green River basin, a low-lying valley dissected by the Green River. The basin is characterized by sandstone and shale deposits (Chronic 1980).

THE MODERN CLIMATE

Colorado's weather conditions are affected by a number of factors. Most important are latitude, continental position, topography, elevational variability, and prevailing wind patterns (Griffiths and Rubright 1982; Siemer 1977). Each of these factors is discussed below.

Because it lies between 37 and 41 degrees north latitude Colorado experiences a number of seasonal extremes. Summer days have an average of 15 hours of sunlight, whereas winter averages only 9.5 hours (Griffiths and Rubright 1982). Combined with Colorado's continental position, this results in hot summers and cold winters. Colorado's continental position, at some distance from large bodies of water, also results in an arid to semi-arid climate (Armstrong 1972; Siemer 1977).

The effect of topography is even more noticeable. The Rocky Mountains form a north–south barrier that moisture-laden storm clouds cannot pass over. The result is a double rain shadow in which the western portion of the state receives most of its precipitation from storms originating in the Pacific Ocean whereas the eastern part of the state receives most of its precipitation from storms from the Gulf of Mexico. The mountains receive the greatest precipitation as clouds are forced to dump their moisture before they can pass over the high peaks (Huber 1993; Siemer 1977). This results in different rainfall patterns and precipitation rates in the plains, mountains, and plateau.

An added factor controlling not only precipitation but also temperature is elevation, which ranges from 3300 feet on the eastern edge of the plains to well over 14000 feet in the mountains. Generally speaking, for every 1000 feet in elevation increase, temperature decreases approximately 3.6 degrees Fahrenheit (Armstrong 1972; Siemer 1977). This results in more days when dew forms at higher elevations. However, there is also a decrease in the number of frost-free days at higher elevations. The combination of shorter growing seasons and higher moisture levels greatly affects plant and animal resources.

The final factor influencing weather is the prevailing winds. Constant winds increase aridity, particularly on the plains where high winds are common throughout summer and early fall, and the mountain peaks where they are present year-round. Additionally, prevailing continental wind patterns are related to the movement of major storm systems, which bring moisture to the state. In winter the jet stream often crosses Colorado, resulting in westerly air patterns and storms originating in the northern Pacific Ocean. In summer, however, the jet stream tends to pass to the north, and prevailing winds are from the south, as are the major storm systems (Armstrong 1972; Huber 1993). As a result, most winter storms have high snowfall in the mountain ranges with relatively light snows on the eastern plains.

In summer, rainfall is dependent on storm systems in tropical regions of the Gulf of Mexico and Pacific Ocean. Because these storms form at different times, the eastern and western slopes receive their greatest amount of summer precipitation at different times. Specifically, the plains receives most of its precipitation in early summer and the western slope in late summer (Siemer 1977).

The combined effects of latitude, continental position, topography, elevation, and jet stream location result in a highly complex and variable pattern of temperature gradients, rainfall patterns, and wind velocities (Grieser 1985). Temperature, precipitation, and wind data have been collected by the Colorado state climatologist for more than sixty years, the

TABLE 1.1
Average Temperatures and Length of Growing Season in Colorado

Location	Elevation	January High	January Low	July High	July Low	Number of Frost-free Days
Low Elevation						
South Platte River	4930	43	14	89	58	144
Arkansas River	4370	46	14	92	61	159
Colorado River	5191	38	13	92	57	152
High Elevation						
South Platte River	8363	33	11	77	44	68
Arkansas River	9615	32	4	76	44	65
Colorado River	8656	31	1	76	42	39

Compiled from Siemer 1977.

first forty of which have been compiled and reported on extensively by Siemer (1977). Summary data have been extracted from this report, which illustrates the effects of precipitation, temperature, and length of growing season throughout the state (Tables 1.1 and 1.2).

VEGETATION AND ANIMAL COMMUNITIES

Vegetation and animal communities in Colorado have been included in the Kansas biotic, the Upper Sonoran biotic, the Mountain Forest, and the Subalpine and Alpine Tundra zones (Greiser 1985; Griffiths and Rubright 1982; see Appendices 1, 2, and 3 for detailed lists of plant and animal species). Although continental location and elevation determine the initial placement of an area, there is a great deal of diversity within each of these zones. Therefore, more detailed divisions have been made for Colorado (Armstrong 1972; Huber 1993; Mutel and Emeric 1992). In any biotic zone, the transition from one zone to the next is never absolute or abrupt. There are often large transitional areas, and areas generally designated as one zone type may in fact be a mosaic of several in which one type dominates. The following summary is structured by the divisions outlined for Colorado by Mutel and Emerick (1992).

TABLE 1.2
Average Yearly Precipitation in Colorado

Location			Precipitation	Length of
County	City	Elevation	(in Inches)	Record
Plains				
Yuma	Yuma	3560	17.5	41
Kiowa	Eads	4215	14.2	48
Baca	Springfield	4410	15.0	18
Arapahoe	Cherry Creek Dam	5647	15.8	21
Eastern Mountains				
Fremont	Canyon City	5343	12.5	42
Jackson	Walden	8099	9.6	35
Lake	Leadville	10046	17.9	42
Western Mountains				
Alamosa	Alamosa	7531	7.0	17
Pitkin	Aspen	7928	19.2	44
Routt	Steamboat Springs	6770	23.4	42
Colorado Plateau				
Rio Blanco	Rangly	5216	8.9	21
Mesa	Grand Junction	4849	8.5	74
Montezuma	Cortez	6177	13.2	46

Compiled from Siemer 1977.

Plains Grasslands Zone

The Plains Grasslands zone is restricted to the eastern part of the state and generally lies below 5500 feet elevation. The grasslands is home to twenty-two grass species and twenty-one forbs, eleven of which were used by Native peoples as food sources. The most dominant species are short grasses, particularly buffalograss, blue grama, Junegrass, and needle-and-thread, which cannot be consumed by humans. All are characterized by extensive but shallow root systems that form sod. Dormant much of the year, they grow in late spring and early summer—seasons with the most precipitation. In their dormant state they are a highly nutritious forage and support numerous herbivores including bison, mule deer, and pronghorn as well as large numbers of rodents and birds.

Upland Grasslands and Meadows Zone

Upland grasslands are dominated by grasses and forbs found outside the Plains Grasslands zone and are generally found at higher elevations. Represented by mountain meadows, they are less open and often tightly bounded by other biotic zones. Whereas many of the same species are present, there are fewer grass (fifteen) and forb (eighteen) types in these upland zones than on the Plains. Five of these species were used as food sources by Native peoples.

Because of the higher elevation and more bounded nature of these grasslands, the most dominant species on the Plains—the bison—is not common here (though it may have been present in prehistoric times). Mule deer, elk, and bighorn sheep are the most common here, along with a number of small mammals and birds.

Lowland Riparian Zone

Lowland riparian zones are those in lower elevations on either side of the Rockies and are generally restricted to river- and streambanks. Because of the greater moisture in these regions, numerous trees, particularly cottonwoods and willows, join the grasses, forbs, and shrubs found in their neighboring zones. At least nine species were used as food sources ethnographically. Large numbers of birds (some of which are migratory), shellfish and fish (Appendix 3), and mammal species are present.

Upland Riparian Zone

Upland riparian zones are more varied than those found at lower elevations. They include river- and streambanks, as well as numerous marshes, lakes, and ponds. Some lakes and ponds are frozen during the winter, which affects the fish species. Many of the birds are present only seasonally. The plant life differs from lowland habitats with spruces and aspens as well as cottonwoods dominating. These zones were exploited ethnographically, with at least eight plant species used for food.

Semidesert Shrubland Zone

Semidesert Shrubland is concentrated between 5000 and 7000 feet in elevation and is found most commonly in the southwestern portion of the state, specifically in the lower elevations of the Colorado Plateau. The San

Luis Valley, which is dominated by Semidesert Shrubland vegetation, is an exception.

The lack of moisture and alkaline nature of the soils result in low-lying shrubs and no trees. The most common shrubs include Great Basin big sagebrush, greasewood, rabbitbrush, four-winged saltbush, and shadscale. Eleven plant species were exploited ethnographically in this zone. Animal species include rabbits, mice, and prairie dogs. The most common larger mammal is the mule deer.

Sagebrush Shrubland Zone

As the name implies, the dominant vegetation in this zone is sagebrush, specifically Great Basin big and mountain sagebrushes. Like the Semidesert Shrubland zone, the Sagebrush Shrubland zone occurs in the western portion of the state. The major difference is that Sagebrush Shrubland is at higher elevations (5000 to 8000 feet) and is concentrated in the northwest, but there is considerable overlap. Another difference is the absence of greasewood, four-winged saltbush, and shadscale. As a result, only seven plant types were used ethnographically in the Sagebrush Shrubland zone. Although many of the animal species are found in both zones, a larger variety is found in the Sagebrush Shrubland (Appendix 2).

Mountain Shrubland Zone

As the name implies the Mountain Shrubland zone is found at higher elevations than Semidesert and Sagebrush Shrublands. It occurs on both sides of the Continental Divide, generally in areas with thin soils and rocky surfaces. Gambel oak and mountain mahogany are the most common plants, the oak being one of eleven food sources exploited by Native peoples. Animals include a variety of chipmunks, rabbits, mice, shrews, and mule deer.

Piñon-Juniper Forest Zone

Piñon-juniper forests occur on the eastern and western slopes and represent the transitional zones between the lower grasslands and shrublands and the mountain forests. Piñon-juniper forests, located between 6000 and 7000 feet, consist of piñon pines and one-seed junipers. Tree density and size increase with elevation in this zone. The piñons and junipers are intermixed with a number of shrubs, particularly Gambel oak and mountain mahogany, as well as other low-lying plants. Twelve plant species were used for food ethnographically, in particular the seeds of the piñon pine and Gambel oak.

Animals in this zone are numerous, represented by twenty-nine species of birds and thirty-three species of mammals. Of particular importance to ethnographic groups is a variety of cottontails and jackrabbits, as well as mule deer and elk.

Ponderosa Pine Forest Zone

Ponderosa pine forests are found between 7000 and 8000 feet in elevation, with some as low as 6000 and as high as 9000 feet in protected situations. It is the lowest of the mountain forest zones.

The trees in this zone are almost exclusively ponderosa pine, with a sprinkling of some junipers. The understory includes several shrubs, grasses, and herbaceous plants, although only four species were used as food sources ethnographically. These forests house a variety of animals including migratory and year-round birds, mule deer, cottontails, and bighorn sheep, which often winter here.

Douglas Fir Forest Zone

Douglas fir forests can be found anywhere from 6000 to 9000 feet in elevation, though they are most common between 8000 and 9000 feet. As the name implies, they are dominated by Douglas firs and a sparse understory of shrubs. Because of the lack of variety only four plant species were used ethnographically.

Reptiles and amphibians are absent, probably due to the cool weather in the higher elevations, but birds are common, as are mammals. Most of the thirty-one animal species are small in size, but mule deer and elk can be found.

Aspen Forest Zone

Thick aspen groves occur between 8000 and 10000 feet and are often found in mosaic forests surrounded by ponderosa pine, Douglas fir, and lodge-pole forest zones. Aspen forests are concentrated in wet areas and are accompanied by thick understories of shrubs and herbaceous plants, the most common of which are columbine, geranium, and daisy. Because of the larger number of plant species than in the lower forests, more (nine) were used as food sources by Native groups. A variety of small mammals and birds (some of which are exclusive to the Aspen Forest zone) can be seen here. Larger mammals are limited due to the dense nature of the forest, although mule deer and elk can be found.

Lodgepole Pine Forest Zone

Lodgepole pine forests are the highest of the mountain forest zones and are transitional to subalpine conditions. These forests prefer areas between 9000 and 10500 feet, though they can be found on the north face of slopes as low as 8500 feet. Because lodgepole pines form dense stands, there is little to no understory. Only a small number of berry-producing shrubs that are present were used ethnographically.

The fauna number an impressive twenty-one species of birds and thirty mammals. Large mammals include black bear and mule deer; however, smaller species—squirrels, porcupines, and voles—dominate.

Limber and Bristlecone Pine Woodland Zone

The Limber and Bristlecone Pine Woodland zone is the lowest of the subalpine forest populations. These zones are generally found in exposed ares, which accounts for the trees' stunted growth. Because of cold weather and high winds, there is no undergrowth, and rocky surfaces are often exposed. Animals and plants here are few—fifteen bird and twenty-one mammal species. In spite of this, Native peoples used these woodlands. Of particular importance were the limber pine seeds along with various parts of four other plant species.

Engelmann Spruce–Subalpine Fir Forest Zone

The Engelmann Spruce–Subalpine Fir Forest zone is the last of the alpine forests before the treeline. These forests are found as low as 9000 feet but are most common between 10000 and 11000 feet in elevation. Unlike limber and bristlecone pine, however, they form dense forests. As a result, the understory is limited but does contain numerous berry-producing shrubs. Birds are fairly common, with twenty-seven species residing here. Common mammals include voles, squirrels, martens, and snowshoe hares, though elk and mule deer can be found.

Alpine Tundra Zone

Despite its initial appearance, the alpine tundra is actually a rich and diverse ecosystem. Although there are no trees, low-lying shrubs, grasses, and forbs are numerous. Animals are numerous and include shrews, voles, ermines, and marmots. Larger species include elk and bighorn sheep, which summer in the alpine tundra regions and represented a major food source for indigenous groups.

PALEOENVIRONMENTAL RECONSTRUCTIONS

Although these environmental zones appear to be stable, this has not always been the case. The environment in which prehistoric peoples lived has changed over the past 12,000 years due to Colorado's climatic shifts. These environmental changes are different for the eastern and western portions of the state, because of various rates of glacial advances and retreats during the Pleistocene/Holocene transition and rainfall patterns during the Holocene.

Eastern Colorado

Scholars have studied environmental changes in eastern Colorado using geomorphological, palynological, and ecological data (Brunswig 1992; Butler 1992; Greiser 1985; Wendland 1978). These reconstructions break the past into environmental periods that relate to changes in mean temperature and precipitation and the obvious effects on plant and animal populations (Table 1.3).

TABLE 1.3
Paleoenvironmental Periods in Eastern Colorado.

Climatic Period	Date (B.P.)
Late Glacial	16,000-10,500
Pre-Boreal	10,500-9650
Boreal	9650-8450
Atlantic	8450-4680
Sub-Boreal	4680-2760
Sub-Atlantic	2760-present

Late Glacial period. During the late Glacial period, when human groups entered the New World (see Chapter 2), the environmental regime looked much different from what we see today. Because of the glacial ice sheets, lack of seasonality, lower temperatures, and lower precipitation, current vegetation zones were compressed and found in areas of considerably lower elevations and latitudes than they are today. In Colorado much of the higher elevations of the Rocky Mountains were covered with ice sheets, and forest zones were considerably lower in elevation. As recently as 15,000 years ago, much of the Great Plains consisted of boreal and mixed forests except for a narrow strip of grassland at the 99th meridian (Fig. 1.2; Brunswig 1992; Wendland 1978). Megafauna, including mammoths, giant bisons, camels, and horses, found throughout were exploited by humans. However, the situation was far from stable and by 11,000 years ago the boreal forest had retreated north of 40 degrees latitude along the 99th

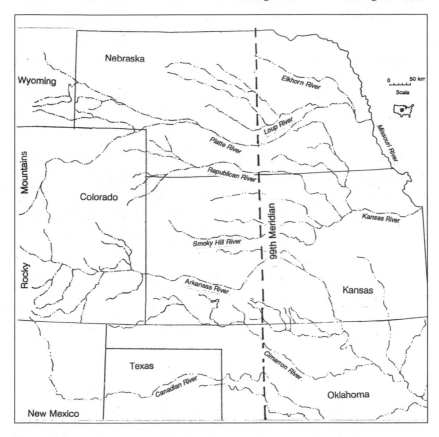

Figure 1.2 Major topographic features on the Central High Plains.

meridian, leaving a mosaic of grasslands, pine, and spruce forests in western Kansas and eastern Colorado (Greiser 1985).

As the glacial sheets began to retreat, we move from Pleistocene into Holocene climate. This transition was neither rapid nor smooth and was characterized by numerous oscillations in the environment and many periods of glacial retreat and expansion before today's conditions were reached. In general, however, temperatures rose, and there was a marked increase in seasonality. Combined with the movement of vegetation zones to current positions, these factors resulted in mass extinctions of megafauna and the expansion of populations of smaller animals. Among the large mammals that remained, such as bison, there were marked changes in their size and behavioral patterns. Modern *Bison bison* is much smaller than its predecessor, *Bison antiquus*, and moves in much larger herds. All these changes had a dramatic effect on human populations as well (see Chapter 2).

Pre-Boreal period. The Pre-Boreal marks the first of the periods in the Pleistocene/Holocene transition. It was characterized by elevational shifts in vegetation and climatic zones. For example, the pine and spruce forests retreated from the Great Plains into the foothills and mountains. This period also was characterized by numerous glacial retreats and advances and temperature and precipitation fluctuations. Overall, however, the climate was considerably cooler and moister than it is today.

Boreal period. The Boreal period is characterized by further retreat of the glaciers of North America, which is particularly noticeable in the Rocky Mountains where ice sheets retreated from most of the eastern slope. This retreat was hastened by higher temperatures, decreased precipitation, and, most important, increased seasonality, which, along with warmer and drier conditions had a dramatic effect on plant and animal communities. The only remaining megafauna were bison, which were much smaller and formed larger herds as the grasslands expanded onto the Great Plains. By the end of this period, most of the modern plant and animal communities were established near their present locations. From the end of the Boreal period on, temperature and precipitation oscillations affected the size of these zones, though not their locations.

Atlantic period. As a whole, the Atlantic period is drier and warmer than previous periods and approaches modern conditions. Researchers have subdivided this period into cool and warm and wet and dry phases. These fluctuations are related to shifts in the jet stream and the amount of moisture brought into Colorado by the westerlies.

The Atlantic period was particularly warm between 7,000 and 5,500 years ago when desiccation occurred throughout the Plains. This period is known as the Altithermal and is characterized by an increase in cacti and woody shrubs on the Great Plains and a decrease in the short grasses that bison prefer. In several areas, including eastern Colorado, bison were absent except for small remnant herds (Butler 1992; Dillehay 1974). However, conditions improved at the end of the period, and by 4,500 years ago, the bison returned in large numbers to eastern Colorado.

Sub-Boreal period. As the name implies, this period represents a return to cooler and moister conditions, resulting in an environment similar to today's. Associated with these climatic changes, the woody shrubs and cacti that had advanced onto the Plains retreated, and the modern limits of the Great Plains were formed.

Sub-Atlantic period. The Sub-Atlantic period began around 2,760 years ago and continues today. Many of the environmental zones have been relatively stable through this period, though localized droughts and/or cooling episodes have had an impact on the size and productivity of plant and animal communities. Between approximately 1,450 and 750 years ago, much of the Central and Southern High Plains underwent a drying trend, resulting in a northward retreat of the bison herds, but this did not seem to affect Colorado's bison population (Butler 1992; Dillehay 1974).

During more recent times (since A.D. 1590), drought was frequently widespread in eastern Colorado. Wendland (1978) reports a number of droughts in the Denver basin that would have had a significant impact on the indigenous groups and early Euro-American farmers. Based on geomorphological data, during the late 1680s the North Platte basin was dry at times. Between 1851 and 1874 eastern Colorado experienced a series of localized droughts. Drought hit again during the 1930s in much of the western United States.

Western Colorado

The climatic periods for western Colorado are more detailed than for the eastern half of the state (Table 1.4). One of the main reasons for this greater resolution is the addition of dendroclimatological data after A.D. 300. This is particularly true in the southwest, where climate has been studied extensively. These data were recently synthesized by Petersen (1988) for the Dolores area. Petersen's data are supplemented in the reconstruction presented here by information from the northwestern part of the state included in La Point's (1987) report on the Little Snake resource area.

The climate on the western slope is characterized by localized variability. The variability in precipitation and temperature is due to glacial advances and retreats as well as modern storm systems. Because of local variability, contradictory reconstructions are sometimes present for areas that are relatively close to each other.

Deglaciation occurred earlier on the western slope than in the east. Data from the San Juan Mountains indicate that glaciers in that area had started to retreat by 15,000 B.P. and by 14,000 B.P. they were restricted to areas above 14000 feet in elevation. However, there have been periods of minor glacial advances in the ice caps above 14000 feet more recently, which affected temperature and precipitation rates.

Reconstructions of the early paleoenvironment are based predominantly on sediment columns from high-elevation (above 7000 feet) lakes and geomorphology. From these columns we get information from pollen, and charcoal samples from natural forest fires can be identified and dated. These macrobotanical data, combined with data on the ratios of piñon pine to spruce pollen have allowed us to reconstruct the upper and lower margins of the spruce forest and the size of the piñon forest (Petersen 1988).

Today spruce is most commonly found between 9500 and 11500 feet, whereas piñon pine grows between 6000 and 7000 feet on the western slope. By using macrobotanical and pollen data, we can chart the changes in the locations of these zones. In general, when the upper margin of the spruce timberline was higher than it is today, it indicates warm summers and wet winters. Conversely, when the lower timberline was lower, it means that it was cooler and drier. Changes in the extent of the piñon forest are related directly to precipitation levels, especially to summer rainfall. Based on changes in these three indices, the following reconstruction has been made (see Table 1.4).

By 14,000 B.P., deglaciation of the Rocky Mountains in the southern part of the state was complete on the western slope. Slightly later, deglaciation was also complete in the northern part of the state. Between 14,000 and 12,000 years ago, there was a continued warming trend, though temperatures were still significantly cooler than they are today; precipitation is greater than in the previous period.

TABLE 1.4

Paleoenvironmental Periods in Western Colorado

Date (B.P.)	Conditions
15,000–14,000	Deglaciation occurred, resulting in warmer temperatures and increased precipitation
14,000–12,000	Further increase in temperatures and precipitation occurred, although it was still colder than today
12,000–8500	Temperatures continued to increase, resulting in conditions that were warmer than today; precipitation decreased
8500–7500	Temperatures decreased slightly, reaching modern levels and precipitation continued to be at low levels
7500–7000	Temperatures and precipitation remained at lower than normal levels
7000–6000	Temperatures and precipitation increased
6000–5000	Temperatures and precipitation were lower than normal
5000–4300	Temperatures were lower than normal but precipitation was higher
4300–4000	Temperature and precipitation levels were higher than normal
4000–3300	Temperatures were lower than normal and precipitation was higher
3300–2700	Temperatures and precipitation were lower than normal
2700–1900	Temperature was lower than normal and precipitation was higher than normal
1900–1450	Conditions were cooler and drier in the south
1900–1350	Conditions were cooler and wetter in the north
1450–850	Precipitation increased and spatial variability decreased in the south; temperatures increase after 1150
1350–950	Temperatures and precipitation increased to modern levels
950–625	Precipitation decreases in both areas with a protracted drought between 625 and 650
650–450	Precipitation and temperatures increase but it is still drier than today
450–250	Conditions are cooler and drier than today
250–present	Modern conditions

Between 12,000 and 8500 B.P., temperatures continued to warm, and for a while were warmer than they are today. Accompanying this warming trend was a drop in precipitation. The result was a movement of vegetation zones toward their modern locations, although spruce was found at lower elevations then.

Modern temperature ranges and vegetation zones were established between 8500 and 7500 B.P. The slight decrease in temperature that this represents was due to hotter summers rather than warmer temperatures year-round, indicating that seasonal swings may have been slightly more intense than today. Precipitation remained at the same low levels of the previous period. These two factors may have caused a decrease in piñon nut production, a food source of humans and animals.

Between 7500 and 6700 B.P., it was cooler but a decrease in precipitation levels resulted in severe drought. This period, often referred to as the Altithermal, was less severe and shorter-lived than in the east. However, piñon nut production was definitely lower. Conversely, the spruce zone (and therefore the habitat of the animals that lived there) may have expanded, particularly downslope, because of the cooler weather. The alpine zone also may have been slightly lower than today because of the cooler temperatures.

Between 6700 and 6000 B.P., average temperatures and precipitation increased, resulting in conditions that were similar to today. The piñon forest and spruce zones expanded and the alpine zone decreased.

Between 6,000 and 5,000 years ago, it was cooler and drier. This period was equivalent with the end of the Altithermal in eastern Colorado. On the western slope, the Altithermal was interrupted by a 700-year period of improved precipitation rates. The cooler temperatures between 6000 and 5000 B.P. in the west are related to increased glaciation in the higher elevations of the Rocky Mountains, resulting in downward compression of the spruce zone. The dryness also caused a decrease in piñon nut production.

Between 5000 and 4000 B.P., cooler conditions remained, as did the increased glaciation; however, the drought ended. In the following 300 years (from 4300 to 4000 B.P.), temperatures warmed and the glacial fingers retreated. The warmer temperatures and longer growing season increased plant production and expansion of the spruce zone into the Alpine Tundra zone.

From 4000 to 3300 B.P., cool and wet conditions returned, which decreased the spruce zone but increased production of piñon nuts. However, the shorter growing season affected the productivity of some plants at higher elevations. From 3300 to 2700 B.P., cooler conditions remained, but the drying trend resulted in less piñon nut production. Precipitation levels and piñon nut production again increased between 2700 and 1900 B.P.

By 1900 B.P., dendroclimatological data can be added to the macrobotanical, palynological, and geomorphological data from previous periods. Therefore, there is greater resolution on spatial variability. What follows is a synthesis of broad temporal patterns, which glosses over some of this variability. However, one must realize that there is considerable local variability within these patterns. The result is that in the southwestern portion of the state conditions may be different in Mesa Verde than along the Utah border. This is particularly true for periods characterized by high spatial variability. Further, local conditions are affected by elevation. For example, weather may be favorable for agriculture at 7000 feet but too dry at 4000 feet.

Between 1900 and 1450 B.P., southwestern Colorado was cooler and drier, whereas the northwest was cooler and wetter from 1900 to 1350 B.P. In the northwest, these conditions were accompanied by high spatial variability, resulting in patchy production, whereas the spatial variability was low in the southwest, resulting in a more homogeneous distribution of high-production patches.

In the southwest, between 1450 and 1150 B.P., precipitation increased to a moderate level with a further reduction of spatial variability. Between 1150 and 850 B.P., precipitation increased further, as did average temperature, resulting in an increase in the length of the growing season. However, spatial variability also increased, which resulted in increased patchiness for both domesticated and wild species.

In the northwest, between 1350 and 950 B.P., temperatures increased, resulting in modern conditions and extending the growing season. The longer growing season was accompanied by more precipitation and less spatial variability, resulting in decreased patchiness and increased productivity of wild and domestic species.

Unfortunately the paleoclimatic data between 950 and 750 B.P. are not well known for the northwest. In general, throughout the western part of the state, conditions were considerably drier. The drought worsened between 650 and 625 B.P. This twenty-five-year period is often referred to as the Great Drought.

Despite the droughtlike conditions in the northwest and west, temperatures were different in the north and south, with the north cooler than today and the south hotter. In the north, this resulted in a shorter growing season, and in the south it exacerbated the drought. The drought, combined with social and political factors, led to the abandonment of the western part of the state, and by 650 B.P. (A.D. 1300) both areas were abandoned and remained so until Numic speakers came into Colorado from the west (see Chapters 4 and 5).

Between 650 and 550 B.P., precipitation increased and temperatures decreased in the southwest. Conversely, the north remained in droughtlike conditions until 450 B.P. After 450 B.P. there was more mini-glaciation in the northern mountains, resulting in lower temperatures and higher precipitation in the northwest. The spruce zone constricted and piñon nuts flourished. In the southwest, this mini-glaciation also was felt in terms of a decrease in average temperature, but precipitation remained low, as did overall plant productivity.

Between 250 and 200 years ago, glacial activity decreased resulting in warmer temperatures in the northwest. There is no noticeable temperature change in the southwest until about 50 years ago. The past fifty years have seen higher temperatures and precipitation levels, accompanied by a high degree of spatial and temporal variability (i.e., cyclical short-term drought).

CONCLUSIONS

The climate, plants, and animals of Colorado are highly diverse both spatially and temporally. However, we cannot assume that the environment or changes in the environment determine the nature of human behavior. Rather, human-environment interaction is a complicated phenomenon in which ecological and cultural factors come into play. The environment may place constraints on options available to individuals and groups, but it does not determine which options will be chosen.

CHAPTER 2

The Paleoindian Period

The Paleoindian period is a dynamic one, characterized by massive population movement and dramatic climatic change. According to the site records at the Office of Archaeological and Historical Preservation (OAHP), 399 Paleoindian sites have been recorded in Colorado. Of these, 278 have been assigned to one of the subdivisions within this period. The remaining 121 sites cannot be identified beyond the general Paleoindian designation.

To understand the complexities of the Paleoindian period in Colorado, we must take a broader perspective. During Clovis and pre-Clovis times, population movements from the Old World into the New World and within the New World are frequent and continental in scope. Therefore, this period must be viewed in the context of the peopling of the New World.

In the Folsom and later Paleoindian periods, Colorado was occupied more intensely, and regional variability became evident as peoples adapted to local environments. During the late Paleoindian (or Plano) period, two distinctly different adaptations are evident in Colorado: an eastern and western, with the dividing line along the Front Range of the Rocky Mountains.

INITIAL OCCUPATION OF THE NEW WORLD

Initial entrance into Colorado was part of a widespread, rapid migration throughout North and South America of peoples from the Old World. How and when the New World was populated is a necessary precursor to early occupation in Colorado and how these early inhabitants lived.

The Three Migration Model

The most recent data indicate that the indigenous peoples of the New World came in three separate migrations across the Bering Strait during the Late Pleistocene when lower sea levels created a land bridge between eastern Siberia and Alaska (Fig. 2.1). This conclusion is based on three separate lines of data and is most clearly articulated by Greenberg and his colleagues (1986). These data sets consist of morphological characteristics in the dentition from both living and archaeological populations and linguistic data and genetic studies of living indigenous peoples.

The first data set is based on the distribution of morphological characteristics, the best understood of which is teeth. These data are the result of dental examinations of twenty-eight key traits on archaeological remains and living Native American, Asian, and European populations by Turner (1983, 1992). His data show that Native Americans as a group have different patterns of dentition than do Asians and Europeans, indicating they have been separated for a long time. However, within the Native American sample, there is also patterned variability. Based on similarities and differences, three categories can be defined.

The largest of these groups is the Amerind, which includes most Native American groups in South America and in North America south of the Canadian border. The second is the Na-Dene. This group corresponds to Native American populations in interior Canada, with the exception of the Athapaskan speakers of the southwestern United States, who are relatively recent migrants from Canada. The third group consists of the Aleuts and Eskimos of Alaska, Canada, and the Aleutian Islands.

The second data set is based on linguistic diversity among living indigenous peoples of the New World gathered by Joseph Greenberg and colleagues (1986). As with the dental data, studies of linguistic relationships are based on the assumption that the more recently that two languages shared a common root, the more similar they are. Conversely, the longer they have been separated, the greater the diversity. The results of Greenberg's study agree closely with Turner's in that all Native American languages can be grouped into three categories that correspond with Turner's geographic distributions.

The final data set is based on a genetic survey of indigenous populations of the New World and is the most recent and weakest of the three (Greenberg, et al. 1986). This survey examines genetic characteristics to determine the amount of similarity and diversity among indigenous peoples. It states that the greater the genetic similarity between two groups,

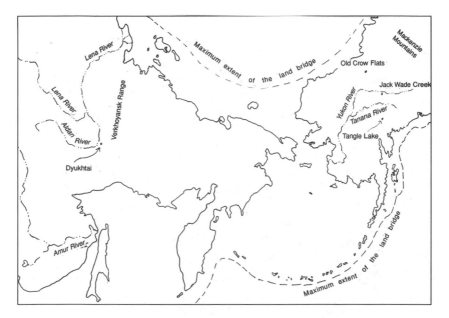

Figure 2.1 Map of the major features and sites of Beringia.

the more recently these groups were part of one larger group in which there was a free exchange of genetic material. Conversely, the greater the diversity, the longer they have been isolated from each other in terms of the exchange of marriage partners. The genetic data agree with the other data sets, indicating that groups within the Amerind category are more similar to each other genetically than they are to the groups in the Na-Dene and Aleut-Eskimo categories.

Given these three data sets, a model of the peopling of the New World has been proposed (Greenberg, et al. 1986; Turner 1992). It should be noted that not everyone agrees with Greenberg and Turner's multiple migration model (see Laughlin 1986 for a criticism of this research and an argument for a single migration). However, the archaeological data appear to support the multiple migration hypothesis. Before proceeding we need to examine the specific migration route and probable adaptive strategies used by these early migrants.

Beringia During the Late Wisconsin Glacial Period

All three migrations occurred across the Bering land bridge during the Wisconsin Glacial period, which is marked by episodes of increased world-wide glaciation and decreased sea levels. Because of the lower sea levels, land bridges existed in several areas of the world that are now flooded, including the Bering Strait. This land bridge, joining eastern Siberia with western Alaska, is referred to as Beringia (see Fig. 2.1).

To understand the paleoecology of Beringia, we need to examine the climatic oscillations that affected it. The Wisconsin Glacial period was not homogenous in terms of climate—there were several periods of glacial retreat and advancement that allow the Wisconsin period to be divided into three intervals (Hopkins 1982). These subperiods include the Happy interval (180,000 to 65,000 B.P.), a time of increased glaciation during which Beringia was its widest. The Happy interval is followed by the Boutellier interval (65,000 to 30,000 B.P.) in which glacial retreat and rising sea levels resulted in partial flooding of the land bridge. The Duvanny Yar interval (30,000 to 14,000 B.P.) again saw increased glaciation and lower sea levels. Beginning in 14,000 B.P., deglaciation began on a worldwide scale. By 10,000 B.P. the sea had reached modern levels flooding the land bridges. Regarding the peopling of the New World, the Duvanny Yar is the most important interval.

Recent geomorphological studies indicate that between 18,000 and 20,000 B.P. sea levels were low, resulting in a sixty-two-mile-wide, unglaciated land bridge from the Yukon into and across Siberia (Wright 1991). From 18,000 B.P. on, deglaciation caused sea levels to rise, but the rate of deglaciation was not constant, and sea levels fluctuated. Large portions of Beringia may have begun to flood as early as 14,000 B.P. (Schweger, et al. 1982). However, the land bridge remained open, at least in narrow sections as late as 11,000 to 10,000 B.P., after which only coastal groups using boats could have moved from northeastern Asia into Alaska (Hoffecker, et al. 1993).

During the Duvanny Yar interval, Beringia extended from the Verkhoyansk Mountain Range in Asia to the edge of the Laurentide ice sheet, west of the Mackenzie River in Canada (see Fig. 2.1). Because of lower sea temperatures, evaporation and precipitation decreased, resulting in an ice- and snow-free Beringia. In some areas the landscape appears to have been cross-cut by glacial streams whereas in other areas sand dunes are indicative of strong and active winds (Schweger, et al. 1982).

Paleoecological reconstructions of Beringia are based on geological, palynological, and macrobotanical analysis of marine sediment cores, but these analyses have yielded contradictory data. Early palynological analysis indicated that Beringia was a steppe tundra with incomplete plant cover and large areas of active dunes. Trees were restricted to the rivers

(Schweger, et al. 1982). Also, whereas spruce forest or forest-tundra characterized either end of the land bridge, much of Beringia itself was cold, dry,
and bare—a polar desert (Wright 1991).

However, early faunal data contradicted this interpretation. There is
good evidence of large and diverse communities of ungulates that could not
have existed if Beringia were in fact a polar desert. Hoffecker and others
(1993) have reexamined the pollen data, combined this information with
more recent sediment core data, and suggested a different reconstruction.

The reanalysis of the pollen data indicates that the Duvanny Yar interval can be subdivided into three phases, or zones. Between 25,000 and
14,000 B.P. is what Hoeffecker terms the herb zone. Based on pollen, the
vegetation during this period was dominated by grasses, sedges, willows,
and sage. From 14,000 to 10,000 B.P. (the birch zone) there is a significant
increase in dwarf birch and willow and juniper pollen, indicating an
increase in precipitation, temperature, and flooding. Between 10,000 and
7000 B.P. alder and spruce increased on either end of Beringia, but the land
bridge itself was flooded.

Based on these data, a new consensus has emerged on the nature of the
Beringia environment. Between 25,000 and 12,000 B.P. there was a complex
mosaic of vegetation that included some steppe communities, particularly
in the river valleys, broad outwash plains, and south-facing slopes, with
tundra and dune areas in between (Hoffecker, et al. 1993). Mammoth,
bison, horse, caribou, mountain sheep, saiga, and musk ox (all gregarious),
as well as a variety of fish and birds, were present (Schweger et al. 1982).

Archaeological Data for the Three Migration Model

Exactly when the various migrations into the New World occurred is a matter of debate. Some scholars have argued for very earlier entrances based on
material recovered from sites with early carbon 14 (C14) dates (Butzer 1991;
Schweger, et al. 1982). Sites in South America (particularly Pedra Furada)
and Alaska (Old Crow Flats and Jack Wade Creek) have been dated to
approximately 30,000 years ago. The South American sites have also produced stone tools including modified pebbles, flakes with microwear, food
choppers, and denticulates. The sites in Alaska have produced no stone tools
but contain bone cores and flakes, whose interpretation is controversial.

In Colorado there are five sites on file at the Office of Historic and
Archaeological Preservation (OHAP) that have been suggested to be very
early and may relate to this debate. The two best known of these are Lamb

Springs and Dutton, both dating to greater than 13,000 B.P. (Rancier, et al. 1982; Stanford, et al. 1981; Stanford 1983). At both of these sites, processed bone similar to that at the early Alaskan sites has been recovered. The sites have produced long bones with spiral fractures, flaked bone, and crushing marks on some of the bones. But the lack of stone tools in good context (there were several flakes at Dutton, and two boulders with crushing marks and a quartzite biface were found at Lamb Springs, but all in equivocal context) leads many to question the validity of pre-Clovis occupation in Colorado. Recent ethnoarchaeological research in Zimbabwe comparing animal butchering and nonhuman taphonomic processes on elephant bones indicates similar fractures and crushing patterns can result naturally, leading to further uncertainty as to the nature of these sites (Fisher 1992).

In addition to the controversial nature of the tool assemblages, the dates from these locations also are highly debatable and may represent contaminated or redeposited material (Toth 1991). Additionally, Hoffecker and others (1993) argue that the vegetation present during the herb zone period (25,000 to 14,000 B.P.) could support ungulates hunted by the early migrants, but that the most likely time of migration is during the birch zone (14,000 to 10,000 B.P.) because before then, there was not enough firewood available to support human populations on the land bridge.

Because of the controversy over the early sites and the limitations of the Beringian landscape, many scholars argue that sites older than 12,000 to 14,000 B.P. do not stand up to scientific scrutiny. The one exception is Meadowcroft Shelter in Pennsylvania with over seventy dates in good context, the earliest of which are at approximately 14,000 B.P. (Adovasio 1980; Adovasio, et al. 1990). However, even with the acceptance of the 14,000 B.P. date of Meadowcroft Shelter, Hoffecker's assertion is not contradicted. Therefore, the birch pollen period *is* the most likely time of the early migrations.

Glottochronological data from linguistic analysis agrees with this possibility, indicating that the Amerind population entered the New World and began to diverge before 11,000 B.P. Glottochronology indicates the divergence of the Na-Dene group at approximately 9000 B.P. and divergence of Aleut-Eskimo groups at 5000 B.P. Because divergence within these three groups occurred after entering the New World, the migrations themselves would have been sometime before this.

The archaeology of Alaska presents convincing data in support of the three migration model. Securely dated sites between 9000 and 12,000 B.P. demonstrate the presence of two vastly different lithic traditions—the

TABLE 2.1

Comparison of the Nenana and Denali Complexes

	Nenana Complex	Denali Complex
Lithics	Flake-and-blade core technology with retouched bifacial teardrop and triangular points; bifaces; unifacial end and side scrapers; wedges and planes; no wedge-shaped microcores or microblades	Wedge-shaped microcores, microblades, burins, lanceolate points; also macroblades, bifical "knives" usually biconvex in form; and boulder-chip scrapers; end scrapers are relatively uncommon
Locations in the Alaska Range	Teklanika Valley (some in Tanana Basin)	Tangle Lakes and Carlo Creek area (some in Tanana Basin)
C14	12,000–11,000 B.P.	earliest is after 10,700 and goes until 2040 B.P. (after 10,700 the microblade technology is widespread in Asia and North America)
Lifestyle	Sites are in the major valleys on terraces to tributary springs; bison, elk, sheep, smaller mammals, birds, and fish are hunted	Sites are in the alpine valleys and high terraces in major valleys; going after the same resources

Nenana and Denali complexes—in the New World (Hoffecker, et al. 1993; Powers and Hoffecker 1989; West 1967; Table 2.1). The earliest material of the Aleut-Eskimo tradition is from the eastern Aleutian Islands, dated to approximately 8000 B.P. From the Aleutian Islands, the expansion of this tradition throughout the Arctic occurs between 6000 and 7000 B.P.

The data from Siberia are equally supportive of the three migration model. Turner (1992) has synthesized the available data from Siberia and combined it with the data from Alaska to produce the following reconstruction.

Initial Amerind Migration. This group, the first in the New World, is ancestral to most Native Americans. No archaeological donor culture is known in Siberia for certain, but there are hints. Between 11,000 and 25,000 B.P., a generalized tool tradition in Siberia consists of basally thinned, bifacial points and knives, similar to those identified as the Nenana Complex in Alaska. The migration route of these peoples probably started in the Lena River basin, then went north to Beringia and across the land bridge (Turner 1992; Hoffecker, et al. 1993).

Initial Na-Dene Migration. The migration of the group that eventually became the Na-Dene is linked to the Paleoarctic culture using microblades and wedge-shaped cores of the Denali complex. Turner argues this group came to the New World around 9000 B.P., based on glottochronology data. However, dates from Alaska indicate the initial migration may be as early as 10,700 B.P. A microblade tradition similar to the Denali complex has been found in Siberia along the Aldan River. It is referred to as the Dyukhtai tradition and is dated between 20,000 and 16,000 B.P. (Toth 1991). It appears that this is the donor group for the Na-Dene migration (Hoffecker, et al. 1993).

Initial Aleut-Eskimo Migration. The earliest Aleut-Eskimo sites are on the Anangula Islands in the eastern Aleutian Islands dated at 8000 B.P. Early Aleut-Eskimo assemblages are similar to the blade-making peoples of the Amur River of eastern Siberia and Hokkaido Island of northern Japan. These coastal-oriented, sea-mammal-hunting groups are believed to have entered the New World along the southern coast of the Bering as it began to flood.

Turner (1992) argues that before 20,000 B.P. these three groups were all one people moving into the uninhabited portions of Siberia. There they separated and inhabited two different river basins—the Lena and the Amur—and the intervening mountains (including areas along the Aldan River) where they diverged culturally and biologically (see Fig. 2.1).

The oldest midlatitude North American complex and the oldest non-controversial complex in Colorado is from the Clovis period (11,200 to 10,900 B.P.), a flake and blade core technology in which microcores and microblades are rare. In this sense it is similar to the Nenana complex. In fact, projectile points from the Nenana complex are similar to Clovis points except for the characteristic Clovis flute. It appears that the peoples associated with the Nenana complex migrated south from Alaska, and developed into the Clovis peoples, who are ancestral to Amerind groups (Goebel, Powers, and Bigelow 1991; Turner 1992). Conversely, peoples associated with the Denali complex migrated east from their original base and became the Paleoartic tradition, and eventually the Na-Dene groups

(Hoffecker, et al. 1993). The Aleut-Eskimo groups expanded from the Aleutian Islands to the northeast along the Arctic coastal margins into their historic territories (Turner 1992). Because only the Amerind/Paleoindian peoples entered Colorado in prehistoric times, our focus is on them.

EARLY PALEOINDIAN ADAPTATION IN THE NEW WORLD: THE CLOVIS PERIOD

Clovis peoples are generally referred to as big-game hunters. However, this does not mean that their diet is exclusively meat. Although these groups rely heavily on hunting—possibly more than most modern hunter and gatherers—carbohydrates are a necessary part of the diet (Speth and Spielman 1983). Therefore, they did not ignore plants and smaller locally available game, but big-game procurement was important and greatly affected their subsistence economy and mobility patterns.

Early Paleoindian occupation of the New World (Clovis period; 11,200 to 10,900 B.P.) is one in which the environment changed rapidly as the transition from the Pleistocene into the Holocene era began. Paleoindian peoples rapidly migrated into uninhabited areas throughout the New World. Archaeologically this period is characterized by homogeneity in subsistence systems and tool technology. Kelly and Todd (1988) present a model to explain this rapid migration throughout the New World (possibly in less than 1,000 years) and the apparent homogeneity in Clovis tool technology and settlement pattern.

Kelly and Todd point out that Clovis peoples entered the New World during a climatically unstable time and did not know the plants and animals in the areas they were migrating into.

Also, local food sources were often unstable and highly variable because of climatic oscillations associated with the onset of the Holocene, which forced animals into seasonal and yearly migrations. Given all these unknowns, Kelly and Todd argue that the rational choice was to concentrate on the things that were known—the migratory game like mammoth, bison, caribou, elk, and deer. In so doing, the Clovis peoples moved rapidly across the landscape, following the migrations of the animal herds. In fact, climatic fluctuations eventually resulted in the extinction of large numbers of species, resulting in long-distance moves by the people who depended on them.

This reaction of animal herds and thus Clovis peoples to the climatic and environmental uncertainty accounts for the rapid movement of Clovis peoples throughout North America and the homogeneity of their technology. The question remains, however, of why the lithic technology looks the way it does. Why is it dominated by bifacial core reduction of high-quality cryptocrystalline material, often from very distant sources?

The Clovis period tool complex contains distinctive fluted projectile points, bifacial knives, steep-edged unifacial end scrapers, spurred scrapers, and tiny- and large-beaked gravers and burins. However, large portions of the assemblage consist of generalized and specialized bifacial forms. Bifaces are beneficial for highly mobile peoples with large territories because they serve both as cores from which new flakes may be obtained, and as tools. Additionally, bifacial knives are easily resharpened and recycled. The multiuse nature of bifaces means that they serve many functions while limiting the number of tools (and therefore weight) that a mobile group must carry. In other words, they are the Swiss Army knife of stone tools (Kelly 1988; Kelly and Todd 1988).

THE CLOVIS PERIOD IN COLORADO

In Colorado, nineteen Clovis period sites are recorded at the OHAP. These sites are dated between 11,200 and 10,900 B.P., as they are elsewhere in the New World. Of these, only one true kill site is known, whereas three isolated finds, one rock art site, ten open camps (many of which contain the remains of animals from kill sites), and four lithic scatters have been identified. A site's assignment to the Clovis period is usually confirmed by the presence of Clovis projectile points. Clovis points are characteristically lanceolate shaped, with the widest part of the point below the midpoint, and contain bifacial flaking (Howard 1990; Irwin and Wormington 1970). On one or both sides is a flute starting at the bottom and extending halfway up the face of the point. Occasionally the flute is formed from multiple flakes (Fig. 2.2).

Faunal remains from Clovis sites include extinct horse and camel, *Bison antiquus*, and several smaller species. However, in Colorado and Wyoming, Clovis peoples are best known for mammoth hunting. Based on kill sites in Wyoming, Frison (1991) argues that a common Clovis hunting technique was to set up hunting stands overlooking tributaries of major streams or Pleistocene lakes and playas. The crucial factor is the presence of areas of slow-moving water with deep mud or marshes, where the animals would congregate.

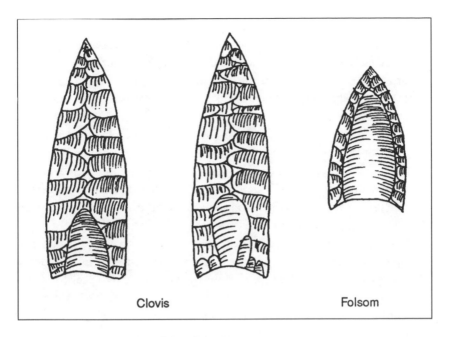

Clovis   Folsom

Figure 2.2 Clovis and Folsom projectile points.

Extensive studies of elephant behavior conducted by Frison (1991) allow us to better understand mammoth behavior and Clovis hunting techniques. Modern elephants move across territories in matriarchies ranging in size from ten to fifty individuals, depending on the season and available resources. These matriarchies contain related females and their offspring. No mature males are found in these groups unless a female is in estrus. This pattern appears to be the same for mammoths as well, although the elephant groups are often smaller (Frison 1991).

Elephant, and presumably mammoth, hide is very thick and difficult to penetrate. Despite this, a dart tipped with a Clovis point can kill an elephant if it is thrown with sufficient force. However, hurling a dart into a charging adult female, which can move with great speed and strength, will fail. Similarly, driving an entire matriarchy into a marshy area and attacking while the animals are trapped in the mud is not likely to succeed. Elephants (and mammoths) are quick and strong and can easily escape. Rather, the best strategy is to kill an isolated individual who has wandered off from the rest of the group, usually one of the young. Mammoth remains from Clovis sites do indicate a preference for hunting juveniles (Frison 1991).

Once the Clovis hunter successfully killed a mammoth, the animal would be butchered using unifacial scrapers, bifacially flaked knives, and large choppers. During butchering, tools became dull through use but were frequently resharpened as is evident by the presence of hammerstones and small resharpening flakes at Clovis period kill and processing sites (Frison 1991).

Butchering followed set patterns, which Frison (1991) has reconstructed based on the faunal remains at both kill sites and open campsites. Clovis peoples would remove prime pieces of meat, apparently drying or jerking some of it, and then move on, leaving the rest of the meat to rot on the bone. Prime pieces of meat usually included the hindquarters and certain internal organs that are high in iron such as the brain and liver. These were almost impossible to jerk and were probably eaten on the spot.

Gathered plants were also an extremely important part of the diet during the Clovis period. Ethnographic research and studies of human physiology indicate that a high proportion of the diet needs to be carbohydrate based (Speth and Spielmann 1983). However because we have not recovered floral remains and tool complexes used for processing, we do not know what plant foods were exploited by Clovis peoples.

THE FOLSOM PERIOD (10,900 TO 10,200 B.P.)

The Folsom period is when Paleoindians stayed in a particular region for longer periods. In Colorado there was an increase in population as evidenced by an increased number—sixty-one—of sites for this period on file at the OHAP. The different site types include six isolated finds, three isolated kill sites, thirty-two open camps (which may include associated kill sites), nineteen lithic scatters, and one stone circle site.

Radiocarbon dates and the presence of diagnostic Folsom projectile points place these sites in the Folsom period. Although there is a great deal of variability in point size, Folsom points can be identified by the following characteristics (see Fig. 2.2; Tankersley 1994). They have a lanceolate outline with parallel or slightly convex sides, concave bases with earlike projections, and often a small nipple at the base. The most distinguishing characteristic is a long flute on both sides that extends the length of the point. The lateral edges near the base are often ground, and they were joined to the dart shaft with a split-stem haft. Based on points found in various stages of production, the manufacturing process was to rough out the shape, flute it, then use pressure flaking around the edges to sharpen the point.

Because the Folsom period occurs after the shift into the Holocene has begun, the resources Folsom peoples used are different from the previous period. In Colorado, the megafauna are dominated by *Bison antiquus* rather than mammoth, which is reflected in the faunal assemblage from kill and campsites. Because *Bison antiquus* live in larger herds than mammoths (though the herd sizes are considerably smaller than modern *Bison bison*), bone beds at kill sites are larger, representing more animals taken at one time (Frison 1991). However, kill sites for *Bison antiquus* vary considerably in size, reflecting differing herd sizes in different areas. For example, the Stewart's Cattle Guard site is a small kill site, probably due to the smaller herd sizes in high-elevation parks as opposed to larger herds on the open plains (Jodry 1987; Jodry and Stanford 1992).

Kill sites are found in marshes, arroyos, box canyons, and snow- and sand-filled basins (Jodry 1987; Jodry and Stanford 1992). As in the Clovis period, most of the hunting activity does not appear to be due to driving the animals over cliffs or arroyo edges. Rather, the animals were herded into areas in which they could be trapped and killed with spears (Frison 1991). The hunters selectively killed members of the herd, probably taking those that were slowest to escape the trap. The most common faunal remains at kill and campsites are juveniles and females (presumably either pregnant or the mothers of the juveniles). The stronger males are less common (Frison 1991).

The larger number of sites, and in particular campsites in which food-stuffs were processed, give us more information on Folsom period subsistence systems than we have for the previous period. There are informal milling stones, which were used for processing plants, as well as evidence for hunting pronghorn, rabbit, fox, and coyote. Clubs and snares were probably used for the smaller animals, though none have been recovered (Wilmsen and Roberts 1978).

We also understand the processing procedures for megafauna better than for the Clovis period. In general, bison butchering took place in specialized processing sites next to big kills and at campsites during the Folsom period. The processing sites were used for first-stage butchering and preparing the meat for transport. First, the meat was cut into large packages, like the hindquarters, to help in transporting them to camp (Jodry and Stanford 1992). Sometimes the femur and tibia would be removed, at a secondary processing site, leaving the metatarsals (the foot bones). The remaining meat was strung on a pole between two people through the ligaments and tendons close to the feet. This reduced the weight and made it easier to carry the meat to a base camp. This is evident in that the hindquarters often are missing from kill sites, metatarsals are found at campsites, and piles of long bones are recovered at the processing sites.

Final processing of meat and other foodstuffs was done at camps that often had multiple activity areas (Jodry and Stanford 1992; Wilmsen and Roberts 1979). Even the smallest camps had multiple-activity areas. The presence of small and large camps may relate to microband and macroband phenomena found among modern hunter-gatherers. Credence for band aggregation comes from large Folsom period campsites like Lindenmeier (Wilmsen and Roberts 1979) and smaller sites like Stewart's Cattle Guard.

Lindenmeier

Lindenmeier is located in Larimer County, 1.75 miles (2.8 km) south of the Wyoming state line in the Lindenmeier Valley. The valley is crossed by numerous small creeks and seeps and lies in the foothills of the Rocky Mountains. It is in an environmentally transitional area that allows easy access to numerous ecozones including the foothills, high mountain peaks, and the plains.

The site was originally discovered in 1924 and excavated from 1934 to 1940 by Frank H. H. Roberts of the Smithsonian Institution. However, the collections were not systematically studied and reported on until the early 1970s when Edwin Wilmsen analyzed the material (Wilmsen 1970; Wilmsen and Roberts 1979). In total, Roberts excavated over 12,000 square feet of the site in three major areas. In the first year (1934) of these excavations, only formal tools were saved, but from 1935 on, all chipped stone material was saved. The result is 5,478 tools and 46,380 pieces of debitage. Unfortunately, fauna and mollusk shells were not saved. It is estimated that between 10,000 and 20,000 pieces of fauna were excavated, but only 700 "representative" pieces were collected. Of the fauna that was saved, nine species appear to have been actively hunted and eaten: box turtle, snowshoe hare, white-tailed jackrabbit, gray wolf, coyote, red fox, swift fox, pronghorn, and *Bison antiquus*. In the original site maps, Robertson lists and plots the presence of a large bison processing area that he refers to as the bison pit, indicating the presence of a nearby kill site, though none has been located (Wilmsen and Roberts 1979).

Roberts had different goals for the different years he excavated at the site, which are reflected in his methodology and what he saved. The rationale for these goals and procedures is detailed in the site report and summarized below (Wilmsen and Roberts 1979).

During the 1934 field season, the major goal was to establish the antiquity of the site and its potential for study. This was important because the antiquity of humans in North America was still in question, as can be seen by the controversy surrounding the finds at the Folsom site in New Mexico eight years before in which Roberts was involved (Roberts 1938). In 1934 he conducted a surface survey of the Lindenmeier site and located an arroyo cut that indicated undisturbed deposits, then excavated several test pits. Because chronology was the main concern, he collected only diagnostic tools. As a result, he established that Lindenmeier was a Folsom period site, but it was not a kill site. The encountered bones were disarticulated, and charcoal was present, indicating a campsite.

The goal in 1935 was to establish the site's stratigraphic deposition and its horizontal extent. Roberts placed a number of trenches across the site and collected all the chipped stone artifacts he found. He demonstrated that most of the site was contained in one buried layer that was associated with extinct megafauna and fluted points. There was a minor secondary deposit (apparently Archaic) above this level.

From 1936 on he looked for living floors at the site by extending hand-dug excavation units from the previous year's trenches. All of the chipped stone artifacts were saved. During these excavations, Roberts found several hearths containing charcoal, but unfortunately we do not have maps or information on their locations. Roberts never successfully defined actual living floors due to disturbance of the deposits. In the 1960s, charcoal recovered from the hearths was submitted to C14 analysis and dated between 11,200 and 10,780 B.P. (Haynes, et al. 1992; Wilmsen and Roberts 1979). During the 1970s Edwin Wilmsen analyzed the artifacts that Roberts recovered, and together they produced the 1979 site report.

There are three major areas of the site designated Area I, Area II, and Unit E (the bison pit). Areas I and II are further divided into units that are related to different living areas. For the most part, Wilmsen believes that all the units are contemporaneous; however, based on the artifacts recovered, the activities in the units in Areas I and II are very different. Specifically, all recovered artifact classes were found in all of the units in both areas, their densities and relative frequencies varied considerably. This led Wilmsen to speculate about specialized activity areas and the possibility of multiple social groups at the site (Wilmsen and Roberts 1979).

To understand the differential distribution of the artifacts and the implications this has for activity areas, we need to describe the tool classes Wilmsen defined. Both ground stone and unworked fauna were encountered during excavation; however, this material was neither saved nor consistently plotted. As a result, its distribution is not well understood. A large amount of worked bone was recovered. Whereas its fragmented nature precludes positive identification, there is evidence of polishing and incising on much of it. Of the pieces that could be identified there are small numbers of bird-bone beads and a large number of awls and needles made from mammal bone.

Lithics dominate the artifact assemblage saved from the site (Wilmsen 1970; Wilmsen and Roberts 1979). Both modified and utilized flakes were recovered. Wilmsen argues that the formal tools because they tend to be much smaller than any of the tools or utilized flakes. Utilized flakes are expedient flake tools with wear and limited marginal resharpening. They are larger than the unmodified flakes and were selected for their thinness and overall size. They tend to be lightweight with acute edge angles and are frequently made out of chalcedony and some chert. The use wear consists of small edge nibbling and unifacial scalar damage. Based on the edge angles and the nature of the wear, they were probably used for skinning animals and cutting meat.

The class Wilmsen identified as single-edge tools includes unifaces and marginally retouched items used as side scrapers. These tools are more formal and have a larger mass than utilized flakes, as well as steeper edge angles due to retouching. Unlike utilized flakes they are made primarily out of quartzite and some chert. The edge wear includes extensive bifacial nibbling and unifacial scalar damage. Due to the steep edge angles and scarring, the tools were most likely used for cutting bone and wood and dismembering carcasses.

Distal-edge tools (also known as end scrapers) have a larger mass than single-edge tools and are believed to been hafted. The edge angles on these tools are similar to single-edge tools, and the wear includes abrasions, striations, and step fractures. The large number of step fractures in this class may be because most of them are made of chalcedony, which is sharp but brittle and breaks easily when the edge angle is acute. The steep edge angles and hafting associated with this tool would have made the edge stronger, indicating they were probably used for rough shaping of hard materials like bone and wood (Wilmsen and Roberts 1979).

Wilmsen refers to the largest tools that were excavated as double-edge tools. They have uniformly steep edge angles and evidence of heavy stress including edge shatter, erosion, pitting, and step fractures. Wilmsen interprets these as handheld scrapers for hard materials like bone and wood.

He identified two additional tool types, each appearing to have a specialized function. The first he refers to as tip tools, which have a sharp protrusion and extensive wear. These were used as gravers and perforators. The second is projectile points, which are often reworked into end scrapers when broken. Fluted and unfluted projectile points were found at the site. With the exception of the flute, they are identical.

Now that we have defined the tool types, we can discuss their distributions. First are the projectile points. Although both types are found in both areas, unfluted points are more common in Area I and fluted ones are more common in Area II. Based on this distribution, Wilmsen argues that there was simultaneous occupation by two groups with overlapping territories whose different environments converged at the site (Wilmsen and Roberts 1979). He argues that these two groups were geographically distinct but interacted and participated in common social and procurement practices while maintaining independence, hence their separation at the site. This implies, though Wilmsen does not explicitly state it, that they were culturally distinct. Conversely, the remains may reflect the presence of two bands from the same cultural group aggregating during a period of plentiful resources at a single site.

Other artifact types are also differentially distributed. For example, bone needles and chalcedony utilized flakes are numerous in Unit H of Area II. Wilmsen suggests that their concentration here may represent a skin-working area. Conversely, Area I (especially Unit B) has an extremely high number of quartzite one-sided tools, tip tools for engraving, end scrapers, and small worked bone fragments, suggesting that this was a bone-working area. Area II has many unworked and fluted flakes, so fluted points, and stone tools in general, may have been made in this area (this could be biasing the projectile point results stated above).

Overall, the Lindenmeier site presents a rich picture of a Folsom period campsite. It appears that the camp space was divided into different activity areas for manufacturing various items from bone, including jewelry. This site demonstrates that Folsom period peoples butchered and ate many different animals including, but not restricted to, bison, although we do not know in what proportions. The presence of grinding stones indicates they processed wild plant foods, probably grains and seeds, though we do not know how much. Also, it appears Folsom peoples aggregated into macroband camps at certain times of year, although it is not clear if they represent two different ethnic groups or two bands from one group.

Stewart's Cattle Guard Site

Stewart's Cattle Guard site is in the San Luis Valley at an elevation of approximately 7600 feet (Jodry 1987; Jodry and Stanford 1992). It consists of a campsite with several bison bone beds representing a secondary processing area. The location of the exact kill site is not known, though the animals were probably ambushed as they fed near several playas.

The processing area consists of five bone piles representing eight animals. The bones are from front and hindquarters as well as rib slabs, which were transported to the site and then further processed (Jodry and Stanford 1992).

With each bone pile is a lithic concentration, one of which has a hearth. All five clusters represent hearth-centered activity areas that hold the full range of domestic tools. "Each area contains debris from a variety of domestic activities of which the rejuvenation and maintenance of hunting gear and the use and resharpening of end scrapers (hide working?) are two archaeological identifiable examples" (Jodry and Stanford 1992: 158).

The distribution of artifacts at this small campsite is evidence that the structure of camp life here was different from that at Lindenmeier. Instead of areas that were task-specific for the whole site (hide-working, point production, and so on), at Stewart's Cattle Guard site families shared a location but pursued the full range of domestic activities at their individual hearth area. The small size and low density of artifacts indicate that this site was used for a relatively short time by a small group (Jodry and Stanford 1992). The difference in the size, length of occupation, and composition of activity areas between these two areas indicate sites associated with both the microband and macroband portion of the seasonal round of Folsom peoples in Colorado.

LATE PALEOINDIAN OCCUPATION IN COLORADO

The late Paleoindian period is often called the Plano period, within which are different phases and associated tool complexes. The presence of these multiple complexes is associated with a period of diversification of Paleoindian adaptation throughout the New World. The technologies and subsistence systems vary considerably across space as people adapted to regionally specific environmental differences.

In the process of fission, migration, and fusion, groups adjust and invent technological and organizational features to accommodate new and different settings. Migration, particularly into empty lands, must have produced a great deal of variation in human mobility and social cohesiveness, with some groups being more adaptable than others, more apt to move, and over longer distances and experiencing greater changes in population growth and size and segmentation (Dillehay and Meltzer 1991: 289).

In other words, if the Clovis period is characterized by the initial colonization of the New World and the Folsom period is a settling of the different regions, then the Plano period is a period of local adaptation and increasing regional differentiation.

There are two different Paleoindian traditions in Colorado (Pitblado 1993). On the plains there is an adaptation directed toward big-game hunting, specifically bison. In the west and the Rocky Mountains, we see a broader-based subsistence pattern. This is obvious in much of the Rocky Mountains, western plateaus, and eastern foothills of the state (Pitblado 1993; Rayne 1994). Interestingly, Wyoming has a similar phenomenon (Frison 1991, 1992; Frison and Grey 1980).

The dividing line between these two groups in Colorado is unclear. Pitblado (1993) argues it is along the continental divide based on the distribution of projectile point style and settlement pattern. She also argues that although there is some limited movement back and forth across the divide, particularly in the mountain passes, the two traditions did not mix and remained distinct. Recent research by Rayne (1995) indicates that whereas Pitblado's reconstruction of two separate traditions is accurate, the dividing line may be farther east, in the foothills of the Front Range.

Regardless of where the line is drawn, their basic characteristics can be summarized in the following way. In the east are individuals that appear more specialized in their subsistence technology, concentrating on megafauna (i.e., bison), whereas in the west are individuals with a more generalized subsistence system, using an even mixture of mammals (including large mammals but not megafauna) and gathered resources. The origin of this western form of Paleoindian adaptation is the Great Basin, but by about 10,000 B.P. it extended into western Colorado (Pitblado 1993).

The reason for the differences in the eastern and western systems is that in the west there are no herd animals or megafauna. Therefore, people in the west concentrated on smaller, nonherd game and gathered resources. Also, because the game that was present in the west had a more limited migration route, seasonal rounds were much more circumscribed. One of

TABLE 2.2

Characteristics That Differentiate the Western and Eastern Paleoindian Tradition

Western (Mountain-Foothills-Great Basin-like)	Eastern (Plains)
Generalized hunting-gathering	Specialized (big game)
Generalized tool kits	Specialized tool kits
Local lithic raw material (quartzite)	Exotic raw material (cryptocrystalline)
Formal tools are rougher and cruder with random flaking	Formal tools are finer with predominantly parallel convergent flaking
Expedient chipped and numerous ground stone tools	Some expedient chipped tools (scrapers) but little ground stone
Points are socket hafts	Points use both split-stem and socket hafts

From Pitblado 1993.

the aspects of the archaeological record of the west at this time is that the overwhelming proportion of the lithic assemblage is of low quality but locally available quartzite and orthoquartzites. This is in direct opposition to the occupation on the plains, where there is a high proportion of high-quality cryptocrystalline rocks, often from nonlocal sources, and reflects use of smaller territories in the west (Pitblado 1993).

In addition to subsistence systems and the type of raw materials used, there were other differences between the eastern and western traditions (Table 2.2). These differences include tool kit makeup and lithic production (specifically, projectile point style). The eastern tradition features a more formal and highly stylized tool kit, which is dominated by bifacial core reduction of nonlocal, high-quality cryptocrystalline material. Although ground stone is present, it is informal and a small part of the overall tool kit. In the west, chipped stone tool kits are much more generalized and expedient, and ground stone is more common (Pitblado 1993).

Differing raw materials and levels of formalization can be seen in terms of lithic style. Flaking patterns on projectile points in the east are often regularized and parallel convergent. Both split-stem and socketed hafts were used (Fig. 2.3). This is in contrast to the western tradition in which only socketed hafts are present and the flaking patterns are much more random and unstandardized.

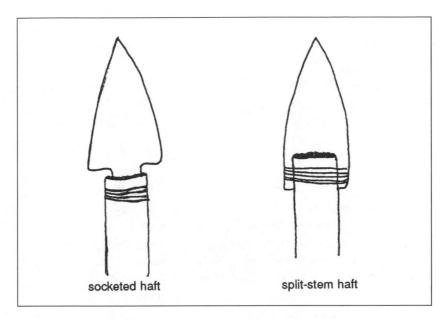

socketed haft   split-stem haft

Figure 2.3 Examples of socketed and split-stem hafting.

Pitblado (1993) relates these differences in projectile point style to the quality of raw material (cryptocrystalline versus orthoquartzite) and the degree of specialization in the tool kit, but there may be a third reason. Brian Hayden (1981) argues that the sophistication and standardization of plains projectile points over extremely large areas may be the result of more than the type of raw material used. He argues that in a situation where animals and people ranged over extremely large areas, cementing political and economic alliances was very important. The exchange of finely crafted and highly prized projectile points may have been crucial in maintaining these networks on the plains on a symbolic level, even when very little in the way of other material is exchanged (see also Wharburton and Duke 1995). Hayden further argues that the increasing regionalization of projectile point styles on the plains during the Archaic period represents an economic and symbolic breakdown of these alliances. This model also can explain the lack of a standardized point style in the west during the Paleoindian period. It may be that the localized nature of the fauna and flora led to little alliance building on a regional level between western Paleoindian groups. Thus there was no need to maintain symbolic links through style.

Based on these characteristics, a number of different complexes can be defined in the east and west for the late Paleoindian period (Table 2.3).

TABLE 2.3

Dates of the Eastern and Western Late Paleoindian Complexes in Colorado

Western Complexes	Eastern Complexes
Western Stemmed 10,800–8200 B.P.	Plainview 10,200–9900 B.P.
Foothills-Mountain 10,000–7500 B.P.	Agate Basin 10,800–10,000 B.P.
	Hell Gap 10,500–9400 B.P.
	Cody 10,000–8000 B.P.

From Pitblado 1993.

They are differentiated by projectile point styles. The remainder of the tool assemblages remains relatively stable, although the exact proportions of individual tool types in the assemblages may vary slightly (Irwin and Wormington 1970). The defining characteristics of the projectile points associated with each of these complexes are described and illustrated by Gunerson (1988), Irwin and Wormington (1970), and Pitblado (1993).

Even within an area (eastern and western), there is overlap in the temporal distributions of the complexes. It is unclear exactly what the differences in projectile point styles between these complexes mean. In some cases, style differences may be due to differences in ethnic group composition, whereas in others it may be due to differences in trade patterns.

All of these complexes contain a variety of scraper and knife types, and on the plains atlatl hooks have been recovered. No atlatl hooks have been found in the west, but it is unknown if this is due to poor preservation or the actual lack of atlatl use. The only clear temporal trend is an increase in the number and size of large kill sites through time in the east, indicating increasing use of communal kills (Frison 1991).

Eastern (Plains) Complexes

The Plainview complex is defined by the presence of Plainview projectile points, which are lanceolate-shaped with parallel or slightly convex sides and concave bases (Fig. 2.4). The flaking pattern is largely parallel convergent but can be irregular on occasion, particularly at the tip. The points are on a split-stem haft. The lateral edges at the base are ground, and there are small thinning flakes at the base.

Sites with Agate Basin points first appeared in northern Colorado in the foothills and eastern parklands of the Rockies. Later they were found in the Front Range, extending onto the plains themselves and eventually expanding south to encompass most of the Central High Plains. Agate Basin points

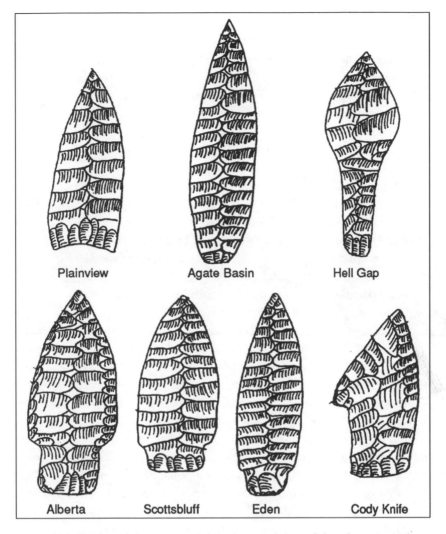

Figure 2.4 Points of the eastern (plains) complexes of the Plano period.

do not represent the entrance of a new group into Colorado; rather, the Agate Basin style is an outgrowth of the Folsom tradition. This is evident in the analysis of stylistic and technological aspects of Folsom and Agate Basin points, and has been used to argue for continuity between the two traditions (Frison and Stanford 1982). The technique of platform preparation is similar in the two point types. The absence of flutes in Agate Basin points either represents an attempt to increase tool completion rates or is a response to changes in hafting techniques (Shelly and Agongion 1983).

Agate Basin projectile points are generally very long and slender. In fact, they can be distinguished from Plainview points by their higher length-to-width ratio. They are parallel-sided with flat to rounded bases. The variability in basal forms ranges from lanceolate to a leaf shape that is rounded at both ends. Occasionally, both ends are pointed. They have fine parallel convergent flaking throughout, with fine marginal retouch and a split-stem haft. The lateral edges are ground at the base but the base itself is not.

The Hell Gap projectile point style developed out of Agate Basin points, both being long and slender (i.e., they have high length-to-width ratios). The Hell Gap points have constricted bases that are straight to slightly convex, but unlike other constricted base styles, they lack defined shoulders. The constricted base indicates that these points may have had socketed hafts, which is further supported by grinding on the base but not on the lower lateral edges. The flaking pattern is often parallel but can be more random, and marginal retouch is common. The cross sections of these points range from thin ovals to diamond-shaped.

The Cody complex is defined by several different projectile point types including Cody, Alberta, Scottsbluff, and Eden. In fact, these may actually be all one point type, their differences due to varying degrees of resharpening. The major differences between these point types are the length-to-thickness ratio, the bluntness of the tip, and how pronounced the shoulders are, all of which are affected by resharpening. All of these point types have the following characteristics in common. The overall shape is triangular or parallel-sided with small shoulders and broad stems. Facial flaking tends to be finely done and parallel, but irregular flaking is present occasionally. They are thick (thicker than Agate Basin) and the cross section is a thick oval (though it can be more diamondlike after extensive resharpening). Finally, the presence of stems and grinding on the stem edges and sometimes bases indicate they were used in socketed hafts.

Also diagnostic of this complex are Cody knives, which are asymmetrical shouldered blades. Below the shoulders the stems are usually basally thinned and may have been used in socketed hafts. They are bifacially worked with fine marginal retouch on the slanted blade edge.

Western Complexes

The Western Stemmed tradition developed as early as 11,100 B.P. in the Great Basin and gradually spread to the east. The earliest indication of this tradition in western Colorado is at approximately 10,800 B.P. When it originally

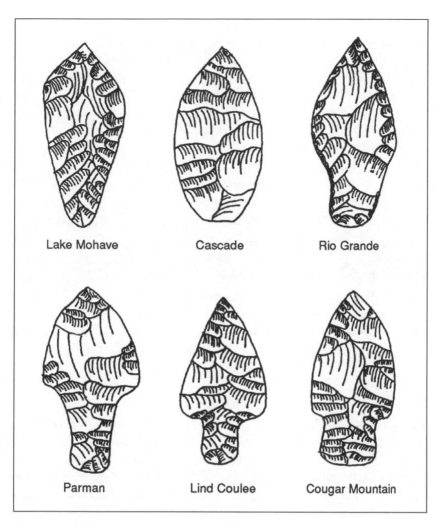

Figure 2.5 Projectile points of the Western Stemmed tradition.

developed, this tradition was contemporaneous with the Folsom period and probably represents a shift in adaptation related to the constraints of the Great Basin environment. However, it does not appear in Colorado until several hundred years later and is in fact never very common in the state (Pitblado 1993).

The Western Stemmed tradition is defined by a number of different point types including Mount Moriah, Lind Coulee, Cascade, Lake Mohave, Parman, Couger Mountain, and Rio Grande (Fig. 2.5). The differences among these points are restricted to shoulder morphology and the type of thinning flakes present. However, they have a number of things in common. The most important is that they were hafted into a socketed shaft, which is not evident on the plains at this time. These points differ from the later socketed types on the plains in that they are thinner but longer, when shoulders are present they are much more distinct, and despite the fact that they are thinner, the flaking patterns are often much more random.

The Foothills-Mountain complex also is closely tied to a Great Basin-like adaptation. However, unlike the Western Stemmed tradition, it is found throughout western Colorado (Pitblado 1993). These sites are common at high elevations, as well as in lower areas. This complex contains several point types, including Pryor Stemmed, Lovell Constricted, Pine Spring, Angostura, Frederick, Jimmy Allen, and Lusk (Fig. 2.6). Although their basal shape differs, they all have a number of things in common. For example, they are roughly made, compared with the points found on the plains, and tend to be very thick. All are leaf-shaped with ground bases. The flaking is usually parallel but also oblique and is not symmetrical through the center of the point (i.e., nonconvergent). In other words the thinning flakes often go all the way across the point. Finally, all are used in socketed hafts.

Adaptation

Based on the site records at the OHAP, 319 Late Paleoindian period sites have been identified in Colorado. Of these, 35 have been further designated as to which complex they belong. These designations are based on the presence of diagnostic projectile points, almost all of which are in the eastern tradition including 20 in the Cody complex, 3 each in the Agate Basin and Hell Gap complexes, and 1 Plainview site. This does not mean that sites are not known for the western tradition—they are, as Pitblado's (1993) study clearly demonstrates. Late Paleoindian sites are present throughout the state, but further research is needed to learn more about the nature of the adaptation in western Colorado and how much it diverged from the Great Basin–type adaptation in this area. Pitblado has ventured some preliminary statements about these peoples based on the data she has collected for the southwestern portion of the state.

Pitblado indicates that lithic scatters, open camps, rock shelters, and isolated point finds have been identified for the late Paleoindian period in the western portion of the state, but kill sites and game drives are rare. Although these sites are found at various elevations, clusters in Pitblado's

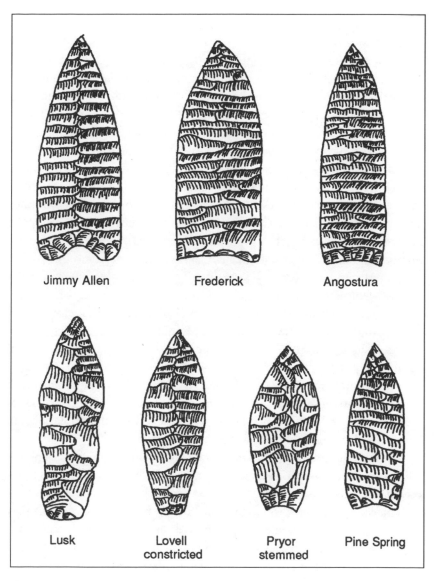

Jimmy Allen

Frederick

Angostura

Lusk

Lovell
constricted

Pryor
stemmed

Pine Spring

Figure 2.6 Projectile points of the Foothills-Mountain complex.

site data indicate a concentration between 5500 and 8000 feet (1993).
Interestingly though, there's no apparent relationship between elevation
and site type. This indicates a broad-based foraging pattern and lack of
specialized extraction patterns.

Our knowledge of the Late Paleoindian period on the plains is more complete due to the excavation of sites in Colorado and Wyoming. Throughout this period, population aggregations like those seen at Lindenmeier, for the purposes of communal bison kills, are common. This may be because both bison herd size and human population were increasing. Also, hunting techniques associated with large kill sites became more diversified as prehistoric hunters varied their methods to make full use of bison-herd behavior, seasonal resource availability, and topography.

Although large kill sites increased during this period, other hunting techniques were used as well. Ground stone in small numbers is evidence that plant foods were processed. The large number of isolated point finds and sites with faunal material other than bison indicates small groups of hunters exploited a variety of species (Wheat 1978). However, because a number of mass kill sites have been excavated, we understand this part of the hunting strategy best. Two large sites—Agate Basin (a winter site) and Olsen-Chubbuck (a summer site)—demonstrate the diversity of communal hunting and processing techniques evident at these sites. However, in order to understand these sites, we need to understand bison behavior.

Bison herd movement is unpredictable and very hard to control because they are fast, agile, and very large. As a result, modern bison ranchers use pickup trucks rather than horses to herd them, because bison will run over a horse and rider (Frison 1991). Given that prehistoric peoples on the plains lacked horses, much less pickup trucks, their manipulation and control of bison herds becomes all the more impressive.

Frison (1991) argues that in small herds (fifteen animals or so) the animals will stampede, but they will change directions rapidly and easily if they perceive danger. Therefore, it is hard to predict how they will react unless they can be funneled into an area where they can go only in one direction. The only way to make sure they go in one direction is to place large impediments everywhere else (they will run over smaller obstacles like a brush fence or person).

Behavior is more confused in larger herds (thirty or more) during stampedes. Specifically, if animals in the front reverse direction quickly, they may run head-on into animals in the back of the herd who have not reacted to the conditions at the front. The result is occasional injury to these animals and a period of confusion that prehistoric hunters could take advantage of if they had planned carefully.

Grazing behavior also was exploited. Bison grazing varies from season to season as does the herd size. In summer, particularly after the rains, short grass is plentiful throughout the plains. Hunters knew to look for bison in rich grass areas that also had a water source such as rivers and playas, where herds aggregated.

In winter, heavy snowstorms scatter herds into subherds (approximately 100 animals) along major river bottoms where there is water and plentiful grass, even after the first snows. As the river bottoms are grazed and trampled, these subherds break into smaller groups and move up the tributaries in search of forage. However, although the tributaries have water they usually lack grasslands, forcing the herds onto the surrounding windswept ridges. Which ridges the herd uses is dependent on prevailing winds, which create snowdrifts—minimal drifting is preferred. The bison feed by pushing the snow out of the way with their heads. They eat until full, then lie down in the same spot until they are hungry again (Frison 1991).

Because of seasonal availability of forage and water, as well as herd size and the constraints of the local topography, hunting techniques had to be modified to fit the situation. Because of differences in season and topography, different hunting methods were used at the Agate Basin and Olsen-Chubbuck sites.

Olsen-Chubbuck is a summer kill site excavated by Joe Ben Wheat of the University of Colorado Museum (1972) and is associated with the Cody complex. The kill site is in an arroyo in a dissected area of eastern Colorado on the Kansas border. The arroyo—associated with the Big Sandy, a tributary of the Arkansas River—has plentiful water and rolling grasslands capable of supporting a large herd. The arroyo is deep with very steep sides. The lip of one side is higher than the other, rendering the drop into the arroyo invisible if approached from the right direction.

Prehistoric hunters took advantage of this topography. The hunters started a bison stampede while the herd was on the blind side of the arroyo. Bison will stampede at full speed away from the source of confusion toward open space. Planning, coordinated labor, and patience were needed to maneuver the animals into a position where they would run blindly over the arroyo edge.

At Olsen-Chubbuck, this planning and patience were rewarded. The bison ran toward the arroyo, and the first animals over the steep edge went head-first into the bottom, breaking their necks. They were then crushed by the animals that landed on top of them (Wheat 1972). This process continued until the pile was either high enough that the rest of the herd could see and changed direction or until they could run over the top of the pile. Those bison that were on top and still alive were killed with spears. More than 200 bison, representing both sexes and all ages, were killed this way.

After the animals were killed, the group skinned and butchered the animals that were on top. Those that could not be reached were left to rot. In the archaeological remains, the animals on the top of the pile were disarticulated, and their bones are found in a processing area near the site. The animals on the bottom of the pile were still articulated and in place at the bottom of the arroyo (Wheat 1972).

The hunters removed and processed the skins and jerked as much meat as they could carry, leaving behind the heaviest elements and those with the least amount of meat, like the skulls. It is unknown how long a group could provision itself on the meat from a summer kill. We do not know of a long-term campsite near Olsen-Chubbuck, though there may be one near the river. We do know from other sites that meat processing and the length of stay at sites varied considerably. For example, at the Jurgens site, during each of its three occupations, the site was used for different activities and for different lengths (Wheat 1972, 1978, 1979).

In area three of the Jurgens site, activity was restricted to secondary butchering. Material removed from kill sites like Olsen-Chubbuck in the primary butchering process was brought to these secondary sites. The bone evident at secondary butchering sites is restricted to body parts that had a high meat-to-bone ratio. Most important among these are rear and front leg units and thoracic vertebrae (from the removal of the hump meat). Also, foot bones are numerous, apparently from stripping the muscle mass away from the leg bones and carrying the meat away by stringing a pole between the foot bones and ligaments still attached to the muscle.

This area can be contrasted with areas one and two at the Jurgens site, which represent camps used for varying lengths of time (Wheat 1978). These campsites contain faunal material from a variety of species—bison, pronghorn, elk, mule deer, rabbit, rodents, and fish—indicating that within any one area a variety of hunting techniques were used.

It is unclear how long a group stayed in one place, be it a campsite or a communal kill site. The length of stay was probably dependent to a large degree on how long the jerked meat lasted. The group had to move to a new hunting area for fresh meat because there was no way to store it in the summer. Paleoindian groups may have cached meat and stayed for a long time at winter kill sites such as Agate Basin.

Agate Basin is in Wyoming near the South Dakota border. The site has evidence of use by Clovis, Folsom, Agate Basin, and Hell Gap peoples, but the largest component of the site is of the Agate Basin complex. The site was dug by the University of Wyoming and the Smithsonian Institution under the direction of George Frison and Dennis Stanford (Frison and Stanford 1982). Agate Basin was used repeatedly to kill winter subherds ranging from 30 to 100 bison.

Agate Basin is in the Moss Agate arroyo, a tributary of Moss Agate Creek, which in turn is a tributary of the Cheyenne River. The arroyo is short and begins as a shallow and flat-bottomed drainage with a meandering stream. It becomes wide and deeper with steep sides as it approaches the confluence of Moss Agate Creek. As such, it is a perfect habitat for bison in late winter because it has easy access to the creek, plentiful grass, and no snowdrifts. When the grass is used up it is easy to get out of the upper end of the arroyo onto the surrounding ridges.

The topography at Agate Basin is different from Olsen-Chubbuck in that it does not have a blind side that the animals could be driven over. Additionally, because winter bison behavior is different from summer behavior a different strategy was used. The prehistoric hunters maneuvered behind the herd at the upper end of the arroyo where it is shallow and drove them toward the river where a barrier could be raised. The timing for the raising of the barrier was crucial. If the barrier was raised too soon, the bison would turn around and go up the arroyo walls and back out the way they came. If it was raised too late, the bison would run over it. However, if timed correctly, the bison would be in the arroyo where the sides are high and very steep. When they turned to run back out, the ones at the front would run head-on into ones in the back. The result is confusion. When confused, bison charge at everything they see, including each other and the arroyo walls At this time, the hunters could use spears to kill the animals that had been hurt in the confusion or that were still confused and charging blindly (Frison and Stanford 1982).

After the kill, the meat was processed differently than it was at Olsen-Chubbuck. Because no tailbones were recovered in the arroyo bottom, it appears that all of the animals were skinned. Then they were butchered into sections and several caches placed at the upper end of the arroyo. To protect the meat from scavengers, the caches were placed on prepared surfaces and covered with hides reinforced with small timbers. The hides were then covered with snow, and the piles were glazed with ice (Frison and Stanford 1982). These "refrigerators" allowed the group to stay in the area for a long time—at least as long as the meat stayed frozen. The kill site is near a protected forested area and permanent water so it would have been an ideal winter camp, though no habitation site has yet been identified.

Frison and Stanford developed their model of storage based on ethnographic analogy with historic bison hunters and Inuits. This model is supported by the lack of drying racks (patterned postholes and hearths) in the processing areas, floors that lack the posthole patterns normally associated with houses, and piles of bones from caches that were not tapped before the group moved on.

Sociopolitical Organization

Both of these communal kill sites indicate a sophisticated hunting technology and organized labor. If historic Great Plains groups, as well as hunters and gatherers elsewhere in the world, can be used as a model, these groups probably had a political structure of task-specific leaders. Otherwise, decision making was by consensus. The microband/macroband phenomenon of Folsom times at sites like Lindenmeier is probably at work during later times as well, even though no habitation sites the size of Lindenmeier have been excavated for the Plano period. However, it would require many people to supply the labor needed to start and direct stampedes like the ones at Agate Basin and Olsen-Chubbuck. The human population aggregations associated with mass bison kills are not evident in the next period and new organizational and subsistence systems are evident.

CONCLUSION

At approximately 6000 B.C., a new projectile point style is found in a number of areas. Specifically, corner-notched points, representing a new hafting technology, are found and mark the end of the Paleoindian period and the beginning of the Archaic period.

Throughout the Paleoindian period, massive migrations and adjustments to basic strategies occur as individuals adapted to new environments in a climatically unstable period. In Colorado this adjustment and readjustment result in two very different adaptations late in the period, a broad-based western pattern and a highly specialized eastern tradition. From the end of the Paleoindian period on, increasing diversification becomes evident and it is no longer possible to discuss a period for the entire state. Therefore, the remainder of the time periods will be discussed here in regional context.

CHAPTER 3

Plains Adaptation During the Holocene

As with the Paleoindian period, to understand prehistoric Holocene occupation of eastern Colorado, we need to take a broader perspective. The eastern plains are part of the Central High Plains culture area. The borders of this area as defined by Gunnerson (1987) are 41 degrees latitude on the north and 35 degrees on the south. The eastern boundary is the eastern woodlands (at approximately the 99th meridian) and the Front Range of the Rocky Mountains on the west. The western Central High Plains includes eastern Colorado, southwestern and south-central Nebraska to approximately the South Platte River, western Kansas, the northeastern corner of New Mexico to the Canadian River, and the panhandles of Oklahoma and Texas (Fig. 3.1). There is no sharp dividing line between east and west within this area, but rather a broad transition area with differences in rainfall, elevation, and vegetative communities that affect the fauna. In the eastern portion, the tallgrass prairies are generally less arid and lower in elevation. The western portion is higher in elevation, drier, and dominated by short grass (Johnson and Wood 1980).

Sites in Colorado cover three broad periods, the first of which is the Archaic. During this time, adaptation in the eastern and western portions of the plains diverged (Johnson and Wood 1980). This is followed by the Woodland, or Ceramic, and the Historic period.

Dating of the different periods in the Central High Plains region (Table 3.1) is controversial. Differences in the dating schemes may be due to the fact that the Plains is a large area, and changes in subsistence, technology, and mobility are not consistent throughout. Clearly, better definition of the temporal periods and understanding of the relationship between

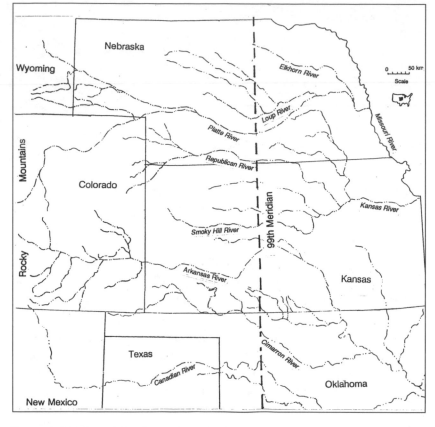

Figure 3.1 Map of the Central High Plains.

diagnostic artifacts and absolute dates are needed. A project to clarify these aspects is under way (Rayne 1995).

THE ARCHAIC PERIOD ON THE CENTRAL HIGH PLAINS

The Archaic period (ca. 6000 B.C.) begins with the appearance of corner-notched projectile points and ends with the introduction of pottery. It coincides with the second of the Altithermal droughts and Dillehay's first bison absence period (see Chapter 1). Coincidentally, there is a decrease in the number of sites found on the high plains, which along with deteriorating environmental conditions has led some scholars to argue that the western

TABLE 3.1
Chronologies of the Central High Plains

Period	Gunnerson 1987	Johnson and Wood 1980	Cassells 1983	Anderson, et al. 1994
Late Ceramic	A.D. 1850–1500	A.D. 1850–1450		A.D. 1750–1450
Middle Ceramic	A.D. 1500–900	A.D. 1450–900		A.D. 1450–950/850
Early Ceramic	A.D. 900–500	A.D. 900-0	A.D. 1000–100	A.D. 950/850–150
Late Archaic	A.D. 500–500 B.C.	0–8000 B.C.	A.D. 100–1050 B.C.	A.D. 150–1050 B.C.
Middle Archaic	500–3000 B.C.		1050–2050 B.C.	1050–3050 B.C.
Early Archaic	3000–6000 B.C.		2050–3000 B.C.	3050–5550 B.C.

portion of the Central High Plains was abandoned. Benedict (1979) proposed that the plains inhabitants fled the area for the better-watered areas of the Rocky Mountains. This is supported by an apparent increase in population in the mountain regions.

However, since Benedict proposed his "mountain refugia" scenario, research has led to a reevaluation of this model. Black (1991) examined Archaic period materials recovered in the higher elevations for technological and stylistic patterning. Based on his research and the investigation of sites predating the Altithermal, he concludes that occupation in the mountain areas extends into Paleoindian times. A stylistic and technological continuity in the lithic assemblages, settlement pattern, and site layout indicates indigenous development of a "mountain tradition" during the Paleoindian period with, ultimately, Great Basin roots (see also Pitblado 1993). There is no evidence of a migration from the plains into the mountains during the Early Archaic period (see Chapter 6).

The question remains then, why are Archaic, and in particular Early Archaic remains so scarce in eastern Colorado? Part of the problem may be sampling bias (Frison 1991). If shifts in land-use patterns occurred during the Altithermal, the sites may be located in very different topographic settings. For example, in the Republican River area of southern Nebraska, Early Archaic sites were more heavily concentrated along the major river systems than in either earlier or later periods (Wedel 1986). Also, because of their alluvial settings, many of these sites are buried and often missed during pedestrian surveys. If a similar shift in settlement pattern occurred in eastern Colorado, Early Archaic sites could be underrepresented in the existing database. Further, Archaic sites may be less visible on the plains because hunting techniques changed with periodic shifts in faunal resources. For example, if bison were more dispersed during the Altithermal because of poor pasture lands, mass kill techniques, such as those at Olsen-Chubbuck (see Chapter 2), for large herds may not have been used as often. Instead individual animals were stalked and only very small bison herds were exploited through mass kills. The result is decreased visibility of the sites, despite the continued presence of people in the area.

The lack of Archaic period sites on the plains in Colorado has led many to rely on reconstructions of culture history from adjacent areas, specifically the Front Range of the Rocky Mountains and eastern prairies. It has been argued that the plains of eastern Colorado saw a number of trends noted elsewhere in the United States at this time, including increased reliance on gathered resources at the expense of hunting, increased regional population levels, decreased mobility, and increased regionalization of lithic styles. This represents the transition from Binford's forager-type to a collector-type adaptation (Binford 1980). The traditional cultural history of the plains region dates the Archaic period from 6000 B.C. to A.D. 500 and breaks it into three subperiods: Early, Middle, and Late (Cassells 1983; Gunnerson 1987).

The Early Archaic period is dated between 6000 and 3000 B.C. During this time the first architectural structures—pit houses—appeared in the eastern Central High Plains. In addition to architecture, sites commonly had slab-lined storage pits that represent an increase in the reliance on stored goods and longer stays at base camps.

The Middle Archaic (between 3000 and 500 B.C.) is a continuation of the trends begun during the Early Archaic, particularly decreasing mobility. Architecture, in the form of stone circles and pit houses, is more common, and formal grinding stones suggest increasing reliance on gathered resources. Because of this shift in subsistence adaptation, roasting pits and stone-lined storage pits are more common. An increase in the number of sites also probably represents an increase in population.

The Late Archaic is dated between 500 B.C. and A.D. 500. It is characterized by occasional seasonal villages with pit houses and stone circles, as well as a heavy reliance on plants and small game.

Some scholars feel that adaptation in the eastern and western areas of the Central High Plains began to diverge at this time. It has been argued that although the eastern half of the Central High Plains underwent an Archaic-type adaptation, this shift is not evident in the western plains. Rather, the western area had a subsistence economy similar to that of the late Paleoindian period (Johnson and Wood 1980). There is evidence from the Dutch Creek and Massey Draw sites in eastern Jefferson County that this is an accurate reconstruction (Jepson and Hand 1994; Anderson, et al. 1994). Both of these sites have hearths and appear to be short-term camp-sites. Additionally, a bone-processing area in Massey Draw contains the remains of bison, deer, and a variety of small rodents. Both sites are multi-component and comparison of materials from different periods demonstrates remarkable stability. This adaptation represents a highly resilient, broad-spectrum hunting-and-gathering system throughout the Holocene occupation of the area, with changes restricted to lithic style. These lithic changes may be from technological innovation (i.e., introduction of the bow and arrow at the end of the Late Archaic period) or stylistic preferences that are not understood (Butler 1986). However, the same subsistence techniques are used, though there may be slight shifts in hunting strategies due to shifting resources.

This continuity in economy and basic organizational principles through time has forced us to reexamine the period names for the culture history of the Great Plains. Michlovic (1986) has argued that the Early, Middle, and Late Archaic carry the connotations of specific economic, settlement, mobility, and technological organizations (i.e., Archaic-type adaptation) and are inappropriate because of the dual meaning of these labels as both temporal divisions and adaptive strategies. This is particularly true in an area like the Great Plains where there is abundant evidence for stability throughout the Archaic period. In Colorado the phase divisions are based solely on shifts in projectile point styles rather than shifts in adaptive strategy (which are assumed rather than demonstrated). To quote Michlovic, "An evolution from one stage of culture to another is more than a matter of minor changes in the artifact inventory, or simple stylistic variation" (1986: 209).

He further argues that slight shifts in economic orientation at some sites and at certain periods in the prehistory of the Great Plains "do not represent a new life way, but a simple and understandable variation on a basic Plains pattern" (1986: 212). This pattern is dominated by a foraging strategy concentrating on big game, which continued from late Paleoindian times until the adoption of settled village life and horticulture during the Woodland period in the eastern part of the Plains and until abandonment of the area in the 1400s in the west.

Michlovic does not argue that divisions signaled by the appearance of artifacts associated with these categories should be done away with. Rather, he argues that these divisions are strictly temporal. Therefore, loaded culture history labels like Paleoindian and Early, Middle, and Late Archaic may be inappropriate.

Given these arguments, what can be said about the Archaic period in the Central High Plains? William Butler (1986, 1988) argues that eastern Colorado should be included in the western Plains Archaic tradition, which can be divided into a number of local phases based on projectile point styles. In terms of the rest of the material culture assemblage, there is remarkable continuity through time and across space. The tool complex is specialized, with a heavy emphasis on bifacial core reduction, indicating a high degree of mobility. He argues that the end of the western Plains Archaic is transitional, "reflecting a wide range of internal developments and increasing external relations" (1986: 206). Unfortunately he does not elaborate on what these developments include.

There are some specifics in the Archaic period adaptation in eastern Colorado in terms of land-use patterns, subsistence, and tool technology. Despite sparse data, it appears sites are more restricted in location than in previous periods, at least in the northeastern part of the state. Access to water was a major concern because of the area's increased aridity. As such, campsites are often located on terraces of major rivers and streams and are protected from prevailing winds (Greiser 1985).

Favored locations reveal repeated, if somewhat sporadic, use. Anderson and colleagues (1994) argue that Archaic period hunter-gatherer

> groups often use landscapes and regions as the focal point for many resource procurement decisions, rather than for specific site locations. Although the seasonal availability of certain types of resources in the Massey Draw area may have been highly predictable, the specific locations where mobile game resources could be encountered would have been variable. Slight year-to-year variation in resource productivity can easily result in some changes to specific locations where game could be found and procured [due to variations in water and pasturing]. . . . Over the long term, however, such yearly variation should, at some places on the landscape, tend to average out. . . . Over a long period of time, however, such periodic use would lead to a

patterned accumulation of archaeological materials in certain places and more diffuse scatters in others. (1994: 247)

It is possible that the attraction of an area is not limited to environmental factors. Sites that were frequently reused also could be important ritual or political points on the landscape. This becomes increasingly obvious for the eastern Central High Plains in the next period. In addition to continued reuse of small sites, the population aggregations evident in the Paleoindian period are absent, although the territory an individual group occupies increases in size (Greiser 1985).

The lack of aggregation is also evident in the patterns of animal exploitation. Whereas there is continuity in what fauna are used, the manner in which they were harvested is more restricted (Anderson, et al. 1994). The mass kills of earlier times are absent during the Archaic period, due to the smaller herds of the Altithermal (Wedel 1986). These herds were harder to control and could abort or change the direction of a stampede quickly. Interestingly, mass kills on the scale seen during the Paleoindian period do not reappear after the end of the Altithermal in Colorado, when bison herds should have regained their pre-Archaic size. In fact they are largely absent until the protohistoric period on the plains of Colorado, though they are found elsewhere on the Great Plains (Southwell 1996; Frison 1991). Therefore, changes in the labor organization needed to carry out a mass kill also may have occurred. Partial evidence for this can be seen in a breakdown in the long-distance trade networks and the manufacture of highly stylized projectile points associated with them at the end of the Paleoindian period (Hayden 1981). In other words, if social alliances were transforming, the large aggregates of people needed to coordinate and carry out a mass kill may not have been available (Bamforth 1988).

Rather than mass kills, ambush and stalking techniques were employed. These methods could be used on bison, deer, and pronghorn by one or a few individuals and did not result in large bone beds (Greiser 1985).

Continuity through the Archaic period also can be seen in the tool technology. Scrapers, knives, gouges, and nonformal grinding stones are common throughout the Archaic period. What does vary is projectile point style. The Early Archaic is signaled by the appearance of large corner- and side-notched points. Their size indicates they still were used as dart points (Anderson, et al. 1994; Gunnerson 1987).

The McKean Point complex is generally designated as the diagnostic point complex of the Middle Archaic (Frison 1991). The McKean Point

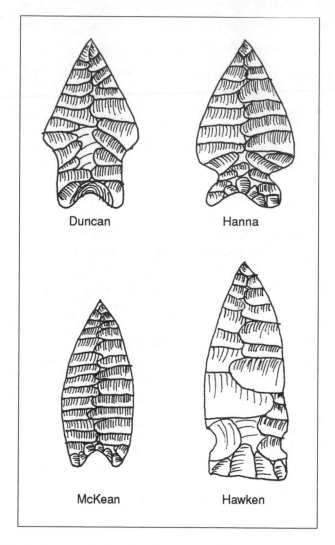

Figure 3.2 Archaic period projectile points of the Central High Plains.

Complex includes the McKean, Duncan, Hanna, and Mallory points (Fig. 3.2), which are often lumped into one type (Butler 1988; Gunnerson 1987). They are characterized by constrictions on the sides of the point near the base that range from shallow indentations to deep notches. The bases are concave and either are deeply indented or have true basal notches.

The McKean complex findings are interpreted in various ways, two of which are contradictory and are outlined by Gunnerson (1987) and Butler

(1988). Gunnerson argues that the presence of a large number of grinding slabs and roasting pits at some McKean sites indicates the McKean complex had a diversified subsistence system in which plants were more important (1983; Frison 1991). Butler argues that the tool complex actually became more specialized with the increased number of point types, indicating a nondiversified subsistence system in which hunting bison was even more important (1988). The floral and faunal data are of little help in this debate. Clearly, this is an issue that needs further study.

The Late Archaic period is equally confusing. Anderson (1994) argues there is continuity in chipped stone assemblages, though ground and pecked stone tools increased in diversity. Additionally, corner-notched points became more common, particularly those with large expanding bases.

THE POST-ARCHAIC PERIOD
ON THE CENTRAL HIGH PLAINS

Pottery, small corner-notched projectile points used with a bow and arrow, and expanding base drills appeared at the end of the Archaic period on the Central High Plains (Butler 1988). The Post-Archaic era consists of three periods: Early, Middle, and Late Woodland, or Ceramic. The Woodland nomenclature is based on affiliations of the eastern prairies with the Woodland areas they border. This affiliation decreases considerably as one moves farther west until it becomes relatively unimportant. As a result it could be argued that the Woodland terminology is inappropriate for the western Central High Plains because it implies a cultural continuity that is absent. Rather, the eras should be referred to as the Early, Middle, and Late Ceramic (Ellwood 1995; Gunnerson 1987). Because of the ambiguity inherent in the traditional woodland taxonomy, the less-meaning-laden Ceramic is used here.

The division between the Early, Middle, and Late Ceramic periods is distinguished by projectile point styles, pottery, and in some areas subsistence and architecture (Cassells 1983; Gunnerson 1987). During each period, there are several regional variants known variously as aspects, foci, or phases. Therefore, the taxonomic classifications can be confusing (Butler 1988). Also, the cultural manifestations in each regional variant are different. Therefore, each is addressed separately.

Note that throughout this period, most of the changes are related to indigenous development and the exchange of goods and ideas from adjacent areas (particularly from the eastern woodlands and the Southwest).

The greater the distance from these sources, the less change in the local area. Although there may be some movement of people within each area, there is very little between areas until later in the Ceramic period. In effect, what may have occurred with the rise of regional variants is ethnogenesis. This is supported not by the differences in material culture but by the differences in concepts of the afterworld, social organization as indicated by site layout and house structure, and patterns of cooperation and competition. The specific behaviors in each area represent a combination of different environmental constraints, particular histories, and different choices in ritual, economics, and social organization.

Early Ceramic Period

As the name implies, the major shift in material culture at this time is the introduction of pottery, apparently from the eastern woodlands. This assertion is based on the fact that it first appears in the eastern prairies and is technologically and stylistic similar to eastern woodland vessels (Ellwood 1995; Gunnerson 1987; Wedel 1986).

Ceramic typology for eastern Colorado has been compiled by Priscilla Ellwood (1995), whose type designations are used here. Vessels are constructed through the paddle-and-anvil method in which coils of clay are built up into a jar form, with a conical base. The coils are securely joined by hitting the exterior of the vessel with a paddle while a small anvil is held on the inside. The paddle is often cord-wrapped, resulting in a roughened, or cord-marked surface. Vessels were low-fired. Temper varied depending on the location of manufacture and availability of material, though crushed rock and sand were the most common.

Lithic technology also witnessed a transformation (Fig. 3.3). In addition to the full ranges of knives and scrapers, there were small projectile point styles with corner-notched and straight to convex sides and bases. Their smaller size is interpreted as the introduction of the bow and arrow. The presence of large points indicates continued use of the atlatl (Anderson, et al. 1994; Butler 1988; Cassells 1983; Gunnerson 1987).

In the eastern Central High Plains, corn was introduced. The species of corn indicates it came from the east (Gunnerson 1987; Wedel 1986). However, its appearance had little impact on settlement patterns and subsistence activity until after A.D. 1000 (Johnson and Wood 1980). In fact, as one moves west, the evidence of corn diminishes, and it is completely absent in some areas of the Central High Plains (Gunnerson 1987).

Plains corner notched

Figure 3.3 Early Ceramic period projectile points of the Central High Plains.

Despite maintaining a hunter-gatherer lifestyle, mobility decreased in the eastern Central High Plains. Evidence for this occurs in the form of shallow pit houses at some base camps (Gunnerson 1987). These base camps may have been used for an entire season.

In the western area (including eastern Colorado) a high degree of mobility continues with habitation restricted to small, temporary campsites. Shallow basins at some sites indicate shelters (Ellwood 1995). Additionally, the subsistence system remains relatively unchanged from the Archaic period throughout eastern Colorado (Butler 1988; Eighmy 1994). This also is true of the lithic assemblage and settlement pattern.

Regional variants are defined based mostly on projectile point and ceramic styles. However, there are also differences in the burial patterns with the eastern areas having ritual mortuary traits reminiscent of the eastern woodlands, particularly in the use of ossuaries. However, as Cassells (1983) indicates, these can be found (though on a smaller scale) as far west as Colorado. Gunnerson (1987) has defined six regional complexes for the Central High Plains, two of which are in Colorado (Fig. 3.4). In general, sites in the eastern area are concentrated along rivers and reflect the continued use and diversification of subsistence strategies started during the Archaic period. Conversely, sites in the western areas are found in the same areas as those of the previous Archaic period and appear to reflect a continuation of the hunting-and-gathering strategies of earlier times with a

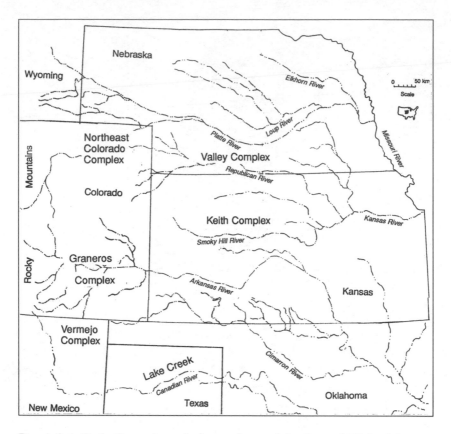

Figure 3.4 Early Ceramic period complexes of the Central High Plains.

concentration on bison (Gunnerson 1987; Eighmy 1994; Johnson and Wood 1980; Krause 1995).

The Valley Complex. The Valley complex is restricted to south-central Nebraska—in particular, the area north of the Republican River. As during the Archaic period, most of the habitation sites are seasonal, with sites positioned to maximize access to raw materials, subsistence goods, and important political or ritual areas (Anderson, et al. 1994).

At most habitation sites, hearths and pit houses are common. Pit houses are generally shallow pits surrounded by postholes and range 3.4 to 7.3 meters (11 to 24 feet) in diameter (Gunnerson 1987). However, the small depressions and insubstantial nature of the superstructure, indicated by the posthole arrangement, do not argue for a substantial decrease in mobility. Rather, these structures represent skin-covered houses that could be moved easily. That is, pit houses were part of a repertoire that was well suited to the mobile hunting-and-gathering existence of the early Ceramic period (Johnson and Wood 1980).

The Keith Complex. The Keith complex is an eastern complex that dominates western Kansas. It is found both north and south of the Smoky Hill River and at a few sites along the Arkansas River. Most sites, however, are on the Republican River. Its close association with the Valley complex can be seen in site layout and pit house structure. At many of these sites, there is evidence of repeated short-term occupations similar to those of the Archaic period. This is particularly evident in the sacred use of the landscape (see below).

Pottery decoration distinguishes the Keith from the Valley complex. Specifically, Keith complex sites have fabric-marked pottery as well as cord-marked ceramics (Gunnerson 1987). This texturing technique is created by wrapping woven fabric around the paddle rather than cordage, resulting in a fine checkerboard pattern.

One of the most diagnostic aspects of the Keith complex is the mortuary practices and the implications they have for ritual, concepts of death and community, and territoriality. At many sites burial remains show a mixture of concepts regarding proper mortuary ritual. At some campsites there are primary burials in individual pits. At most, however, secondary bundle burials are found, while at still others, ossuary and burial mounds are found. Grave goods are highly variable, though beads made of both freshwater mussel and marine (primarily *Olivella* and *Marginella*) shells from the Gulf of Mexico are common, as are tubular bone beads. Rarely, in eastern sites, there is sheet mica, red ocher, and shell gorgets similar to those used by the Hopewell peoples of the eastern woodlands (Wedel 1986). However, the farther west the site, the fewer and simpler the burials.

The most spectacular and complex burial displays are found in Kansas and Nebraska (Gunnerson 1987; Wedel 1986). In the east, where the Republican River drops south into Kansas, these sites contain both ossuaries and burial mounds. Conversely, along the river in Nebraska, the mounds are missing.

Mounds are usually on bluffs overlooking rivers and appear to serve numerous campsites scattered on the floodplain below. They range from 6 to 15 meters (20 to 50 feet) in diameter and 2 meters (6.5 feet) in height. All are earth filled and overlie a circular or oval basin. At some mound sites, burial areas are paved with stone beneath the bone. The shallow basin serves as an ossuary in which the bones of numerous (often twenty or more) individuals are mixed together. These bones are often highly fragmented and frequently partially burned, although the cremation did not occur at the burial mound. Often a single articulated individual is found at the ossuary (Wedel 1986). After interment, the basin was covered with fill.

Sites to the west lack mounds but have ossuaries consisting of either a series of pits that hold one or two individuals, shallow basins of up to sixty individuals, or both (Gunnerson 1987; Wedel 1986). Sometimes a large ossuary may have a single articulated burial. As with the mound sites to the east, these sites are usually on bluffs and terraces overlooking campsites but are not associated directly with campsites at this time (though they are during the Middle Ceramic period).

In both mound and nonmound ossuaries, subadults and adults as well as males and females were buried the same. Partially articulated material indicates that the ritual process did not last over a standard length of time. Rather, the varying levels of articulation represent periodic, or calendric, ceremonies in which all those who had died since the last ceremony were interred, regardless of when they died.

The traditional interpretation of mound and nonmound sites is one of a diffusion of elaborate mortuary practices west from the Hopewell heartland (Cassells 1983; Gunnerson 1987). Whereas the dates of the Early Ceramic period generally agree with those of the Hopewell phenomenon, there are problems with this proposal. First, although postmortem manipulation of body parts did occur in the Hopewell core area, ossuaries are not found. Instead, disarticulated skeletons were interred in individual secondary or bundle burials (Braun 1979). Additionally, the ritual symbols and extensive trade networks that accompany the Hopewell system are absent in the Central High Plains sites (Braun 1986). Therefore, mortuary ritual in the Keith complex should be seen as an indigenous development, with minimal influence from the eastern woodlands.

Why then did the mortuary ritual change in this area during the Early Ceramic period? Krause (1995) argues that we should view Ceramic period mortuary behavior as an active stage of symbolic manipulation. Ritual transformation may relate to changing views of interpersonal relationships and the renegotiation of social and political networks. He states that this is part of a social transformation in which economic cooperation changes from the level of the family to a larger corporate group and finally to the community level. Krause's study deals specifically with Middle Ceramic mortuary ritual, but his ideas can be expanded to include Early Ceramic remains.

In many ways the Early Ceramic represents a period of transition along the Republican River in Kansas. Subsistence shifted from hunting and gathering of the Archaic period to horticulture and foraging in the Middle Ceramic period. Mobility also changed, resulting in the sedentary villages of the Middle Ceramic period. But this shift could not occur without changing perspectives of landscape and place, land use, and territoriality. Burial practice of the Early Ceramic period may be integrally tied to, and necessary for, this transformation.

At the end of the Late Archaic and beginning of the Early Ceramic periods, reuse of important points on the landscape for economic reasons is evident. Therefore, ritual reuse of a point on the landscape, as ossuary sites in the area represent, is an extension of an existing pattern. We can assume that ossuary sites saw long-term and repetitive use by a group because of the large number of individuals buried at the site and superposition of features.

However, the reuse of the landscape is more than just an extension of an economic activity, because a ritual change is also present—specifically, an increased formalization of the relationship between the living and their ancestors through the use of cemeteries. This relationship is often associated with an increased connection of a group with specific plots of land, both spiritually and economically (Charles and Buikstra 1983; Saxe 1970). Formal cemeteries tie a group to a specific locale by symbolizing the ancestral claims of a people to use the area (Stone and Howell 1994). These cemeteries are markers that spiritually and ritually tie the group to the area through mortuary rituals. The change in rituals at this time is an integral part of social group formation and territoriality (i.e., ethnogenesis), rather than a nebulous diffusion westward of an idea from a people and area (the Hopewell core area) that are dramatically different.

Northeast Colorado Complex. The economic adaptation of the Northeast Colorado complex shows little or no difference from the Archaic period. Groups are relatively small and highly mobile. Hunting and gathering concentrates on bison, deer, and antelope, procured mostly through stalking. Projectile points and conical-shaped, cord-marked pottery distinguish it from other periods (Eighmy 1994; Gunnerson 1987).

Because it is a mobile and specialized subsistence system, sites are found in more diverse areas. Not restricted to permanent water sources, open sites are found on south-facing slopes away from rivers. This affords protection from the wind while allowing a view of the surrounding area (Gunnerson 1987). Rock shelters were often used as winter dwellings, almost always facing south or southwest to absorb solar heat.

However, winter sites were much less common than warm-weather ones (Greiser 1985). Wedel argues this is because of a lack of edible plants and, most important, firewood in the winter. He concludes that there was a "probable seasonal abandonment of the Colorado portions of the Republican drainage and withdrawal eastward . . . to lower sections of the main [Republican River] valley" (1986: 94).

Graneros Complex. The Graneros complex is on the western edge of the Central High Plains. It dominates central and southern portions of eastern Colorado, though it is most common along the Arkansas River and the Chaquaqua Plateau. Little is known about the economic, political, or social organization, although investigations indicate a hunting-and-gathering society (Gunnerson 1987).

As in northeastern Colorado, it is distinguished from the periods that proceed and follow it by projectile point style, pottery, and the presence of architecture (Baugh 1994; Gunnerson 1987). Specifically, round architectural structures, from 2.4 to 4.6 meters (8 to 15 feet) in diameter, constructed of several courses of dry-laid masonry with plastered floors are present. In many ways these structures resemble later rock-ring structures, though they can be distinguished by their higher density of building stone and plastered floors (Gunnerson 1987).

Because data for agriculture are extremely limited, it is unclear what these structures represent (Gunnerson 1987). The presence of architecture is normally interpreted as an increase in sedentism, whereas the lack of corn pollen and macrobotanicals indicates hunting and gathering. It is possible that mobility decreased due to factors other than changes in subsistence, but we do not know what these factors were.

Vermejo Complex. The Vermejo complex is located in the western foothills of the Sangre de Cristo Mountains near Cimarron, New Mexico, and north through the Raton pass to the headwaters of the Purgatory River. This area is particularly interesting and confusing because of the presence of Southwestern-like pit houses. Additionally, the ceramics are different from elsewhere in the Central High Plains in that they are manufactured in the coil-and-scrape technique of the Southwest rather than the paddle-and-anvil method common to the Great Plains. Some of these ceramics may be tradewares, although many appear to be manufactured locally (Mitchell 1996). The architecture consists of more formal and substantial dry-laid masonry structures than those found in the Graneros complex and in many ways is similar to that of the northern Rio Grande area. Many scholars argue that these Southwestern traits represent a northern expansion of Northern Tiwa peoples (i.e., Taos) into the area (Gunnerson 1987). This has been challenged, however, in southeastern Colorado and the Lake Trinidad area (Gunnerson 1989; Mitchell 1996). These studies argue that there were no migrations into the area during the Ceramic period, but that changes in mobility, subsistence, and architecture reflect indigenous developments and changing trade patterns. During the Early Ceramic period, the trade relations in this area were directed south and were initiated, at least in part, by the peoples of Colorado. The reasons for adoption of Southwestern traits are not clear but may relate to internal competition for status and solidification of contacts with trade partners to the south.

Lake Creek Complex. The Lake Creek complex, centered in the Texas panhandle along the Canadian River, contains a mixture of the characteristics that define the Vermejo and Graneros complexes—conical base, cord-marked paddle-and-anvil, and coil-and-scrape pottery. Unlike the Vermejo complex, however, much of the coil-and-scrape pottery represents trade with Southwestern peoples in the El Paso area rather than the northern Rio Grande or local manufacture (Baush 1994; Gunnerson 1987; Gustafson 1994). The ceramics in Lake Creek sites are a result of trade between people of the Texas panhandle with those to the south and west as part of their yearly rounds. These individuals were highly mobile, with a subsistence pattern of broad-spectrum foraging, with bison representing only a minor component (Baugh 1994).

During later times (A.D. 1200 to 1700), there is considerable evidence for exchange between the Pueblo peoples of the Rio Grande area and Great Plains peoples along the Canadian and Red Rivers. This evidence is in the form of Puebloan pottery recovered from Plains sites in northern Texas and alibates flint from Texas at Pueblo sites (Baugh 1994; Schroeder 1994). The Southwestern pottery found in Lake Creek sites during the Early Ceramic period may represent an earlier trade pattern that was directed north and south, perhaps in conjunction with yearly rounds following bison migration. Later, as bison migrations shifted north (see Chapter 1), these routes also shifted, resulting in an east–west orientation (Spielmann 1983).

Middle Ceramic Period

The Middle Ceramic period is a dynamic one, witnessing further diversification of the subsistence, mobility, and social patterns that began during the Early Ceramic period. The divisions between eastern and western Great Plains groups are more noticeable as eastern groups became sedentary with economies that focused on bison hunting, gathering, fishing, and corn farming. As would be expected, villages were largely restricted to terraces and bluffs overlooking the tributary systems where floodwater farming was practiced (Gunnerson 1987; Wedel 1986). These were ideal locations because of plentiful fauna (birds, fish, deer, and bison) throughout the year. Also, the risk of flooding was much lower than on the rivers (Wedel 1986).

The reasons for this shift in the east are not totally clear. Researchers have argued for migrations of one group or another into the area, in particular the expansion of Hopewellian groups or Caddoan speakers from the eastern woodlands (Vehik 1994). However, many believe this is an indigenous development due to a number of different factors, the most important of which is the onset of the Pacific climatic period that resulted in warmer, drier conditions and shifts in bison migrations (Gustafson 1994). In other words, agriculture and gathering became increasingly important as bison herds shrank in size (Gunnerson 1987; Gustafson 1995; Roper 1995).

The western groups continued, for the most part, with a hunting-and-gathering lifestyle dominated by bison procurement. Continued bison hunting was possible in the western half of the Central High Plains because the bison absence period on the southern Plains, and to some degree in the eastern high Plains, is not evident in eastern Colorado (Butler 1992). It should be noted, however, that mass kills are not evident and hunting probably was still through stalking and ambushes of individual or small groups of bison (Wedel 1986).

There is good evidence that the differences in ritual and social and political organization, which began in the previous period between different regions, were more marked at this time (Gunnerson 1987). In other words, the process of ethnogenesis continued.

Certain characteristics allow the Middle Ceramic designation to be applied throughout the Central High Plains despite spatial variability (Anderson, et al. 1994; Cassells 1983; Ellwood 1995; Gunnerson 1987). In particular, projectile points are small and contain either side notches or lack notches entirely (Fig. 3.5). These points are associated with the dominant bow-and-arrow technology. The lithic assemblage contains distinctive

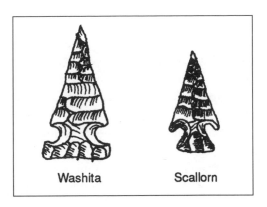

Figure 3.5 Middle Ceramic period projectile points of the Central High Plains.

diamond-shaped knives with alternating beveled edges. Expanding base drills and scraper forms of the previous period continue to be used.

The ceramics are morphologically and stylistically different from the previous period. In general, vessel form is more globular than conical, with northern and southern variations (Butler 1988). In northern Colorado, along the South Platte and Republican Rivers, ceramics are associated with the Upper Republican complex. In southern Colorado, along the Purgatory and Arkansas Rivers, they are associated with the Panhandle complex. Upper Republican ceramics are characterized by short necks and vertical flaring or "collared" rims (Ellwood 1995). The collared rims are thickened and overhang the neck, accentuating the constricted area. The rims on these vessels are occasionally incised; otherwise, vessels are cord-marked, though plain surface vessels also are found. The most common temper type is coarse quartz sand or crushed granite (Ellwood 1995).

Panhandle complex pottery is usually cord-marked or striated; plain surfaces are rare (Ellwood 1995). Occasionally the rims are decorated and almost always flared. They are distinguished from Upper Republican ceramics by the use of grit temper.

In addition to the distinction in material culture on a north–south axis, there are east–west differences. Areas in the eastern Great Plains commonly contain deer and bison scapula hoes and tibia digging sticks as well as stone elbow pipes. These are uncommon in the west, particularly in Colorado (Anderson, et al. 1994; Gunnerson 1987). Also found at eastern sites are deer and bison mandible sickles and corn shellers. Ground stone is more common and formalized in the east. Also, fish hooks have been recovered from permanent villages along the rivers.

A further spatial distinction exists in subsistence, settlement pattern, and site layout. The Plains Village pattern is established in some areas with formal architectural structures and a substantial commitment to agriculture. Related to the increased reliance on corn agriculture and sedentism, most habitation sites are now on rivers and major tributaries. This increased commitment to horticulture may be due to the introduction of corn species that are drought-resistant, and therefore more productive, on the Great Plains from the Southwest (Gunnerson 1987).

However, there is a great deal of variation between the northeastern and southeastern areas of the Central High Plains, indicating major differences in ritual, social, and political organization. In the west, there is also variation in the prehistoric record. In general, it can be argued that the village complex was never really established in Colorado, though some would argue that a "dilute form of the plains Village Pattern" occurs in the northeast portion of the state where stone circles are evident (Anderson, et al. 1995: 24).

As mentioned above, there are two general axes of variability. There is an east–west axis with agriculture increasing in importance in the eastern areas. The approximate dividing line between eastern and western areas is at the Colorado border (Ellwood 1995; Gunnerson 1987; Johnson and Wood 1980). The north–south axis relates to differences in trade patterns (Butler 1988; Ellwood 1995). Groups to the south traded more frequently with the Pueblo groups to the southwest, whereas northern groups directed more of their trade toward the Mississippian cultures of the eastern woodlands. The closer to these sources an individual was, the more intense the trade relations (Gunnerson 1987).

Based on the differences in these axes, Gunnerson (1987) has defined five major variants for the Central High Plains during the Middle Ceramic period (Fig. 3.6). Each of these is discussed below.

Upper Republican Complex. The Upper Republican complex is found along the Republican River, particularly in southern Nebraska and northern Kansas. Aspects that characterize this complex are a formalization of those found in the Valley and Keith complexes of the previous period. These formalizations are associated with the changing social dynamics related to increasing sedentism and an increased reliance on horticulture. They are especially evident in terms of site structure and mortuary ritual.

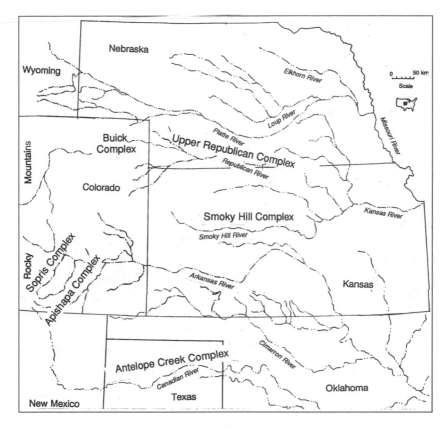

Figure 3.6 Middle Ceramic period complexes of the Central High Plains.

Architecture is more substantial than in the previous period (Gunnerson 1987; Roper 1995). Domestic architecture is dominated by structures built on cleared ground that may extend several inches below the surface. They are either oval or square with rounded corners. The oval structures are quite large—11 to 14.6 meters (37 to 49 feet) in length, whereas the square houses average 8 to 8.5 meters (27 to 28 feet). They have a long covered entrance facing away from the prevailing northwest winter winds (Wedel 1986). A central hearth, four center post supports, and bell-shaped storage pits 1.5 meters (5 feet) deep are typical (Gunnerson 1987; Wedel 1986). The large structures are referred to as earth lodges and are similar to those used in eastern Kansas and Nebraska at the time of contact (Holder 1970). The lodges probably housed extended families, or lineages, whereas a single family occupied the smaller structures.

Unlike historic times, however, the villages were relatively small and dispersed (Roper 1995). Most sites contained a single or a small cluster of lodges. In general, the farther east the site, the larger the village. In the east, villages held up to twenty-two lodges, although they may not have been occupied at the same time—the life of an earth lodge tends to be less than ten years (Wedel 1986). Conversely, the farther west the site is on the Republican River, the more likely the site is to consist of an isolated lodge. In northeastern Colorado there are no sites with permanent habitation structures, but stone circles are present (Ellwood 1995; Gunnerson 1987).

Mortuary ritual also tends to be more formal and elaborate than in the previous period. Burial mounds were built over basin ossuaries on bluffs overlooking habitation sites throughout the area (Wedel 1986). There is some size diversity in the mounds and in the amount and type of grave goods included in the ossuaries (Gunnerson 1987; Krause 1995). However, formal cemeteries are more common and are found at most habitation sites. In other words, multiple communities no longer shared a single cemetery, even though individuals may have attended mortuary rituals in adjacent villages.

The existence of mounds and artifacts with iconography similar to that found in Mississippian sites has been used to argue for further diffusion of mortuary ritual from the east (Gunnerson 1987; Wedel 1986). However, Krause's (1995) study of twenty-three burial mound sites on the Republican River in Kansas challenges this interpretation.

These mounds date to the Middle Ceramic period and are found in isolation or, in larger sites, in clusters. All show periodic use and exhibit the addition of soil, grave offerings, and bodies. Beyond this, however, there is a great deal of variability. They range from 1.8 to 17 meters (6 to 57 feet) long and 28 centimeters to 3.7 meters (11 inches to 12 feet) high, averaging 7.09 meters (23.6 feet) and 69.4 centimeters (27 inches), respectively (Krause 1995).

There also is considerable variability in the nature of the burials. Almost all are ossuaries, although bone processing and selection varies considerably. Additionally, while some have evidence of burning and chopping, in others it is missing. Formal crematoriums are absent in all the sites (Krause 1995). The variability in postmortem treatment of bone is similar to that in the Keith complex of the Early Ceramic period, indicating the ritual continuity in this area.

There is also continuity in grave goods. The most common offerings are shell disk beads from freshwater mussels, as well as *Olivella* beads, tubular bone beads, ceramics, projectile points, stone pipes, and pendants.

As with the previous period, the exact makeup of the mortuary assemblage varies from cemetery to cemetery.

The major difference between the ossuaries of the Early and Middle Ceramic periods is the addition of mounds throughout the area and the long-term use of larger mounds in the Middle Ceramic. Burial mounds served as community shrines and symbols of community identity. Periodic rituals of community purification probably were performed at them. Krause (1995)argues that the addition of the mounds and their ceremonial use represents their continuation in the social renegotiation that began in the previous period. As sedentism increased, this renegotiation was intensified, and the importance of expanding corporate group size and individual and group cooperation became even more important. The sponsoring of mortuary rituals and mound construction are interpreted by Krause as an attempt by family leaders to manipulate relationships of social debt with other individuals. That is, burial mounds and mortuary ritual are "the means for creating, and the conduit for distributing, power and authority" (Krause 1995: 142) in the area.

Buick Complex. Whereas the Republican River extends into northeastern Colorado, the Upper Republican complex does not, though Colorado may have served as a resource area for its Upper Republican peoples. Therefore, dependence on agriculture, permanent villages, and elaborate mortuary rituals are not found in eastern Colorado. Instead, the Buick complex, which is centered along the South Platte River and throughout northeastern Colorado, is a continuation of the hunting-gathering adaptation, with a concentration on bison hunting seen during the previous period (Butler 1988; Eighmy 1994; Ellwood 1995; Gunnerson 1987). This does not mean that Buick complex people were unaware of their Upper Republican neighbors. Some stone circle and nonarchitectural sites in northeastern Colorado have been interpreted as evidence of hunting parties from the Upper Republican core area (Anderson, et al. 1995). However, the contacts were minimal, and there is little evidence of exchange of goods or ideas between the two groups.

Because the Buick complex was a mobile hunting-and-gathering society, sites are small and ephemeral. Pit houses and stone circles are occasionally found, but most sites were short-term camps lacking formal architecture (Butler 1988; Ellwood 1995; Gunnerson 1987). Based on ethnographic analogy, sites with stone circles were winter sites. Stones were used by many ethnographic groups to hold down the edges of skin-covered structures when the ground was frozen. In summer the poles were secured with pins or stakes driven into the ground (Kingsbury and Gabel 1983). Wintertime use of stone circle sites is further supported by the presence of hearths in many. Stone circles dating to the Middle Ceramic period in northeastern Colorado range from 4 to 6.5 meters (13 to 22 feet) in diameter. Sites contain anywhere from one to twenty rings, suggesting fluid group membership and periodic aggregations in winter (Morris, et al. 1983).

Most sites were near permanent water, but on smaller tributaries rather than major drainages (Ellwood 1995). Southern exposures and locations with good views of the surrounding prairies were preferred (Butler 1988). In general, this period represents continued use of a highly resilient and stable adaptation first established during the Early Archaic period in the area.

Smoky Hill Complex. The Smoky Hill complex is found along the Smoky Hill River in western Kansas. It does not extend into eastern Colorado. As with the Upper Republican complex, Smoky Hill is a regional variant of the Plains Village pattern, with a dual economy directed toward raising corn and hunting bison. Burial mounds were used but in a different way than in the Upper Republican area. Rather than ossuaries, the burials represent individual primary burials, with no evidence of postmortem handling of the body. This pattern is similar to that found in the Caddoan branch of the Mississippian complex (Gunnerson 1987). Despite this similarity and the fact that both areas were inhabited by Caddoan speakers at the time of contact, the nature of the contact between the two areas in prehistoric times is unclear.

The second difference between Upper Republican and Smoky Hill complex burial mounds is that the Smoky Hill mounds are not located in the habitation sites, but are outside the village limits (Gunnerson 1987). This physical separation of domestic and sacred areas indicates a different relationship between the living and spirit world and the transition between the two.

The remaining difference relates to the architectural style and does not represent differences in social and economic organization. Specifically, square long houses, averaging 16 meters (53 feet) each side, are found in the Smoky Hill Complex, but they are not subterranean.

Antelope Creek Complex. The southernmost of the eastern complexes, Antelope Creek is located along the Canadian River in the panhandles of Texas and Oklahoma. Antelope Creek is similar to the other eastern complexes in that the sites are located on major river systems, are occupied year-round, and are occupied by individuals participating in a dual economy. It differs from the Upper Republican and Smoky Hill complexes in site layout (which relates to family and corporate group structure), mortuary ritual, and evidence of extensive trade between Antelope Creek and the Southwestern Pueblos.

Settlement pattern shifts significantly from that found during the Early Ceramic period (Lake Creek complex). As the inhabitants of this area became more sedentary due to a decreased reliance on bison, site location was more restricted. Habitation sites on the terraces above creeks and tributaries were surrounded by smaller hunting-and-gathering camps (Gunnerson 1987).

Architecture consists of multiroom structures of rubble-filled masonry early in the sequence, with isolated rooms becoming more common later on (Baugh 1994; Gunnerson 1987). Room size indicates nuclear families as opposed to the extended-family lodges of the north. Conversely, architecture at most sites is stone and multiroomed, which may indicate an economically cooperating group (i.e., a corporate group). The structure of the relationships between individual families is undoubtedly different from that found in the earth lodge villages to the north.

These multiroom structures range in size from one to thirty-five rooms and are generally constructed of stone slabs set on edge in parallel rows about 1 meter (3 feet) apart. The space between these rows is filled with earth. The walls are generally several courses, reaching a height of about 1.5 meters (5 feet), becoming thinner with each course and ending in a width of approximately 30 centimeters (12 inches) at the top (Gunnerson 1987). Ventilator shafts are common in the rooms, as are wall niches and what appear to be clay altars.

The multiroom masonry construction and use of ventilator shafts, wall niches, and clay altars were originally interpreted as an indication of a westward expansion of Pueblo peoples. However, transitional sites between Lake Creek– and Antelope Creek–type adaptation argue for indigenous development as a result of decreased bison herds (Gustafson 1995; see also Chapter 1). There is a great deal of evidence for trade relations between Antelope Creek and Pueblo peoples, but it is unclear if this contact was direct or through a third, more mobile, group in the southern Plains (Baugh 1994; Schroeder 1994; Spielmann 1983). The presence of these extensive trade networks is a continuation and formalization of trading patterns found in the previous period, although the trade networks shifted somewhat north.

Sopris Complex. The Sopris complex is located along the Purgatory River (a southern tributary of the Arkansas River) and south through the Raton Pass into New Mexico. Variability in population density, mobility, subsistence, and trade patterns has led some, including Gunnerson (1987) and Baugh (1994), to subdivide this area into two regions: Sopris and Cimarron. However, these divisions are chronological rather than geographic and the characteristics noted by Gunnerson and others are due to temporal variability. Therefore, they do not justify a geographic division.

The major source of variation throughout time is the amount of interaction the local population had with adjacent areas (Baugh 1994). This interaction is not merely a borrowing of traits from adjacent areas but rather a shifting of alliances and a manipulating of trade relations (Mitchell 1996).

Despite shifting relations throughout the region, it does not appear that peoples moved into the area. Instead, demographic continuity is evident in site layout and gradual changes in architectural style arising from the masonry structures of earlier periods (the Vermejo complex). Throughout this area, architectural features at habitation sites consisted of circular or square structures with rounded corners. Construction techniques and materials included jacal, adobe, and dry-laid masonry (Baugh 1994; Butler 1988; Ellwood 1995; Mitchell 1996). The number of structures at any given site ranges from one to thirty-seven. Generally, the structures were individual, though some were contiguous (Cassells 1983). Although rarely used, rock shelters had interiors that were subdivided with masonry walls (Gunnerson 1987). Burials were flexed and usually found under house floors and in storage pits (Mitchell 1996).

Continuity also occurs in site placement and in the subsistence pattern. Sites were generally restricted to high terraces or isolated mesas overlooking well-watered valley floors. This was a hunter-gatherer society that also practiced limited horticulture (Baugh 1994; Butler 1988; Gunnerson 1987), though agriculture was more common south of Raton Pass. Hunting focused on individual bison, pronghorn, and a variety of smaller mammals (Ellwood 1995).

This area has been subdivided according to differences in ceramics, both locally made and those that were traded. Sites north and south of Raton Pass (what Gunnerson calls the Sopris and Cimmaron areas, respectively) contain coil-and-scrape Taos-style ceramics of local clays and ceramics manufactured in the Taos area (Mitchell 1996). The style and manufacturing techniques have led many to argue that occupation in the area represents a northern expansion of peoples ancestral to Taos (Ellwood 1995; Glassow 1980; Gunnerson 1987).

Recently, however, this interpretation has been called into question. Mitchell argues that the local inhabitants of the Purgatory River area maintained constant and reciprocal relationships with their neighbors. To understand these relationships, we must reassess concepts of cultural boundaries as well as the trade and chronometric data (Mitchell 1996).

Southwestern ceramics appeared south of Raton Pass as early as A.D. 900. It has been argued that the greatest distribution of Taos-style ceramics occurred between A.D. 1100 and 1225 (Baugh 1994; Gunnerson 1987; Schroeder 1994). However, recent recalibration of archaeomagnetic dates with the revised Southwest Archaeomagnetic Master Curve indicates considerable contact between A.D. 950 and 1050. Ceramic cross-dating indicates continued, significant contact between the Taos and Upper Purgatory areas until A.D. 1225, after which occupation along the Purgatory River was sparse. Mitchell (1996) argues that when the Upper Purgatory River basin was abandoned, the inhabitants, who now thought of themselves as Southwestern rather than Plains peoples, moved closer to Taos.

The trade relations between the Taos and Upper Purgatory River region must be examined from both a Taos and Sopris perspective to be understood. Before A.D. 900, occupation in the northern Rio Grande area, including the Taos region, underwent a number of changes. Sites consisted of a few seasonally occupied, shallow pit houses (Cordell 1989; Glassow 1980). By A.D. 900 we see increased sedentism and reliance on corn agriculture. Evidence of trade with groups to the south is sparse and limited to down-the-line trade. Between A.D. 1000 and 1100/1150, occupation in the Taos area was low, but sedentism and agricultural dependence increased. Sites shifted to a PI-type configuration with multiple-room, aboveground adobe and masonry structures (see Chapter 4). During this time several large trade networks, including the Chaco phenomenon, operated in the Southwest. Although trade in the Chaco area by Taos inhabitants was limited, the amount of trade northward from Taos increased. These trade relations were extended and strengthened between A.D. 1100/1150 and 1225, corresponding with the rising population in the Rio Grande area, which is particularly noticeable near modern-day Albuquerque and Santa Fe. The reasons for the population increase are a matter of contention and may be related to indigenous growth or migration from the San Juan basin (Cordell 1989). Schroeder (1994) argues this population increase may have resulted in social and demographic pressure on the southern edge of the Taos area starting as early as A.D. 1100. If migration into the Rio Grande did occur and resulted in the kind of pressure Schroeder refers to, expansion of trade relations by Taos to the north could have been an attempt to stabilize its position by expanding and formalizing alliances with peoples with whom it previously had limited contact. But to confirm this, we need to understand the demographic shifts throughout the Rio Grande region better.

Trade ended between Taos and southeastern Colorado in A.D. 1225, possibly as a reaction to migrants into the Taos area. Beginning in A.D. 1225 and rapidly expanding after 1275, the Four Corners area was abandoned because of a protracted drought (see Chapter 4), during which the inhabitants migrated to the Rio Grande (Cordell 1989; Lekson and Cameron 1995). A new social dynamic of relations and boundaries had to be negotiated. This negotiation occurred at the same time as droughtlike conditions occurred in the Taos area. In response, Taos contracted its northern trade relations to shore up its position in the Rio Grande region.

Throughout Taos's expansion and formalization of trade relations to the north, the inhabitants of the Purgatory River experienced a number of changes. After A.D. 900 they became increasingly sedentary and somewhat dependent on horticulture. Additionally, trade relations shifted away from other Great Plains groups and concentrated on their southern neighbors. From A.D. 1100 to 1225, most of the ceramics found at Sopris sites are from the Taos area (Ellwood 1995). Mitchell (1996) argues that the changing settlement pattern, subsistence regime, and trade relations resulted in shifting social identities in the Upper Purgatory River area and that Sopris peoples came to think of themselves as part of the northern Taos frontier. Therefore, when Taos began to contract its trade relations in reaction to changing demographic and social factors on the Rio Grande, Sopris people contracted in kind and moved south of the Raton Pass.

If this reconstruction is correct, why did the inhabitants of southeastern Colorado agree to participate in trade relations with the people of Taos in the first place? The use and maintenance of long-distance trade relations by individuals to enhance personal status is one possibility. Using trade rather than traditional methods to enhance personal status is not unexpected given the need to renegotiate personal relationships with increasing sedentism (Saitta 1991). However, more research is needed on the early phase of the Sopris complex to understand this process.

Apishapa Complex. The Apishapa complex is found along the Apishapa River, a southern tributary of the Arkansas River in southeastern Colorado, to the east of the Purgatory River. The Apishapa complex is generally viewed as a local manifestation of the Upper Canark regional variant, which includes the Antelope Creek complex (Baugh 1994; Lintz 1986), although Gunnerson (1989) argues for a closer affiliation with Upper

Republican material. As in the Sopris area to the west, Apishapa complex settlement appears to be an outgrowth of earlier local adaptations, specifically the Graneros complex.

Continuity between the Graneros and Apishapa phases is evident in settlement patterns of sites located on terraces and isolated mesas overlooking well-watered valley floors. Additionally, although small-scale horticulture was part of the subsistence economy by the Middle Ceramic period, hunting-and-gathering still dominated (Gunnerson 1989). In fact, Apishapa sites may not represent year-round occupation but rather base camps to which hunter-gatherers were tethered and where horticulture was practiced to supplement wild resources (Baugh 1994).

Apishapa complex sites are identified by single-room masonry structures and globular-shaped, cord-roughened pottery made by the paddle-and-anvil method (Ellwood 1995). These sites appear as early as A.D. 1000, though the heaviest occupation is from A.D. 1250 to 1400 (Baugh 1994; Gunnerson 1989). Trade relations intensified with areas to the southeast, specifically with other groups of the Upper Canark regional variant, including the Antelope Creek complex. After A.D. 1400, the area was abandoned when Apishapa peoples moved to the east with the onset of drought.

Abandonment. By the mid-1400s, much of eastern Colorado was abandoned for approximately fifty years, though this is not true of Kansas and Nebraska. This abandonment is usually linked to environmental factors, specifically a drought that began in A.D. 1350 (Baugh 1994). Occupation in marginal areas was even more precarious because of local climatic variations and three severe droughts at the end of the Pacific period in the mid-1400s (Schroder 1994). The more sedentary nature of settlements in southeastern Colorado and the reliance on agriculture in western Nebraska and Kansas further limited the prehistoric inhabitants' ability to follow the bison herds during this period. The result was a movement to the east along the major river systems and a consolidation of linguistically related groups. The outcome was a coalition of Caddoan-speaking groups (Pawnee and Wichita) living in villages on the eastern edge of the central Plains at the time of European contact (Gunnerson 1987, 1989; Schlesier 1994; Wedel 1986).

In A.D. 1500 the onset of the neo-boreal climate resulted in increased precipitation and the return of bison to the area. Eastern Colorado was reoccupied, though not by the original inhabitants, but by Athapaskan-speaking Apaches. This occupation is known as the Late Ceramic period.

Late Ceramic Period

In the mid-1500s Plains Apache groups entered the Central High Plains as bison-hunting nomads from the north (Gunnerson 1987). They expanded their territories south to the southern plains adjacent to the Rio Grande Pueblos by the late 1500s (Wilcox 1981). By the 1640s Apachean groups still in eastern Colorado had concentrated along the Republican River in semi-sedentary villages. This occupation is referred to as the Dismal River aspect, which dominated the western Central High Plains in the 1600s (Cassells 1983; Wedel 1986).

Gunnerson argues that before 1640, nomadic Apaches were friendly with Caddoan farmers to the east and lived near them in the winter, trading western plains products for corn. The Dismal River sites may be either a mixture of Caddoan and Apachean groups or Apaches who adopted a Caddoan-like lifeway. This lasted until the late 1720s when hostile pressure from Utes to the west and Comanches to the north pushed the Apache groups to the south (Gunnerson 1987).

The subsistence economy in the Dismal River aspect relied on bison hunting with a secondary emphasis on corn farming and the hunting and gathering of other wild resources (Gunnerson 1987). Despite the reliance on bison hunting, ambush techniques rather than mass kills appear to have been used (Wedel 1986).

The differences between Caddoan and Apache groups go beyond hunting and horticulture. In addition to ceramic and lithic styles, numerous differences in site structure allow us to designate the Dismal River aspect as Athapaskan. Subsistence on fish is totally absent (as opposed to the earlier Caddoan groups), and fish taboos are common among southern Athapaskans today (Gunnerson 1987).

Dismal River village structure is highly dispersed and consists of earthen-floored buildings with wood-and-earth roofs. These are relatively small—6 to 6.7 meters (20 to 22 feet) in diameter—compared with the lodgelike structures of the Caddoans. The difference in size may be indicative of a different kin structure, at least in terms of family size. These houses had five central post supports that supported a wooden frame, which was then covered with brush and earth, similar to Navajo forked-stick-and-earth hogans (Gunnerson 1987; Wedel 1986).

Also common are deep roasting pits with constricted mouths. The roasting pits (1 meter [3 feet] deep by 1.5 meters [5 feet] wide) have large amounts of fire-cracked rock and the remains of roasted corncobs. Often they find secondary use as trash pits. Conversely, the bell-shaped storage pits common among Caddoan farmers are absent (Gunnerson 1987). In fact, storage units in general are rare in Dismal River sites (Wedel 1986).

The lack of storage pits may be because Apache groups were primarily bison hunters and corn farming was secondary. Aside from the faunal remains in Dismal River sites, this contention is further supported by the presence of Apache sites away from the Republican River. In fact, Apache sites, identifiable by their lithic and ceramic remains, are found in a variety of locations. On the open plains these sites are limited to lithic and ceramic scatters with occasional roasting pits and burned rock middens (Gunnerson 1987). Their open and ephemeral nature suggests highly mobile hunting-and-gathering peoples.

In other areas, particularly on the Chaquaqua Plateau in southeastern Colorado, sites are less ephemeral, though apparently still related to a mobile existence. Some contain stone rings dated as early as the mid-1500s, which averaged 3.7 meters (12 feet) in diameter, which is reasonable for dog transport (Gunnerson 1987; Kingsbury and Gabel 1983). There is no evidence for a transformation into a horse nomad way of life at this time.

Plains Apache remains are found throughout the Central High Plains until 1700, when the Apaches were pushed south by Comanche groups. The Comanche and later groups are discussed in Chapter 7.

CONCLUSION

Holocene adaptation on the Central High Plains is variable. Some parts of the area were occupied by highly mobile hunter-and-gatherers while other areas witnessed the rise of settled village life and a reliance on agriculture among the indigenous peoples of the area. In the mid-1400s, eastern Colorado was abandoned by the indigenous occupants to be replaced by new migrants from the north. These groups were, in turn, pushed south by other groups during the historic period.

CHAPTER 4

Southwestern Colorado and the Four Corners

Southwestern Colorado is in the northern San Juan branch of the Anasazi (Cordell and Gumerman 1989; Fig. 4.1). Although there are adaptations that are unique to the Four Corners area, this region is also affected by larger regional networks that connected it to the remainder of the American Southwest. As such, the culture history of the area uses the categories of the Pecos classification for the northern Southwest. The time periods associated with these in Colorado are outlined in Table 4.1.

THE ARCHAIC PERIOD

The Archaic period begins in southwestern Colorado with the establishment of the Holocene at approximately 8000 to 8500 B.C. (see Chapter 1). During this period aridity increased, forestlands retreated, and deserts were formed, to near modern standards. Seasonal extremes (i.e., temporal heterogeneity) increased and were combined, with a patchy resource distribution (i.e., spatial heterogeneity). Prehistoric use of the landscape reflects this as different methods of harvesting resources are used at different times of year. Whereas Archaic remains are limited in southwestern Colorado, sites are common in northern New Mexico, Arizona, and southwestern Utah (Kane 1986; Matson 1994). In general, the Archaic tradition in the northern San Juan basin is a variant of the Southwestern Archaic tradition known as the Oshara (Irwin-Williams 1973; Vierra 1990).

It is unclear exactly when the Archaic period starts and how it develops. Some researchers argue that Archaic settlement patterns are found at sites

Figure 4.1 Map of the landmarks and Anasazi culture areas in the American Southwest.

TABLE 4.1

Southwestern Colorado Chronology Using the Pecos
Designations by Rohn (1989) and Lipe (1993)

Period	Rohn	Lipe
Archaic	8000–500 B.C.	6500–1500 B.C.
Basketmaker II	500 B.C.–A.D. 450	1500 B.C.–A.D. 500
Basketmaker III	A.D. 450–750	A.D. 500–750
Pueblo I	A.D. 750–900	A.D. 750–900
Pueblo II	A.D. 900–1150	A.D. 900–1150
Pueblo III	A.D. 1150–1300	A.D. 1150–1300
Abandoned	post-A.D. 1300	post-A.D. 1300

containing Jay, San Jose, and Pinto points whereas others argue these sites are Paleoindian in nature (Parry and Smiley 1990; Stuart and Gauthier 1981; Vierra 1990). Still others argue that Paleoindian peoples left the area, moving to the Plains to continue a specialized hunting strategy. The area was then reoccupied by Archaic peoples (Irwin-Williams 1973).

Part of this debate hinges on the definition of the Archaic as either a time period or a type of adaptation (Vierra 1990, 1994a). If it is a period, the onset of the Holocene at 8000 B.C. seems a reasonable starting point. If it is an adaptation, the taxonomic classification becomes increasingly muddled because recent studies of the Paleoindian period in southwestern Colorado demonstrate a generalized hunting-and-gathering (i.e., Archaic) adaptation. To simplify the argument, we will use Archaic as the period here. Also, due to the apparent continuity in adaptation demonstrated by Pitblado's study (1993), it is argued that this is a continuation and modification of an adaptive pattern established early in the area's occupation.

The major modification was a response to the temporal variability associated with the onset of the Holocene. Different mobility and subsistence patterns were followed at different times of year. Vierra (1990, 1994b) argues that during spring, summer, and fall, Early Archaic peoples were highly mobile, with very large territories. The seasonal round started in the lowlands and moved into higher elevations as upland resources ripened (Toll and Cully 1994). One of the main resources in the uplands was game. In the lower elevations, *Sporobolus*, cacti, chenopods, and sunflower seeds were gathered (Matson 1994). Based on the types of raw materials in the chipped stone assemblages, seasonal rounds may have encompassed approximately 3,000 square kilometers (1,863 square miles) (Vierra 1994b). This is supported by similarities in projectile point style and rock art over large areas. In the winter, Archaic groups were more sedentary, living off occasional hunting forays and food stores collected during the fall (Vierra 1990). Macrobotanical and coprolite data indicate that rice grass, chenopodium, dropseed, goosefoot, and prickly pear were used at winter sites, but interestingly, piñon nuts were unimportant (Kohler 1993). Faunal assemblages are dominated by rabbit, with smaller amounts of mountain sheep and pronghorn (Parry and Smiley 1990).

Winter camps are larger than those used during the rest of the year. However, these sites may not have had more people but represent frequent reoccupation of favorite locations (Vierra 1990). To take advantage of crucial water sources, these sites were established in canyon heads near permanent springs. In the vicinity of the winter camps, smaller special-purpose sites served as hunting stations to supplement winter stores (Irwin-Williams 1973).

This pattern of seasonal subsistence did not develop overnight. Winter camps were always present and occupied longer than during other seasons, but the length of stay increased through time, resulting in a sedentary winter population that was accompanied by increased reliance on stored plants (Irwin-Williams 1973; Vierra and Doleman 1994). This shift is evident not only in increased storage but also the appearance and formalization of ground stone. Small basin metates and associated hand stones became an important part of the tool assemblage around 3000 B.C.

By 2500 B.C., gathered grains and cereals were a major part of the diet, but a new plant appeared: corn. Corn is not indigenous to the Southwest. It was domesticated in the Mexican highlands approximately 5,500 years ago, or 3500 B.C. (Smiley 1994). Corn, beans, and squash are complementary plants of the Upper Sonoran Agricultural complex. Beans contain the amino acid lysine, which enables efficient digestion of corn's protein (Ford 1981). Also, whereas corn depletes the soil's nutrients, beans return nitrogen to the ground. Consequently, when corn and beans are planted in the same field, nutrient depletion is minimized.

The first evidence of corn in the archaeological record in the Southwest is at approximately 2500 B.C. at Bat Cave in southwestern New Mexico and Three Fir Shelter in northeastern Arizona. Most of the early dates are from rock shelters in the Mogollon highlands of southern and central Arizona and New Mexico (Smiley 1994). This distribution may be a result of peoples moving to higher elevations during the dryness of the Altithermal (Matson 1994; Wills 1988). Alternatively, it may be that corn thrived in the Mogollon highlands' elevation (Fig. 4.1).

The corn at these early sites is Chapalote corn, a type of popcorn with small cobs. Chapalote corn is diverse, and through experimentation by Southwestern peoples, different varieties developed.

But how did corn, beans, and squash get to the Southwest in the first place? Cordell (1984) argues that the plants of the Upper Sonoran Agricultural complex were grown by nonsedentary peoples in northern Mexico prior to their introduction to the Southwest. "Within the context of mobility and periodic interaction among groups of people, it is likely that knowledge of particular plants and specimens of potentially useful plants would be readily exchanged" (Cordell 1984: 173).

Early domesticates were not very productive, so why did Archaic peoples in the Southwest accept this technology? Most studies agree that horticulture is more labor-intensive than hunting-and-gathering, but there are certain benefits to domesticates. First, if corn, beans, and squash are planted above 6000 feet elevation in the Southwest, there is sufficient rainfall for it to grow with little or no attention. However, if the fields are not weeded and protected from animals, productivity is limited (Cordell 1984). Conversely, although productivity would be limited, domesticates would be an additional resource that would not require changes in the mobility and socioeconomic organization of a group (Wills 1988). Additionally, planting domesticates changes the ecozones in which they occur by increasing the presence of other edible annual seeds (like cheno-ams), which prefer disturbed soils (Ford 1984).

Early experimentation with domesticates may have occurred in the Mogollon highlands for two reasons. First, plants in the Upper Sonoran complex prefer the highlands' elevations of 5000 and 7000 feet. Second, Ford (1984) suggests the constraining factor for population growth in the highlands is calories rather than water because resources were scattered. By planting a field of corn, squash, and beans, a resource could be concentrated into an easily exploited patch. Also, if one resource is low in a given year, the advantage of having a concentrated stand, even of a crop with limited productivity, becomes obvious, particularly if it increases the production of wild resources, such as cheno-ams as well. Finally, both the domesticates and the cheno-ams are storable, increasing the length of their use.

However, adding agricultural products to the subsistence regimen did have consequences. Wills (1988) argues that what little information we have about the early agricultural period, based on research on site organization, suggests that this may actually have been a dynamic time and that different strategies were used by people in different areas. For example, Wills's reanalysis of several cave sites indicates that changes in the social, economic, and mobility patterns occurred early in this process. The early sites of Tularosa Cave, Bat Cave, and Cienega Creek demonstrate this diversity despite their similar ages (Early and Middle Archaic levels) and proximity.

Bat Cave was used both before and after the introduction of domesticates. In strata where domesticates are present, several differences are evident, specifically large storage pits; thick, compacted floors; dense deposits of domestic debris; and changes in the lithic assemblage are present. In contrast, preagricultural deposits have almost no cultural material, with the exception of sporadic hearths and broken projectile points.

At Tularosa Cave, the density of corn recovered (several thousand cobs) is much higher than at Bat Cave where 300 cobs were found. Also, Tularosa

Cave features large storage pits that are excavated directly into the bedrock floor of the shelter. This demonstrates that agricultural production was neither minimal nor unimportant at all the early cave sites.

Cienega Creek is an open-air, stratified site. The pre-Ceramic levels contain numerous pits, hearths, and cremations, as well as large amounts of corn pollen. This location was used repeatedly during the pre-Ceramic period for mortuary ritual. Ethnographic studies indicate that a redundant pattern of mortuary behavior in a single locale is a territorial link between the locale and a particular social group (Charles and Buikstra 1983). This is the earliest evidence of a territorial social system that demonstrates a major change in concepts of resource ownership and land tenure.

Wills (1988) indicates evidence of long-term use of sites in numerous places outside the Mogollon highlands. Patterns of redundant mobility involving settlement reuse and dwelling construction throughout the period from the adoption of agriculture to the beginning of ceramic manufacture are common. Conversely, there is little evidence of site reoccupation in the Mogollon highlands.

Although no cave sites have early evidence of agriculture in southwestern Colorado, Three Fir Shelter on Black Mesa in northeastern Arizona does have early dates (Smiley 1994). When agriculture spread to southwestern Colorado, it was accepted into the existing hunting-and-gathering pattern. Rather than dramatically altering the mobility pattern, it seems to have reinforced it, as winter camps become longer-lived and more formal. In addition to wild resources, corn was used as a stored good. The ground stone used to process corn became more formal, as small trough metates were added to the assemblage to compensate for the amount of time spent processing corn. These changes coincide with the beginning of the Basketmaker II period.

BASKETMAKER II

The Basketmaker II period has been classified as a transition between the hunting-and-gathering groups of the Archaic and the Basketmaker III periods in which a significant commitment was made to growing corn. We do not know why agriculture increased, but population growth is a possibility (Lipe 1993). Technologies were introduced, allowing intensification of traditional subsistence patterns, the most obvious of which are more formalized ground stone and, late in the period, the bow and arrow (Janetski 1993). We see the beginnings of clay figurines and clay basket linings, although true pottery does not appear until Basketmaker III (Janetski 1993; Lipe 1993). Associated with these changes in subsistence and technology are the renegotiation—sometimes peacefully, sometimes not—of social relations.

Pit houses, found throughout the Southwest, are the main defining characteristic of the period. In the Four Corners area, they vary in depth (with earlier structures being deeper), but all are round. The superstructure consisted of four main support posts that supported a pole frame, which was then covered with small branches and mud, though cribbed roofs were used in some late Basketmaker II sites. Entry was through a doorway on the south or southeastern side (Lipe 1993).

Pit houses are winter residences rather than year-round habitations (Kohler 1993). The people who occupied them lived off stored goods in the winter and returned to a more mobile lifestyle in the summer. The settlement pattern consisted of late fall, winter, and early spring pit house villages and small, late spring, summer, and early fall foraging (or short-term collecting) camps, which are represented by the numerous lithic scatters dated to this period (Gilman 1987; Rohn 1989). The introduction of pit houses is not a dramatic change from the Archaic period mobility pattern. Rather, winter camps became more formal and were used for longer times. There are, however, a number of differences between the Basketmaker II and Archaic periods, including landscape use, intercommunity relationships, and changes in the subsistence economy.

Although Basketmaker II sites are uncommon in Colorado, patterning is evident in their location. Rather than being limited to canyon heads, Basketmaker II villages are located in areas where several ecozones converge (Lipe 1993). Specifically, they are located in areas that had access to wild resources, and locations favorable for agriculture were preferred.

Villages ranged from six to eleven structures, although isolated pit houses are known. As opposed to the Archaic period, larger villages meant larger populations. Hearths and storage pits were located inside and outside the structures (Lipe 1993; Rohn 1989). Interior and exterior storage units indicate that storage and resource pooling occurred at household and community levels, but formal communal space and centralized storage are absent.

There were no formal cemeteries and burials are generally found in midden areas, under house floors, or in storage pits (Rohn 1989). Grave goods are rich in these burials, with differences in content and amount related to the age of the individual, indicating a prestige system. Grave goods often include trade items such as marine shells, ornaments out of nonlocal minerals, and nonlocal lithic material (Lipe 1993).

Despite the presence of trade, often used to cement social and political alliances, competition, and at times conflict, arose between local groups (Hurst and Turner 1993). The reason for this competition is not clear, but Basketmaker II is a dynamic period in which the relationship of individuals to the land and concepts of land tenure changed with the increasing importance of corn agriculture. The competition could be a result of the renegotiation of social relationships and boundaries this entailed. Support for this can be found in Lipe's (1993) argument that increasing use of anthropomorphic figures in the rock art is related to the veneration of ancestors. Ancestral claims are often an important part of establishing and maintaining group control over territory (Charles and Buikstra 1983).

Finally, during the Basketmaker II period, the subsistence system changed, with an increased commitment to both growing corn and collecting piñon nuts (Janetski 1993). As corn became more important, more types of locations were exploited. Because early Basketmaker II farming was based on floodwater and runoff techniques, sites were restricted to canyon bottoms, but later in the period upland dry farming was conducted on mesa tops (Lipe 1993). The increasing importance of corn also is supported by changes in the ground stone assemblage. Early in the period, ground stone was a mixture of informal basin and small trough metates, whereas late Basketmaker II sites contain formal trough metates with larger grinding surfaces (Lipe 1993; Stone 1994a). However, wild seed and nut crops did remain important, as evidenced by a wide variety of conical collecting baskets and winnowing trays (Lipe 1993).

The introduction of pottery signals the end of Basketmaker II and beginning of Basketmaker III. This period is accompanied by other changes as sedentism and the reliance on agriculture increases.

BASKETMAKER III

As in Basketmaker II, the basic long-term settlement type is the small village with one to eight pit houses. Unlike the previous period, however, these sites are more complex, indicating longer periods of use. Pit houses are larger and antechambers have been added. Additionally, exterior space is more formal with outdoor ramadas and work areas. At a number of sites in the Dolores area, small jacal rooms with dome or "beehive" roofs may have served as external storage areas (Kane 1986). At some villages, unusually large pit houses have been identified as ritual structures, or proto-kivas (Rohn 1989).

In addition to the villages are limited activity sites—resource processing areas—consisting of small lithic and sherd scatters (Rohn 1989). Some scholars suggest that Basketmaker III villages were year-round establishments, others argue that Basketmaker III villages were cold-weather villages, the lithic and sherd scatters representing warm-weather foraging camps (Gilman 1987; Kohler 1993).

It is clear that there is an increasing commitment to agriculture at this time. The most direct evidence for this is from coprolite analysis. Minnis (1989) has synthesized the coprolite data from the northern Southwest for this period, identifying a number of patterns. One of the most interesting is that some resources that were important earlier, like dropseed and cactus, are unimportant during the Basketmaker III period. Also, three plants are found only in Pueblo or Basketmaker III times. Cotton seeds are common in Pueblo III coprolites but absent from the Basketmaker III assemblage, and piñon and beeweed are common in Basketmaker III but rare in Pueblo III coprolites. However, with the exception of these plants, the Basketmaker III and Pueblo III coprolites are remarkably similar in content and rank orders of the various plant types.

From Basketmaker III on, corn dominates the assemblage, but it is more ubiquitous during the Pueblo than in the Basketmaker III period. Ubiquity represents the number of coprolite samples in which the plant is found, and it is assumed that the more ubiquitous a plant is, the more important it is in the diet. However, it should be noted that a high ubiquity of corn does not mean other resources are unimportant during Basketmaker III times. Evidence for a varied diet lies in ubiquities between 20 and 40 percent for ground cherry, goosefoot, purslane, piñon, and prickly pear (Minnis 1989).

Basketmaker III is noted for the introduction of true pottery: undecorated jars and bowls made of naturally tempered alluvial clays through the coil-and-scrape method (Kohler 1993; Wilson and Blinman 1995). Although alluvial clays are brown, these vessels are classified as gray-wares because the clays are indigenous and because of the similarity in manufacturing and firing technology to the gray-ware tradition. In Colorado the most common type is Twin Trees gray, dated from A.D. 400 to 700 (Wilson and Blinman 1995).

True gray-wares, usually associated with the northern Southwest, did not appear until after A.D. 550, when gray and white clays were used (Kohler 1993). These clays were higher quality but required temper to be added. In Colorado the initial use of these clays can be seen in Chapin gray dated from A.D. 575 to 950 (Wilson and Blinman 1995). Chapin and Twin Trees grays overlap, and both have been found at Basketmaker III sites.

Chapin black-on-white bowls, also found at these sites, date from A.D. 575 to 900 (Kane 1986). This style is characterized by mineral paints, with some organic paints showing up in the western portions of the region. The most common designs are lines, triangles, "Z"s, and dots (Wilson and Blinman 1995).

PUEBLO I

The Pueblo I period of southwestern Colorado is characterized by above-ground structures in year-round villages, a rise in population, population aggregation and dispersion, and style changes in signaling group affiliation (Kane 1986; Kohler 1993; Plog 1989; Schlanger 1986; Wilshusen 1991). The rise of aggregated villages was restricted to the Four Corners area, whereas style changes were widespread throughout the northern Southwest.

Early in the Pueblo I period, A.D. 750 to 860, the most dramatic change in village structure and architecture was the appearance of aboveground structures, which were two rooms deep and one or two rooms wide; generally the room in the back (to the north) was used for storage (Fig. 4.2). In front (to the south) of the structures were rows of deep pit houses (Kane 1986). Work areas, occasionally with ramadas, were between the structures and pit houses. The surface dwellings were made of jacal, with sandstone slab bases. The superstructures were built from soil excavated during construction of the associated pit house (Rohn 1989; Wilshusen 1989b).

This change in architecture is probably related to changes in mobility, which in turn is related to increasing reliance on agriculture. Corn agriculture required more storage space, which was difficult to add to subterranean pit houses, so aboveground buildings solved the problem. Also, as corn farming increased, so did processing time: grinding and cooking were labor-intensive. Interior activity areas were needed, and square, aboveground structures were easier to subdivide (Gilman 1987). Additionally, although pit houses were easier to construct than pueblos, they were more difficult and expensive to maintain for long periods, making them unappealing to sedentary peoples (McGuire and Schiffer 1983).

Early Pueblo I villages are larger than those of the Basketmaker III period. Most pueblos in southwestern Colorado have approximately twelve household units (a household is defined as an aboveground storage and

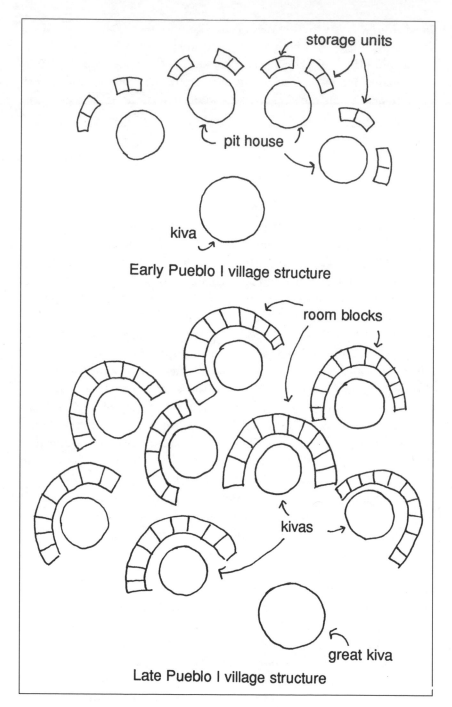

storage units

pit house

kiva

Early Pueblo I village structure

room blocks

kivas

great kiva

Late Pueblo I village structure

Figure 4.2 Pueblo I village structures.

habitation room with a pit house). Larger villages usually have great kivas; smaller villages (two or three households) do not (Kane 1986; Rohn 1989). Although small and large villages were linked ritually, economically, and socially, their relationship is unclear.

By A.D. 800, regional movement caused a population increase in the Dolores area of southwestern Colorado (Kane 1986; Schlanger 1988). Individuals moved from the lower elevations into higher elevations, near 7000 feet, which were more favorable to rainfall and therefore to agriculture (Schlanger 1988).

Architecture also changed. Although jacal structures were still present, masonry room blocks became the norm, and pit houses used for habitation disappeared (see Fig. 4.2). Village structure consisted of an arc of rooms, often two rooms deep, with a kiva in front (Kane 1986; Rohn 1989).

Villages were larger, containing between 30 and 140 extended families after A.D. 840. The McPhee village site, dated between A.D. 860 and 880, is one of the best studied; it housed between 640 and 850 people (Wilshusen 1989a, 1991). Households had a habitation room and at least one storage room in a site that consisted of a series of arcs, each associated with a kiva. Sometimes several households were joined in an arc of continuous rooms. Semi-subterranean great kivas were integrative facilities for the village as a whole (Wilshusen 1991).

The purpose of the smaller kiva (often called the clan kiva) is more controversial. Lekson (1988, 1989) argues that they should be considered part of the household rather than the ritual structures associated with the word *kiva*. He bases this on the fact that although some ritual activity may have occurred here, there was considerable domestic activity as well (Varien and Lightfoot 1989). Additionally, Lekson asks if family groups really needed to be integrated through ritual—the term kiva implies that they did. Conversely, it can be argued that ceremonies to maintain and reinforce family solidarity were conducted in kivas. This solidarity was vulnerable during initial aggregation when social boundaries were renegotiated (Saitta 1991; Stone 1994b). Therefore, based on current data, it is probably best to think of clan kivas as places where groups of three to six nuclear households participate in common economic and ritual activities (Varien and Lightfoot 1989; Wilshusen 1991).

One of the most interesting questions for the late Pueblo I period, however, is why aggregation started in A.D. 840 and ended in A.D. 900. Aggregation tends to occur in situations of low-population densities, not in areas where groups are approaching the carrying capacity of the region(Adler and Wilshusen 1990). Wilshusen (1991) points out that the movement between aggregation and dispersion and the formation, break-up, and reformation of villages demonstrate that this process is dynamic and nonlinear. He states that people always work within multiple organizational structures (particularly when coordinating labor) and emphasize different principles at different times. From this perspective, it would be wise to examine what organizational principles were emphasized that lead to village aggregation.

In terms of organizational principles, families must decide when to compete and when to cooperate with each other. This depends on existing conditions and what their ultimate goals are. There is in fact an uneasy balance between competition and cooperation, and people go back and forth between the two at different times and at different levels (the individual, family, group, and so on). Suprafamily cooperation did occur at some level before aggregation. Specifically, Great Kivas are located in the center of dispersed villages prior to A.D. 840 and temporally limited aggregation occurred at that location, probably for calendric ceremonies. Temporally limited aggregation for ritual purposes is common among dispersed horticultural and hunter-gatherer societies and serves as a time to exchange information, goods, and mates as well as the metaphysical aspects of the ritual (Stone 1994b).

Aggregated villages can be viewed as a form of cooperation among people on a more permanent and formal level. Then, the crucial question is, under what circumstances is cooperation encouraged beyond the level of the household, resulting in village formation? Economically there are certain conditions in which competition or cooperation is favored.

At A.D. 840, the Dolores River area was attractive to the regional population as a source of permanent water and for rainfall runoff horticulture (Schlanger 1988). Cooperation at the suprafamily level had several benefits (Wilshusen 1991). First, it reduced competition over land between members of the group while increasing the group's competitive position relative to other groups. That is, bigger villages can control and defend claims to the land more effectively and therefore have an advantage over neighboring groups. Second, cooperation facilitated the formation of task-specific labor forces during labor bottlenecks, such as when both domestic and wild resources needed to be harvested at the same time. Task-specific labor groups gave individuals and families the advantage of organized labor while still maintaining economic and political autonomy.

When do these benefits result in increased cooperation and aggregation? Late in the Pueblo I period precipitation increased, though it was variable, and good agricultural soils were differentially distributed. According to Wilshusen (1991), economic cooperation within suprafamily groups that were already cooperating on a ritual level was favored, and competition for control over the differentially distributed soils between villages increased. With environmental changes at the end of the Pueblo I period, the selective advantage of cooperation at the suprafamily level disappeared, and the villages dispersed.

If this model is correct, several things should be evident. First, villages would be located on the best agricultural land within settings that maximize precipitation and length of growing season (130 to 140 days), and settlement in a big village should give control over prime land and competitive advantage over others. Second, family autonomy needed to be balanced with village integration. This social balance should be evident in the storage and ritual facilities. Third, there should be competition between villages. Finally, when the selective advantage for aggregation disappears, the population should disperse.

The data support Wilshusen's model. First, large villages dated to this period in the Dolores project area are located in these areas, usually right above a location of potable water such as the Dolores River (Kane 1986; Wilshusen 1991). Additionally, larger stretches of prime agricultural land above 6000 feet in elevation are occupied by the largest villages. Small hamlets are restricted to less desirable locations. Household and village structure also support the model. Storage rooms are attached to habitation rooms, indicating that storage is at the household rather than in the village level. Additionally, ritual structures are at the corporate group (small clan kivas associated with several households) and village (the Great Kiva) levels (see Fig. 4.2).

Data also support competition between villages. Large villages maintained buffer zones of ten kilometers (6 miles) of open space between them. Toward the end of the period, this spacing was not enough and many villages were burned.

Further support of Wilshusen's model is that villages dispersed whenever there were at least three years of low precipitation, and then re-formed when higher levels returned. Aggregation was abandoned completely when moderate precipitation levels returned, and spatial variability decreased for the region as a whole in A.D. 900 (Schlanger 1988).

Between A.D. 900 and 1150 (Pueblo II period), aggregated villages are not found in southwestern Colorado, and the Dolores River and McElmo Creek are not used by the prehistoric inhabitants to the same degree

(Kane 1986; Lightfoot 1993). The area was not abandoned, but site locations did change. Although villages are more dispersed, site clusters are found and represent a continuation of the suprafamily cooperation at some level.

PUEBLO II

After approximately A.D. 900, population decreased in the Dolores River area and increased to the south and west (Varien, et al. 1996). By A.D. 1000, the Dolores River area was abandoned (Kane 1986; Schlanger 1988).

In addition to shifts in location, sites during Pueblo II times were more dispersed (Varien, et al. 1996). However, inhabitants in nearby sites maintained contact and were linked through economic, kin, and ritual ties, which is particularly noticeable after A.D. 1050, when new architectural features appear (Rohn 1989).

Most sites consisted of masonry and jacal structures in continuous room blocks with an accompanying small kiva. Kivas are still semi-subterranean, but are now round and (in later times) lined with masonry. Semi-subterranean grinding rooms, with numerous grinding bins, appear to be tied to the ritual system (Mobley-Tanaka 1997; Rohn 1989).

By A.D. 1050, a new type of site appeared across the landscape. Based on the architecture, location, layout, and artifactual assemblage, these have been identified as Chacoan outliers. Outliers are planned sites with a high proportion of ritual to domestic space, including Great Kivas. Buildings are two stories high with core and veneer masonry. The best known outliers in Colorado are Escalante, Lowry, Ida Jean, Wallace, Yucca House, and Chimney Rock (Judge 1989).

These sites are part of a social and ritual network that encompassed much of the northern Southwest between A.D. 1050 and 1150. The center of this network is Chaco Canyon, which is in Chaco Wash, a tributary of the San Juan River (see Fig. 4.1). Although the canyon gets only four inches of rain a year, the entire basin drains into Chaco Wash, making corn farming possible (Judge 1989).

To understand the relationship between southwestern Colorado and Chaco Canyon, we must address the developments in the canyon itself. Before A.D. 900, sites in the canyon were dispersed farming villages (smaller than those found along the Dolores River at the same time), averaging seven households (Judge 1989, 1991).

After A.D. 900, two distinct types of habitation sites emerged (Judge 1989; Lekson 1991). The first were small, masonry villages of about ten rooms and a small kiva similar to those found throughout the Anasazi region. The masonry stone is generally unshaped and the room blocks are rectangular, two rooms deep and one story high.

The second type is generally referred to as towns, which are considerably larger than the villages. The room block is arc-shaped, creating a central plaza, which has a Great Kiva. The back row of the arc is two stories high and contains storage rooms.

Three towns were founded in A.D. 900, all at the confluence of Chaco Wash and a major tributary: Penasco Blanco, Pueblo Bonito, and Una Vida. Between A.D. 900 and 1000 these sites grew, and two more towns were founded in the canyon: Hungo Pavi and Chetro Ketl. Pueblo Alto—the first outlier—was founded on the canyon rim, and by A.D. 1050 there were several more. Town and outlier expansion continued until A.D. 1150.

The meaning of these architectural differences is heavily debated, as is the organization of the Chacoan system as a whole (Judge 1991, 1993; Sebastian 1991; Vivian 1991; Wilcox 1993). We do know that extensive trade of ceramics, chipped stone, and turquoise occurred between the villages, towns, and outliers (Toll 1991). Also, much labor was involved in constructing towns in Chaco Canyon and at the outliers. Masonry stone was quarried and dressed and ponderosa pine roof beams had to be transported over long distances.

On one hand, it is suggested that Chaco was a highly centralized system in which tribute payments were extracted from local people by elites living in the outliers. These tribute payments were then funneled back into the towns in Chaco Canyon. On the other hand, scholars argue that Chaco was a large trade system based on reciprocal interaction between trade partners bound by religious beliefs.

At the edge of this system lies southwestern Colorado, which served as one of the sources for building materials, particularly ponderosa pine. The relationship of the outliers in Colorado to Chaco Canyon is varied and is strongly related to the system as a whole in terms of complexity (Matlock 1993).

In the 1970s Frank Eddy investigated this relationship, centering on the outlier of Chimney Rock between Durango and Pagosa Springs (Judge 1989; Matlock 1993). His research focused on the way goods from Colorado were moved to Chaco Canyon and the sociopolitical organization at Chimney Rock.

There was considerable trade between the Four Corners and Chaco Canyon. Chimney Rock supplied construction timbers for the canyon (Toll 1991). The relationship between the canyon and outlying areas can be seen in the four ways goods were moved: direct procurement expeditions, establishing procurement outliers to control the source, trade, and establishing captured outliers (Kane 1993).

In direct procurement expeditions the inhabitants of Chaco Canyon went to the source area, personally extracted the resource, and transported it back to the canyon. The advantage of this for Chaco Canyon is that procurement was controlled by the canyon and could be intensified when needed. However, it required numerous trips to the source areas, and access to the resource could be denied by individuals living nearby.

If direct procurement expeditions were mounted for timbers at Chimney Rock, a number of indications should be present in the archaeological record. First, because procuring and dressing timbers was time-consuming, temporary habitation sites should be present at Chimney Rock. "Such camps would be characterized by temporary, low cost shelters, and refuse attributable to the consumption and tool maintenance activities of the crews involved in procuring the resource" (Kane 1993: 47). Because the sites would be abandoned with the intention of returning later, caches of timbering tools (axes and wedges) also should be present.

Procurement outliers would establish a permanent base in the source area and guarantee constant control over timber production. These outliers would be settled by colonists from Chaco Canyon. However, indigenous inhabitants may object to the colonists. One way to overcome these objections would be to draw them into the Chacoan system.

If Chimney Rock was an outlier, a number of archaeological indicators should be evident. First, one or more Chaco-style structures to house the colonists should be present. To ensure and reinforce the position of the colonists as elites, these structures should be near landmarks or visible from a distance. A force of transient workers would also need housing, but because of their low status, the housing would not have to be as substantial as that of the elite (Kane 1993). Kane suggests that local populations would be encouraged or lured into settling near the outlier to provide subsistence goods for the colonists in return for status goods and ceremonial expertise. These settlements would be similar to indigenous architecture found in other areas of Colorado.

If a substantial indigenous population is present, direct procurement or establishing a procurement outlier may not be possible, but trade relations

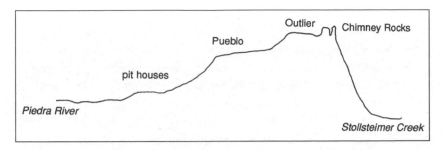

Figure 4.3 Schematic of the Chimney Rock site.

may have developed. Procurement through trade requires a relationship between individuals in Chaco Canyon and individuals at Chimney Rock to exchange timbers for other goods or services. The advantage of this system is that inhabitants of Chaco Canyon would not have to establish procurement camps. The disadvantage is that they could not control the source area or the amount of timber produced.

A formalization of trade relations and further incorporation of the indigenous population into the Chacoan system may have occurred by establishing a captured outlier. Areas are "captured" into the Chacoan system not by force but by incorporating them into the ritual and larger political system. Indications of this in the archaeological record include the construction of Chacoan structures in existing communities.

At times, all four procurement methods have been argued to have occurred in Colorado. Kane (1993) argues that based on the architectural diversity within the site, Chimney Rock was probably a procurement outlier in which managerial elites lived with lower-status laborers. However, this interpretation is not unanimously accepted. Jeannette Mobley-Tanaka (1993) questions the presence of a managerial elite overseeing tenant laborers and local populations at Chimney Rock. She argues that Chimney Rock may be the incorporation of the local population into a widespread religious and economic network (voluntary captured outlier). To support her idea, she looked at two data sources: architecture and ceramics.

Chimney Rock contains three architectural zones located on three benches above Devil's Creek (Fig. 4.3). On the first bench above the river is a cluster of jacal pit houses, and cobble masonry structures. On the middle bench is a cobble masonry structure that lacks Great Kivas and core and veneer masonry. On the highest bench is a two-story Chacoan structure with core and veneer masonry containing forty ground-floor rooms and two Great Kivas.

Based on dendrochronological dates, all three of the architectural components are contemporaneous. Kane (1993) used this fact to argue that the components were occupied by different segments of the procurement outlier society. Conversely, Mobley-Tanaka (1993) argues that differences in architectural style may be related to function. Specifically, Chacoan structures may be ceremonial rather than the domiciles of an ethnic enclave, and architectural variability alone is insufficient to determine the existence of colonizing elites.

Architecture organizes space and controls the movement of people (Hegmon 1989). Differences in concepts of space and its use may reflect ethnic differences and can be examined across masonry style. Mobley-Tanaka (1993) states that the architectural space at Chimney Rock relates to the amount and kind of storage in different parts of the site. At the Chacoan structure, with its compact and interconnected rooms, we see extensive control over access to storage rooms. Control of access is not as great in the structures on the middle bench, and even less so on the lowest bench, where storage rooms were separate from domestic structures.

In contrast to the storage facilities, there is no differentiation in the space within habitation rooms or in the activity areas (e.g., milling stones and knapping stations) within them. Mobley-Tanaka further argues that the overall use of space crosscuts architectural style (suggesting the continuation of local tradition in all of them), and the only differences are in the degree and kind of storage and style of masonry.

She combines these data with information on the ceramics at the site. If the Chacoan structure was inhabited by an ethnic enclave, there should be imported, high-status ceramics. Throughout the site, the dominant ceramic is local Mesa Verde wares. Chacoan ceramics represent a small proportion of the total assemblage. Additionally, Chacoan ceramics are present in all three areas in the site in approximately equal amounts. However, an analysis of Mesa Verde ceramics at the site produced some interesting patterns.

According to Polly Wiessner (1988), style variation comes from passively used cultural traditions (isochrestic style), personal choices and preferences in decoration (assertive style), and purposefully manipulated symbols of group affiliation (emblematic style). These different styles can be identified by their distribution in the assemblage and their degree of visibility.

The designs on Mesa Verde black-on-white ceramics are variable. But hatched bands, which are present on less than 40 percent of the vessels, are similar to those on the Chacoan ceramics. When these appear on local ceramics elsewhere in the Southwest, they represent the emblematic style associated with the Chacoan ritual system (Plog 1988, 1989).

Mesa Verde ceramics with this motif occur in higher than expected frequencies in the Chacoan structures (55.8 percent of Chacoan vessels). Mobley-Tanaka (1993) argues this represents a use of emblic style signaling affiliation with Chaco on local vessels (Plog 1988, 1989).

Based on the ceramic and architectural information, she states that Chimney Rock was a captured outlier and the area's economic center. Activities at the great house on the mesa played an integrative role within the Chimney Rock community, housing communal ceremonies, trade, and storage. The high concentration of hatched band motifs on ceramics at the Chaco structure indicates its ceremonial centrality and its inhabitants' participation in a wider trade network. According to Mobley-Tanaka, the people living at the Chacoan structure were the same ethnicity as the rest of the community, but they may have had higher status, maintained larger interaction networks, and functioned as religious leaders and sponsors of long-distance trade expeditions. Because of this they maintained greater storage areas where goods could be collected for trade expeditions. This could be carried out either in a competing big man or in a more centralized system. Big men are individuals who achieve their position due to their talents rather than through inheritance. Therefore, multiple big men can be present in a community. A big man interpretation is more likely, given that storage is in individual households in the Chacoan structure rather than in a single or limited number of places.

A model arguing for a lack of centralized control at the site is hindered by one fact. Many scholars argue that the Chacoan system is more complex than the model put forward by Mobley-Tanaka and that Colorado must be viewed in terms of the larger Chacoan system and the goods that moved from Chimney Rock to Chaco Canyon (Tucker 1993). A strong argument for Chacoan ties and centralized decision making is the procurement and movement of large amounts of ponderosa pine over long distances representing considerable organization of labor (Kane 1990).

With the collapse of the Chacoan system between A.D. 1130 and 1150, another dramatic change in the settlement pattern takes place in southwestern Colorado. Communities aggregate and several new communal structure forms appear (Rohn 1989).

PUEBLO III

Pueblo III (A.D. 1150 to 1300) is characterized by population growth, aggregation, and regional abandonment. Settlement pattern and ceremonial structures differ from the previous period. Great Kivas become very formal, resulting in a distinctive keyhole shape. Also, multiwalled structures, plazas, and towers appear for the first time. Despite these changes, the basic family structure remained relatively stable. A residential unit still consists of a round room (small kiva) and several square rooms (Rohn 1989). These residential units are often referred to as kiva units, groups of which make up aggregated communities.

Rohn (1989) argues that based on site size and structure, three basic site types can be identified. The largest of these are towns with more than sixty kiva units housing between 1,200 and 2,500 people. One or more specialized ceremonial structures are present at these sites, and plazas and shrines are common. Towns are near permanent springs, washes, and water management facilities such as reservoirs.

Most large towns are in the Montezuma Valley, to the north and northeast of Cortez. Yellow Jacket ruin is one of the largest, with 160 kiva units, 2 plazas, a Great Kiva, 2 streets, several lanes, shrines, a possible concentric wall structure, and a reservoir with a dam and spillway. Of the eight other large towns in the valley, one of the most extensively excavated is Sand Canyon ruin (Rohn 1989). Sand Canyon has ninety kiva units, fourteen towers, an enclosed plaza, a D-shaped multiwalled structure, a Great Kiva, and various peripheral structures and features. It was constructed between A.D. 1250 and 1285, although a substantial population was in the area before this (Adler 1992; Lipe 1992). It sits near the head of a canyon, with most of the construction below the canyon rim. A spring feeds a stream that flows through the site and divides it into eastern and western sections (Bradley 1992). In addition to its protected location, a masonry wall on the southern edge suggests that defense may have been a concern.

The second site type are villages containing from seventeen to forty kiva units, housing between 200 and 500 people. Villages have water management facilities and at least one community-wide ceremonial structure. Many of the sites in Mesa Verde are this type.

The third type is a hamlet, which contains between one and six kiva units, but lacks communal ceremonial structures, although they are often near isolated towers and kivas or sites that contain them. The Hovenweep district contains several hamlets that have been investigated. All are located on springs that have been artificially enhanced by reservoirs or from clearing and widening the spring opening (Rohn 1989).

In addition to these site types, field houses and agricultural features are scattered across the landscape. Field houses are structures that can be used to store agricultural tools or as shelter when individuals are at outlying agricultural fields. However, they also serve as tangible markers to reinforce land claims by families or corporate groups (Kohler 1992; Preucel 1990; Rothschild, et al. 1993).

These sites, as well as the agricultural fields, were not distributed equally across the landscape during Pueblo III times. The highest populations were in the Montezuma Valley where villages and hamlets cluster around towns, forming community clusters (Adler 1992; Lipe 1992). Community clusters may have formed during Pueblo II times around outlier communities, but after A.D. 1250 they became more compact (within a 10- to 15-kilometer area [6 to 9 miles]; Lipe 1992). Sites within a cluster cooperated economically and ritually. Communication and cooperation between different sites in clusters may have been facilitated by a road and trail system that linked them (Rohn 1989).

The reasons for aggregation and community cluster formation in southwestern Colorado are unclear. Many view Pueblo III times as similar to Pueblo I (Varien, et al. 1996) as an organizational structure that increases the competitive stance of a community to others while at the same time minimizes conflict within communities (Kohler 1993). Others have argued that aggregation is the result of sharing and cooperating beyond kin lines, which is encouraged during periods of high productivity (Kohler 1993). In other areas of the Southwest, defense, population concentration around scarce resources, and ritual reorganization have been offered as explanations (Stone 1994). What is clear, however, is that towns and community clusters are found where productive agricultural soils are concentrated (Van West 1990).

By A.D. 1250 population levels in the Four Corners area were extremely high, although well below the carrying capacity of the area (Van West and Lipe 1992). The population in the Montezuma Valley, including the adjacent outlying areas and Mesa Verde, was approximately 30,000 (Rohn 1989). By A.D. 1300, the area was abandoned, populations having migrated to the northern Rio Grande.

Extensive data indicate that between A.D. 1276 and 1299, Four Corners was subject to a long, severe drought (Varien, et al. 1996), which would have had serious repercussions for a population so dependent on corn.

Coprolite studies indicate a decrease in diet breadth from early to late Pueblo III times, with decreased ubiquity of most plants other than corn (Minnis 1989). Van West's study of agricultural productivity indicates that there was sufficient arable land to feed the population, even during the drought, in terms of absolute amounts (Van West 1990). However, if "mobility and access to productive resources were severely restricted and extensive inter-community food sharing was not regularly practiced, then there would have been times when the demand for maize by some populations . . . might not have been met by their agricultural production" (Van West and Lipe 1992: 118).

Several social factors may have limited mobility and food sharing. First, reduced productivity associated with the drought would have required that more distant and less-productive lands be brought under cultivation. Inhabitants of the Four Corners region may have considered abandonment and relocation a more attractive alternative to the increased work this would have incurred (Van West 1990). A shortage of potable water, firewood, or animal protein also may have made the Four Corners area less attractive (Van West and Lipe 1993).

Additionally, a breakdown in the cooperative bonds between individuals and exchange between communities may have limited the individual families' ability to cope with subsistence shortfalls. Kohler (1993) suggests that during times of average production coupled with high temporal and spatial variability, as during the drought, the incentive for families to cooperate economically is low.

Aside from environmental conditions, disruption of social alliances may have hindered economic cooperation. Dean Saitta (1991) has argued that multiple ritual structures indicate multiple organizational principles in a village, which may be associated with the rise of competing interest groups (Stone and Howell 1994). As organizational principles were established in different community clusters, the lines of communication between clusters may have been broken. Interference in communication leads to a breakdown in cooperation and interaction, which would have exasperated economic stress brought on by the drought.

In addition to all the "pushes" in the Four Corners area, a number of "pulls" in the Rio Grande area were responsible for the migration. These include abundant agricultural land and water, access to game both along the Rio Grande and on the southern Great Plains, and the development of a new ritual system among the inhabitants, the Katchina cult (Cameron 1994; Lekson and Cameron 1995).

One of the problems with a model of migration from the Four Corners to the northern Rio Grande is that population growth on the Rio Grande between A.D. 1275 and 1300 was not sufficient to account for the influx of 30,000 people from Four Corners. Also, there is general continuity in architecture, with no evidence of site unit intrusions in the Rio Grande area (a site unit intrusion is a site with traits that are foreign to the area and identifiable with the origin area). Conversely, Linda Cordell argues that site unit intrusions into areas that are already occupied are rare in prestate societies and that when people migrate into an occupied area they tend to go places where they have relatives or trade partners (Cordell 1989). Trade networks established between the Four Corners and the Rio Grande regions during Pueblo II times increased during Pueblo III, as is evident by the amount of obsidian from the Jemez Mountains in the Four Corners area (Cameron 1993). Increases in the amount of nonlocal lithic material like obsidian indicate not only the location of trade partners but also the intensity of contact. Interaction is evident in the actual trade and styles of ceramics over large areas. If small groups of people moved into existing communities where they had trade partners, site unit intrusions would not be evident. Instead we would see stylistic similarities as are present with Mesa Verde and Galisteo black-on-white (Cordell 1989).

As for the Four Corners abandonment, Cameron (1994) argues that previous migration studies looked at the migration issue as a single, unilineal event rather than a process with antecedents and long-term consequences (Lekson and Cameron 1995). Everyone in the Four Corners region did not pick up and move to the Rio Grande in one day. It was a decision made by individuals due to a combination of factors—pushing and pulling. Additionally, the reasons for migration differed through time as kin and social ties were added to economic reasons later in the process.

Cameron suggests back-and-forth migrations may have begun as early as A.D. 1200, which became unidirectional after A.D. 1275 (Cameron 1994) when conditions worsened in the Four Corners area. As increasing numbers of migrants stayed in the Rio Grande area, the pulls became even stronger for those remaining in the Four Corners region due to kin ties with those who had already migrated.

Archaeological data support the concept of multidirectional movement early in the abandonment process (Cameron 1994). We have evidence of increasing amounts of goods moving between the two areas. Also, if Cameron is correct, past population estimates may have been too high because people moved back and forth, maintaining residences in both places. The Four Corners region was not reinhabited until Numic speakers entered the area several hundred years later (see Chapter 5).

CONCLUSIONS

Holocene adaptation in southwestern Colorado witnesses changes in the subsistence patterns and the manner in which individuals interact with each other and the environment through time. The first major shift was the adoption of corn agriculture and the implications it had for mobility. Once sedentism and agriculture were established, inhabitants of southwestern Colorado went through cyclical periods of aggregation and dispersion, though the causal factors may have varied each time. Finally, the nature of the relationships individuals had with people in other areas of the Southwest (Chaco Canyon and the Rio Grande) had profound impact on the local settlement pattern. Occupation of the area by indigenous groups ended by A.D. 1300, with subsequent reoccupation by Numic speakers.

CHAPTER 5

Holocene Adaptation in Northwestern Colorado

Although not within the Great Basin of the American West, northwestern Colorado is usually considered part of the Great Basin culture area, and as such uses the same terminology (Aikens and Madsen 1986; Cassells 1983; Grayson 1993; Jennings 1978; La Point 1987; Marwitt 1986). The Holocene occupation of northwestern Colorado is generally divided into the Archaic, Fremont, and Numic periods. When tied to regional events due to trade or climatic shifts, occupations in adjacent areas are discussed here, particularly evident during the Fremont and Numic periods.

The Great Basin culture area includes two physiographic zones (Fig. 5.1). The first is the actual Great Basin, 165,000 square miles of land on the eastern border of California, the southeastern corner of Oregon, all of Nevada, the eastern half of Utah, and the southern border of Idaho. The topographic boundaries are the crest of the Sierra Nevada in the west and the Wasatch Mountains in the east. The Columbia and Colorado River drainages form the northern and southern boundaries, respectively (Grayson 1993).

The second physiographic zone is the northern Colorado Plateau (Marwitt 1986). The western boundary of this zone is the Wasatch Mountains, and whereas the Rocky Mountains form the eastern boundary, the Colorado River marks its southern extent, and the Uinta Mountains form the northeastern boundary.

Both zones are highly variable in their environmental settings. The Great Basin features north–south-trending mountain ranges interspersed with low-lying valleys. The Colorado Plateau consists of highland regions dissected by rivers and narrow canyons (Grayson 1993; Marwitt 1986).

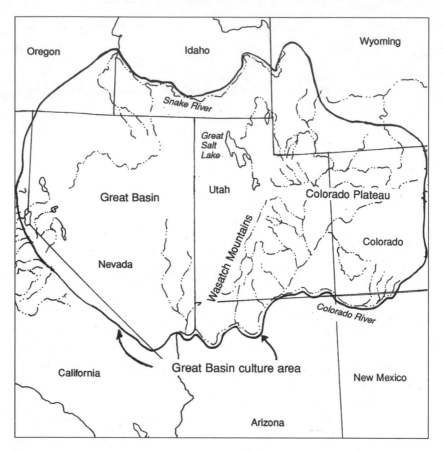

Figure 5.1 Physiographic zones in the Great Basin culture area.

THE ARCHAIC PERIOD

Holocene climatic conditions were well established by 5500 B.C., marking the area's transformation into the Archaic period (La Point 1987). The Archaic lasted until the introduction of maize agriculture, which signals the beginning of the Fremont period. The date of the transition between these two periods varies within the Great Basin cultural region: A.D. 450 is the date most often cited in northwestern Colorado (Marwitt 1986).

With the onset of the Holocene, the foraging adaptation of the Paleoindian period expanded (Pitblado 1993). A truly broad-based foraging system with an increase in harvesting small fauna, like rabbits, waterfowl, and rodents, along with the larger mule deer, mountain sheep, and prong-horn, is evident after 4000 B.C. (La Point 1987). Animals were hunted using a variety of methods, in particular, spears for larger animals and snares and traps for smaller prey. Rabbits were hunted individually or in large drives in which they were caught in nets stretched across access routes and then killed (Aikens and Madsen 1986; Grayson 1993; Jennings 1987).

Increased exploitation of plants is evident in digging sticks, basketry, and ground stone (Grayson 1993; La Point 1987). Coprolite and macro-botanical specimens recovered from adjacent areas of Utah, in which pickle-weed is ubiquitous, also support the idea of the increased importance of plants during the Archaic period (Aikens and Madsen 1986; Jennings 1978).

Increases in ground stone and seed processing are particularly interest-ing, because processing the available seeds (particularly pickleweed) was labor-intensive. But because of the drying trend associated with the onset of the Altithermal, water-intensive plants such as cattails disappeared, making seed processing an attractive option (Aikens and Madsen 1986). Upland zones became more important for hunting mountain sheep, increasing the exploitation of upland grasses.

However, within this general Archaic adaptation there is considerable variation across space and through time (Aikens and Madsen 1986; Madsen and Berry 1975). The Great Basin and the northern Colorado Plateau zones that lie within the Great Basin culture area are heterogeneous environments, and the Archaic exploitation pattern makes use of different seasonal micro-zones. Differences in seasonal and elevational plant availability were exploited in the seasonal round by Archaic peoples in northwestern Colorado (Aikens and Madsen 1986; La Point 1983; Schroedl 1976). The demographic and environmental factors affecting this subsistence economy varied through time. This variation is evident in deposits in deeply stratified sites in eastern Utah and western Colorado. Based on this research, Alan Schroedl (1976) has suggested the presence of four distinct phases. Similar phases can be found in other areas of the Great Basin culture area, though dates vary. However, because events in these other areas did not affect the Archaic period adapta-tion in northwestern Colorado, they are not discussed here.

Black Knoll Phase

The Black Knoll phase is often associated with Pinto basin projectile points (Fig. 5.2), dates between 6350 and 4250 B.C., and is similar to the Wendover phase in Utah (Aikens and Madsen 1986; La Point 1987). The Black Knoll is

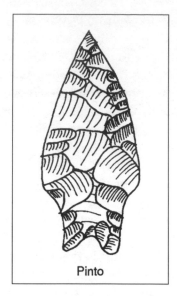

Pinto

Figure 5.2 Early Archaic period projectile points from northwestern
Colorado.

characterized by an increasing population, evident in the increased number of sites.

The subsistence economy was elevationally and seasonally specific.
That is, higher elevations were used during warmer months when large
mammals (mainly mule deer, pronghorn, and sheep) were hunted and
some upland grass species were gathered. In winter months, the lower elevations were used. These sites indicate heavier use of small mammals and
plants, particularly those found along marsh zones (cattail) or dried
Pleistocene lakes (pickleweed) (Aikens and Madsen 1986; La Point 1987).

Castle Valley Phase

The Castle Valley phase dates between 4250 and 2550 B.C. and is witness to a
decrease in the number of sites in northwestern Colorado (La Point 1987).
This decrease is generally interpreted as a decrease in population, possibly
resulting from movement of some of the population into adjacent regions
of Utah. In fact, the same time period in Utah (early Black Rock period) is
characterized by a 400 percent increase in the number of sites (Aikens and
Madsen 1986). Late in the Castle Valley phase (after 3050 B.C.), the number
of sites and population climbs again in Colorado, but Black Knoll phase

levels are not reached. The reasons for the variations in site density are still unclear. Grayson (1993) argues that improved environmental conditions associated with the end of the Altithermal in the Great Basin proper resulted in increased diversity of site location, including use of upland and shallow-water marshes and lakes, and may have resulted in an actual population increase.

Throughout this phase, sites become increasingly formalized. In Utah and Nevada this resulted in the presence of shallow, saucer-shaped pit houses ranging from 10 to 18 feet in diameter (Grayson 1993). In northwestern Colorado it is seen as increasing formalization of features such as slab-lined fire pits (La Point 1987; Schroedl 1976). This formalization can be interpreted as increasing lengths of stay at campsites, although the seasonal round using elevational differences continues.

Green River Phase

One of the most intriguing aspects of the Green River phase (2500 to 1350 B.C.) is the differences in the adaptation between the northeastern plateau area south and east of the Uinta Mountains and the high plateau to the south (La Point 1987). These differences, which are evident at the beginning of the phase and much less noticeable by its end, appear to be restricted to the material culture. But it is unclear whether the differences are from an expansion of Central High Plains groups into the area along what is today the Colorado–Wyoming border, or trade between the two regions.

The most noticeable differences are in the projectile point assemblage (Fig. 5.3). In the northeastern plateau, projectile points are dominated by McKean, Duncan, and Hanna styles identical to those found on the Great Plains at this time. Conversely, the high plateau region is characterized by Great Basin types, in particular Gypsum and San Rafael points (La Point 1987). By the end of this phase, only Great Basin–style points are evident.

Dirty Devil Phase

The Dirty Devil is the last of the Archaic phases defined by Schroedl (1976) and is dated between 1350 B.C. and A.D. 450. Much of the material culture of the high plateau tradition in the Green River phase is still evident, with one technological innovation—the bow and arrow (La Point 1987). Projectile points of this period include the Gypsum, Rose Spring, and Eastgate series (Aikens and Madsen 1987; La Point 1987; Fig. 5.4).

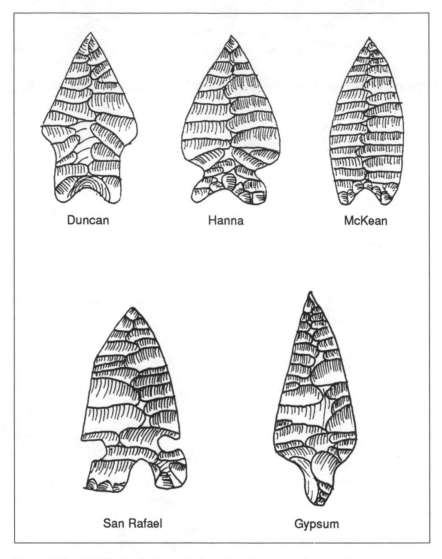

Figure 5.3 Middle Archaic period projectile points for northwestern Colorado.

In contrast to the material culture, there are marked demographic shifts. Population movements were a result of wetter conditions and culminated in the abandonment of several areas of Utah in 1000 B.C. (Aikens and Madsen 1986). More moisture meant higher lake and marsh areas, which affected the shallow marsh resources that were previously exploited. This is particularly noticeable near the Great Salt Lake in Utah and resulted

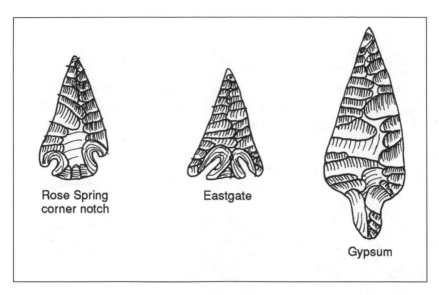

Figure 5.4 Late Archaic period projectile points for northwestern Colorado.

in population movement into upland areas of eastern Utah and northwestern Colorado (La Point 1987).

The end of the Archaic period in general and the Dirty Devil phase in particular signifies the appearance of a number of aspects of material culture generally associated with the Fremont period. The Colorado–Utah border is one of the areas where these changes occurred relatively early (Grayson 1993; La Point 1987; Marwitt 1986).

THE FREMONT

Between A.D. 400 and 1350, much of the eastern Great Basin culture area (i.e., most of northern and central Utah and portions of eastern Nevada and northwestern Colorado) was inhabited by peoples whose lifeways were clearly different from those who came before. These peoples are referred to as the Fremont because they were first investigated along Utah's Fremont River (Grayson 1993; Jennings 1978; Marwitt 1986).

The Fremont area shows a great deal of variability through time and across space. This variability is from adaptation to local environmental conditions that also are evident throughout the Archaic period, differences in the intensity and direction of trade and communication networks, and

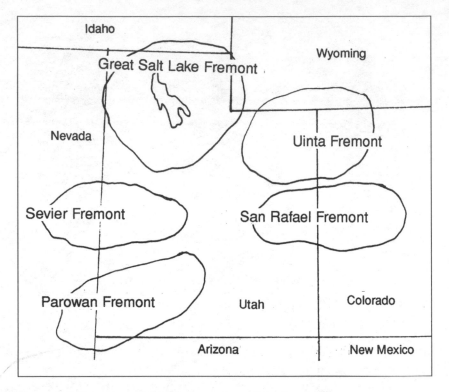

Figure 5.5 Location of the five branches of the Fremont.

demographic factors (Grayson 1993; La Point 1978). Because of the variability, five branches have been defined for the Fremont (Fig. 5.5), three of which are in the eastern Great Basin physiographic zone west of the Wasatch Mountains: the Parowan, centered in the Parowan Valley of southwestern Utah; the Sevier, on the Sevier River in west-central Utah; and the Great Salt Lake of northwestern Utah. Two branches are found on the northern Colorado Plateau east of the Wasatch Mountains: the Uinta Fremont, which is in the Uinta basin of northeastern Utah and northwestern Colorado, and the San Rafael Fremont, located in east-central Utah and west-central Colorado (Jennings 1978; Marwitt 1986; Table 5.1).

Despite the variability of the Fremont period, the different branches are more similar to each other than to groups in the surrounding areas; therefore, they are considered a related adaptation that shares some ritual concepts that differentiate them from the horticulturalist in the Anasazi region to the south. The material culture that characterizes this Fremont adaptation

TABLE 5.1
Summary of the Locations and Dates
Associated with Each Branch of the Fremont

Branch	Location	Dates
Parowan	Parowan Valley, southwestern Utah	Summit phase, 450–1100
		Paragonah phase, 1100–1250
Sevier	Sevier River, west-central Utah	780–1260
Great Salt Lake	Great Salt Lake, northwestern Utah	Bear River phase, 400–1000
		Leeve phase, 1000–1350
Uinta	Uinta basin, northeastern Utah and northwestern Colorado	Cub Creek phase, 650–800
		Whiterocks phase, 800–950
San Rafael	East-central Utah and west-central Colorado	A.D. 700–1200

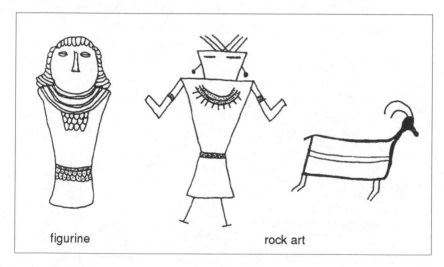

figurine   rock art

Figure 5.6 Fremont rock art and figurines.

includes locally made thin-walled gray pottery, pit houses and aboveground storage structures, distinctive one-rod-and-bundle basketry, moccasins, clay figurines, and rock art. The rock art and figurines can be classified into a number of motifs centering on various animals (particularly bighorn sheep) and plants. The most characteristic, however, are humanlike figures with trapezoidal or triangular bodies, elaborate headdresses and necklaces, and occasionally shields (Cassells 1983; Jennings 1978; Marwitt 1987; Fig. 5.6).

There is also variability in the subsistence system, degree of sedentism, village size, type of architecture, and settlement pattern. To address the defining characteristics of each of the five branches, we need to understand the reasons for the rise of the Fremont adaptation out of the indigenous Archaic base.

Fremont Origins

Despite the superficial similarities between Fremont and early Anasazi, or Basketmaker, sites, there is little relationship between the Fremont and the Anasazi of the Four Corners. Fremont adaptation is an indigenous development that incorporated ideas from the Mogollon region of southern New Mexico and Arizona. The two main ideas are pottery production and maize, bean, and squash horticulture (Grayson 1993; Jennings 1978; Marwitt 1986).

Extensive data show considerable continuity in moccasin, basketry, and lithic styles and technology from the previous Archaic period. This also is true of the ritual system as represented in the rock art. Also, Fremont origins are contemporaneous with early Mogollon villages, which share many characteristics of architecture and ceramic design with the Fremont area, predating their establishment in the Anasazi region. Third, the corn used by the Fremont—known as Fremont Dent—is resistant to drought, environmental extremes, and short growing seasons (Jennings 1978). It appears to have developed in the Fremont area from early species found in the Mogollon highlands but is not the same species found in the Four Corners region.

Given that the Fremont tradition is a local adaptation that borrowed certain ideas from the Mogollon to the south, the question remains, why did this change in settlement pattern and subsistence occur? The earliest indication of horticultural practices and true Fremont adaptation is approximately A.D. 400 in the Wasatch Mountain region.

In addition to a general population increase, in A.D. 400 the Wasatch region experienced a climate change that allowed collecting activities to intensify. This change was the result of northward incursions of very warm, moist air masses with summer-dominated rainfall that lengthened the growing season, which in turn was favorable to horticulture (Grayson 1993). When the incursions ceased around A.D. 1350, so did the Fremont adaptation of mixed horticulture and wild resource exploitation.

Fremont adaptation did not emerge at exactly the same time in all places of the Fremont area. It is probably best to think of the Fremont as a complex patchwork arising from a highly varied Archaic tradition. The result is that the very definition of Fremont is variability (Grayson 1993; Marwitt 1986).

Parowan Fremont

The Parowan branch is centered in the Parowan Valley of southwestern Utah and is distinguished from the other branches of the Fremont by, among other things, village size. Villages are relatively large (ten to twenty structures) and consist of closely spaced pit houses with coursed adobe storage structures (Marwitt 1986).

The pit houses are semi-subterranean with brush superstructures covered in plaster. They vary in shape from circular to rectilinear and are generally about two feet deep. The hearths are in the centers of the pit houses and often contain ventilator shafts to the outside and deflectors. Storage structures are generally aboveground features constructed of jacal. Adobe granaries (about four feet by six feet and three to four feet high) are common. They have cobble and adobe floors and are often subdivided into chambers (Jennings 1978). Subterranean storage pits also are found on occasion (Marwitt 1986).

Midden deposits at Parowan sites are very deep, indicating long-term use, which is further confirmed by evidence of numerous rebuilding and remodeling episodes at most sites (Marwitt 1986). In the midden deposits are large numbers of flaked bone scrapers, bone awls and rings, anthropomorphic figurines, pottery, ground stone, chipped stone, and floral and faunal material (Jennings 1978).

The ceramic assemblage is dominated by local gray-wares including Snake Valley gray, Snake Valley black-on-gray, and Snake Valley corrugated, along with small amounts of Anasazi wares from the Kayenta and Virgin River areas. The chipped stone assemblage includes a variety of bifacial forms including diagnostic Parowan basal notched and Cottonwood projectile points (Fig. 5.7). The floral and faunal material indicates a mixed horticultural and hunting-and-gathering subsistence system. Wild plant resources recovered from granaries include pickleweed, amaranth, piñon nuts, globe mallow, ricegrass, and beeweed (Jennings 1978; Marwitt 1986).

Permanent habitation sites are usually in valley floors, on alluvial fans, or near permanent springs, where floodwater and irrigation farming were practiced and numerous plant resources are available. Seasonal

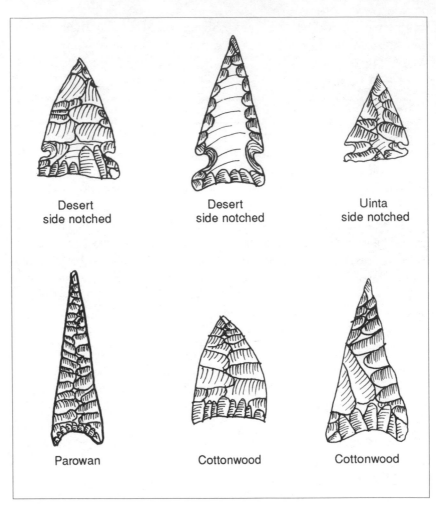

Desert side notched	Desert side notched	Uinta side notched
Parowan	Cottonwood	Cottonwood

Figure 5.7 Fremont period projectile points.

hunting-and-gathering camps are found in caves and rock shelters and are reminiscent of Archaic period sites (Jennings 1978; Marwitt 1986).

Fremont occupation in the Parowan Valley is divided into two phases based on changes in the material culture (Marwitt 1986). The Summit phase dates between A.D. 450 and 1100, during which the pit houses are circular and corrugated ceramics are absent. Anthropomorphic figurines, while present, are unfired and are of simple construction. The Paragonah phase dates from A.D. 1100 to 1250. During this period, house shape is varied, but rectilinear forms are more common. Corrugated pottery is added to the ceramic assemblage, and the anthropomorphic figurines are fired and more elaborate.

Sevier Fremont

The Sevier branch of the Fremont is located in west-central Utah and the adjacent portions of eastern Nevada along the Sevier River. Fremont occupation in this area is confined to the dates of A.D. 780 to 1260, with no internal phase markers.

The Sevier area's geography and material culture are transitional (Jennings 1978; Marwitt 1986). The Sevier branch sits on the boundary of the Great Basin and Colorado Plateau, lending ecological diversity to the area. Whereas sites in its core have definable characteristics, sites away from the core are a blend of the Sevier branch and the branch in the nearest definable area. From this perspective, the typology of the different branches works poorly and should be thought of as a heuristic tool only. The diversity in the Fremont in general and the Sevier branch in particular is a reflection of local choices due to environmental diversity and social parameters. Therefore, the following discussion is relevant to the core area of the Sevier only.

Sites are typically small hamlets (two to three houses) on an alluvial fan at a canyon mouth near a permanent water source, preferably a marsh (Marwitt 1986). They are characterized by rectangular pit houses with several adobe or jacal storage structures. The pit houses are usually about two feet deep with a central basin-shaped hearth. Ventilators are informal and often absent (Jennings 1978).

In addition to the small farming villages, numerous temporary resource extraction sites indicate a heavy dependence on wild resources to supplement the horticultural system. These resources were extracted from distant locations and from adjacent marshes.

The material culture is highly variable. The main diagnostic is Sevier gray-ware, which is distinguished by basalt temper. Both plain and painted forms are found, with wide-mouthed jars and shallow bowls the most common (Jennings 1978; Marwitt 1986).

As with most Fremont areas, bone tools are common, particularly scrapers and fleshers. Bone ornaments, however, are restricted to rectilinear pendants. Diagnostic chipped stone forms mirror the Parowan branch, especially Parowan basal notched and Cottonwood triangular points. Figurines, stone pipes, and ground stone forms are similar to those in adjacent areas (Jennings 1978).

Great Salt Lake Fremont

The Great Salt Lake branch of the Fremont, which surrounds the Great Salt Lake in northwestern Utah, is an area in which horticulture was never fully adopted. Rather, the subsistence economy was based on the exploitation of wild resources—especially bulrush and amaranth seeds, waterfowl, and big game—from the fresh- and saltwater marshes of the area (Marwitt 1986). Occasional findings of corncobs indicate that knowledge and use of agriculture existed, but it was never common here, possibly because the saline levels in the soils were too high for domesticates to grow (Jennings 1978; Marwitt 1986).

But lack of agriculture does not mean the population was mobile. On the contrary, pit house villages with numerous storage pits for marsh resources were common. The sedentary nature of the population combined with several aspects of material culture makes this more a Fremont than an Archaic adaptation. It should be noted, however, that some seasonal movement did occur.

The seasonal rounds include continued use of upland regions as in previous periods. In the warmer months bison, pronghorn, mountain sheep, and deer hunting is especially important. Winter sites are concentrated in lower elevations on marsh edges where wintering waterfowl and seed crops are abundant (Marwitt 1986).

The material culture is different from that of other branches, as would be expected given the differences in subsistence. For example, the ground stone assemblage is dominated by mortars and pestles rather than manos and metates. The chipped stone assemblage differs as well, with slate knives joining bifaces and unifaces. The most common projectile points are Desert side notched (see Fig. 5.7).

Worked bone, common in all branches of the Fremont, is evident in bone awls, fleshers, knives, and saws. Unique to the Great Salt Lake branch are bone whistles and harpoon heads used for hunting and fishing in the marshes. The local pottery is Promontory gray, which can be distinguished by its temper (calcite) and manufacturing technique (paddle-and-anvil). A second gray-ware— Great Salt Lake gray—is characterized by sand temper and coil-and-scrape manufacturing. Trade-wares include Uinta, Parowan, and Sevier grays (Jennings 1978; Marwitt 1986). Also, locally made, unfired anthropomorphic figurines and clay pipes are common.

The Great Salt Lake Fremont period is usually divided into two phases that can be distinguished by architectural changes (Marwitt 1986). The

Bear River phase dates from A.D. 400 to 1000 and features small temporary hunting camps in the uplands and seasonally used pit house villages near the marsh edges. Bear River pit houses are shallow basins with postholes around the edges. The posts converge at a central point above a fire pit, resulting in a conical house that is covered with brush and daub (Jennings 1978). Numerous storage pits are evident at these sites.

The Leeve phase, from A.D. 1000 to 1350, has more substantial architecture consisting of large rectangular structures with clay-lined hearths (Jennings 1978). The substantial nature of the architecture does not correspond with changes in the settlement or subsistence plan, and big-game hunting in upland locations remains important. The other diagnostic of this period is an increase in the number of painted Parowan gray-wares.

Uinta Fremont

The Uinta branch of the Fremont is at the base of the Uinta Mountains in northeastern Utah and northwestern Colorado, and in Dinosaur National Monument. The Fremont occupation of this area was relatively short-lived, being restricted to A.D. 650 to 950 (La Point 1987; Marwitt 1986).

Uinta branch sites tend to be located at high elevations, often on ridges or isolated hills above floodplains appropriate for farming (Jennings 1978; Marwitt 1986). The ceramic assemblage is dominated by Uinta gray, distinguished by its calcite temper and coil-and-scrape method. Trade-wares are limited but include Anasazi types, as well as small amounts of San Rafael and Great Salt Lake gray. Projectile points include Cottonwood, Desert side notched, and Uinta side notched (see Fig. 5.7). The Uinta are unique among the Fremont for not making anthropomorphic figures.

Within this period, two phases can be distinguished regarding settlement pattern and material culture, the first of which is the Cub Creek, dated from A.D. 650 to 800. Sites of this phase are small and represent seasonal rather than year-round occupation. Pit houses are very shallow and have either a single or four central roof supports (Jennings 1978; La Point 1987). Surface storage units are absent, although we find masonry granaries in rock ledges away from sites (Marwitt 1986). There is no evidence of trade-wares, and Uinta gray is limited to plain jars.

The Whiterocks phase (A.D. 800 to 950) is characterized by larger villages with substantial structures of masonry or adobe built into shallow circular pits. Up to twenty of these can be present at a site, particularly in sites near large valleys with abundant farmland (Marwitt 1986). The aboveground storage facilities found in some of these sites and the substantial architecture imply the population is more sedentary (La Point 1987). Alternatively, the same sites may have been returned to year after year. The two best excavated sites have extensive middens and evidence for frequent house remodeling, indicating they were used over many years (Jennings 1978).

The major change in the material culture between the two phases is the addition of textured gray-wares and the use of both bowls and jars. Some Anasazi wares are present at sites dated to the later phase.

San Rafael Fremont

The San Rafael branch of the Fremont is concentrated in east-central Utah and west-central Colorado. This branch is distinguished from other Fremont branches by its architecture, ceramics, and trade patterns. Both pit houses and aboveground masonry (often multiroom) habitation rooms are present. Storage structures and granaries are associated with both (Jennings 1978). Additional storage facilities are found away from habitation sites in small caves and rock shelters (Marwitt 1986).

Pit houses are often slab-lined, whereas the masonry structures are constructed both with and without mortar. In both cases, four central roof supports were used. The structures were plastered on the interior walls, and slab-lined hearths are common. The granaries are often dome-shaped and constructed of adobe (Jennings 1978; Marwitt 1986).

Sites are on hills and ridges overlooking permanent water sources and arable farmland. Agricultural products were a major part of the subsistence system, although hunting-and-gathering were still important.

In material culture, the San Rafael branch can be distinguished from its neighbors by the pottery, the amount of trade-wares, and the elaborate anthropomorphic figurines. The locally made gray-ware, Emery gray, is plain, textured, and painted. Crushed igneous rock was used for temper. The ceramic assemblages at all San Rafael sites also hold considerable amounts of Mesa Verde and Kayenta Anasazi wares. The nature of the trade relations between the San Rafael Fremont and adjacent Anasazi groups are unknown but not unexpected given the proximity of the two areas.

San Rafael is well known for the emphasis on anthropomorphic figures. These rock art and clay figures are found in all the branches of the Fremont except the Uinta, but are most elaborate in the San Rafael area. The figures have detailed facial features, elaborate hairstyles, necklaces and jewelry, and skirts that are appliquéd on the figurines. The unfired clay figurines are painted red, yellow, or green (Jennings 1978). Anatomical detail is sufficient to identify male and female figures.

Fremont Abandonment

By A.D. 1350, Fremont adaptation had ceased throughout the Great Basin and northern Colorado Plateau. The abandonment of this way of life started as early as A.D. 950 in the northeastern edge of the Fremont zone, the Uinta branch (Jennings 1978; La Point 1987). The historical occupants of the Great Basin and northern Colorado Plateau are relatively recent arrivals in the area, which means that not only was the Fremont adaptation abandoned but the region as well. The reasons are unclear, but environmental factors seem to have been important. A gradual retreat of the warm, wet summers that appeared at the beginning of the Fremont period occurred, resulting in a return to a climate that was too dry and cold for horticulture (Lindsay 1986; Marwitt 1986).

Given the increasing unviability of corn agriculture, slight shifts in adaptation occurred. Because hunting-and-gathering had remained important to all of the branches of the Fremont, and in fact was of equal importance for most, it did not require a major organizational shift to return to a more mobile lifeway. This shift could have occurred gradually as groups added pickleweed and piñon nuts back into the diet when domestic crops declined because of the shorter growing season and drier conditions. The result was a return to the use of the topographic relief and variability in resources associated with elevational differences. It was a return to a structure that was heavily exploited during the Archaic period and never totally given up during the Fremont period.

This reconstruction is a plausible explanation for the change in adaptation at the end of the Fremont period, but it does not explain the abandonment of the area by indigenous groups. The reasons for this appear to be related to the entrance of Numic-speaking groups from the east. Numic speakers and indigenous groups may have existed side-by-side for some time, though eventually the Numic groups outcompeted and pushed the other groups to the edges of their previous areas. Protohistoric groups on the northern edge of the Great Basin culture area and possibly in the plains regions along the Colorado–Wyoming border may be remnants of Fremont groups, but the connections are unclear. The ultimate fate of the Fremont simply is not known at this time.

With the abandonment of the Fremont and Anasazi adaptations in western Colorado by A.D. 1350, a new group, Numic speakers, arrived from the western Great Basin. In northwestern Colorado it is unclear if the new emigrants actively interacted with post-Fremont indigenous peoples, or what the level of occupation by indigenous groups was (Grayson 1993; Reed 1995). It is clear, however, that the Fremont period was over and an Archaic-type adaptation was again used by local populations.

The nature of the Numic spread and its timing have been extensively studied. The idea of a recent and rapid spread of Numic speakers from the southwestern edge of the Great Basin throughout the basin and onto the Colorado Plateau was first proposed by linguist Sydney Lamb (1958), based on the distribution of modern linguistic groups. From an archaeological perspective, the Numic spread has been discussed in greatest detail by Robert Bettinger and Martin Baumhoff (1982). Since Bettinger and Baumhoff presented their model, considerable data have come to light that supports their hypotheses (Adovasio and Pedler 1995; Bettinger 1995). It appears that population growth and pressure for territorial expansion among Numic speakers occurred at the same time as territories for horticulture began to contract about 1,000 years ago (Aikens 1995; Grayson 1993). Numic speakers were able to flourish in these areas while indigenous economies were failing because their subsistence system and mobility pattern were different.

Within the Numic language group, there are three branches, each with two languages. These branches begin in Death Valley, on the California–Nevada border and radiate in a fanlike distribution throughout the Great Basin and onto the Colorado Plateau and Rocky Mountains (Bettinger 1995; Grayson 1993; Fig. 5.8). The northwestern branch contains the Mono and Northern Paiute languages, the central branch the Panamint and Shoshoni languages, and the southern branch the Kawaiisu and Ute. Aside from the distribution, one of the most interesting aspects is the degree of homogeneity within a language. For example, the same Shoshoni language spoken in southern Nevada also is spoken on the Snake River, although it differs substantially from the Mono Lake language just a few miles away. Based on glottochronological and archaeological data for the widely dispersed Shoshoni, Paiute, and Ute languages, Lamb (1958) and Bettinger and Baumhoff (1982) argue that a rapid and recent spread of the three Numic divisions occurred, probably within the past 700 to 500 years. During this expansion, indigenous populations were displaced to the

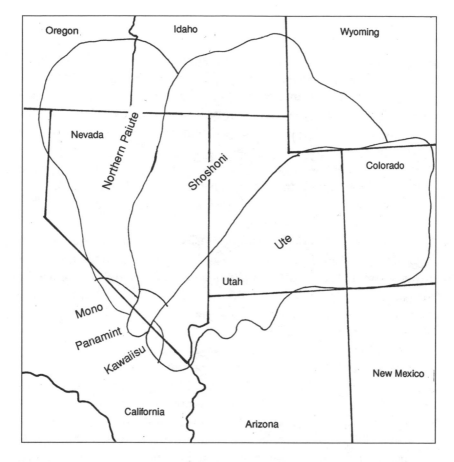

Figure 5.8 Ethnographic distribution of Numic language groups in the
Great Basin culture area.

peripheries of the Great Basin because of increasing population pressure
from new immigrants and deteriorating environmental conditions (Aikens
1995; Bettinger and Baumhoff 1982).

To understand the why and how of this spread, Bettinger and
Baumhoff looked at the archaeological data and concepts of subsistence
efficiency. Bettinger and Baumhoff (1982) argue that the pre-Numic,
indigenous inhabitants of the eastern Great Basin followed a *traveler* strategy "in which high residential mobility and extensive resource monitoring
sustain relatively selective subsistence patterns centered on low-cost, high-
return resources" (Bettinger 1995:46). Traveler strategies are low cost in

terms of resource processing, relying on resources of high quality (i.e., high rank), but incur greater costs in travel time. In northwestern Colorado this is seen in the seasonal movement in elevation and concentration on hunting deer and mountain sheep, before and after the Fremont period.

This strategy contrasts with Numic patterns that Bettinger and Baumhoff refer to as a *processor* strategy, which is "more residentially tethered and supports more people per unit area over a given region" (Bettinger 1995:46). Processors follow a high-cost strategy by relying on resources with high processing costs relative to benefit (i.e., low rank), but they incur lower costs in travel time. This pattern was followed by historic and prehistoric Numic speakers for which resources were considerably higher in cost to procure (such as seeds).

In situations of low-population density with little competition for high-rank resources, the traveler strategies used by pre-Numic speakers are advantageous in the Great Basin and northern Colorado Plateau environments. Conversely, when population density is higher, as it was in the southwestern Great Basin around 1,000 years ago when Numic expansion began, there is an increase in competition for high-ranking resources. In these situations, there is a competitive advantage to the group more willing and able in terms of labor and social organization to engage in high-cost strategies, which the Numic speakers did. Numic speakers had this advantage because they exploited all of the resources that pre-Numic speakers did, thereby increasing the competition for them. However, Numic speakers also exploited resources that pre-Numic speakers did not, thus lessening the competition for these resources and giving the Numic speakers an advantage during periods of environmental degradation and population increase. This resulted in Numic speakers displacing the indigenous pre-Numic inhabitants in the eastern Great Basin culture area (Bettinger 1995; Bettinger and Baumhoff 1982; Grayson 1993).

But if processing strategies were more efficient, given the environmental and demographic conditions, why did change not occur in the pre-Numic speakers' adaptation, as it had in previous times? The answer may be that the time period involved was short due to the influx of new people, and competition was too great for the necessary changes in technology, concepts of land tenure, mobility, resource perception, and labor organization. Pre-Numic speakers were pushed to the edges of their former territories where their previous subsistence strategies could be used. This is clearest on the western and northwestern edges of the Great Basin and less obvious in eastern Utah and western Colorado (Aikens 1995). This may be because we do not understand the ending of the Fremont period and post-Fremont adaptation by indigenous groups very well. Clearly, the period between the Fremont and Numic occupation needs further study.

Data generally support Bettinger and Baumhoff's (1982) argument that Numic speakers are processors who displaced the pre-Numic travelers because of their higher cost strategy in an area of rapidly increasing population density.

If Bettinger and Baumhoff's model is correct, we should see differences in diet breadth and content, as well as settlement patterns for the pre-Numic and Numic speakers. Pre-Numic travelers should use the full range of topography, move often, and exploit high-ranking resources like deer and mountain sheep with a lower dependence on small seeds (Bettinger and Baumhoff 1982). When seeds and nuts are exploited they should be exploited when they are at their ripest and require minimal processing (Bettinger 1995).

Conversely, Numic-speaking processors should concentrate more heavily on seed and nut crops (particularly roots, acorns, piñon nuts, grass seeds, and berries) and game hunting in the areas where these plants are found (Bettinger and Baumhoff 1982). Additionally, they should increase the harvest period to maximize their return (Bettinger 1995) by harvesting some resources while still green, resulting in still higher processing rates.

Second, we should be able to track the spread of the processors based on changes in settlement and subsistence patterns through time and across space. This spread should begin in the Death Valley region and spread across the Great Basin and onto the Colorado Plateau rapidly, corresponding with a retraction of traveler-based settlement and subsistence patterns.

Finally, there should be evidence of differences in social, political, and ideological systems in an area as Numic speakers replace pre-Numic groups. These changes should be particularly noticeable in issues of labor organization and concepts of usable resources. The latter should be evident in ritual context as it relates to ceremonies concerning fertility and hunting success.

The archaeological databases necessary to test the model are numerous. The first implication can be tested with data on the timing and nature of seed harvesting and processing, projectile point distribution, seed-processing technology, and settlement pattern. The second should be evident in the chronological data, and the third in the location and nature of the rock art.

Chronological Data

Most archaeologists agree that the earliest evidence of Numic sites and processor adaptive strategies is on the southwestern edge of the Great Basin, particularly in the Owens Valley, Panamint Valley, and Death Valley between A.D. 200 and 600 (though Aikens [1995] argues the western Great Basin itself is the heartland of the Numic spread). Bettinger (1995) believes that these sites represent the division of inner Numic (Mono, Panamint, and Kawaiisu) and outer Numic (Shoshoni, Paiute, and Ute) groups. The differences in these sites indicate a transition to a processor mode.

Between A.D. 600 and 1000, seed (particularly ricegrass) and nut (particularly piñon) harveting intensified (Bettinger and Baumhoff 1982). Green phase procurement, increased residential length, and bulk storage for winter use appears shortly after A.D. 600, particularly in sites in the White Mountains on the eastern edge of the Owens Valley (Bettinger 1995). From the White Mountains, these sites spread to the east. By A.D. 1350, similar sites are found in the eastern Great Basin physiographic zone (Grayson 1993).

Seed Harvesting and Processing

Bettinger (1995) states that whereas the use of pickleweed dates back to the early Archaic period, use of a more extensive seed, grass, berry, and piñon complex is restricted to Numic times. Also, harvesting and processing methods are distinctly different between the two groups.

Seed and nut harvesting by pre-Numic groups is restricted to ripe seeds, or what Bettinger refers to as *brown phase procurement* (1995). This results in many resources becoming available at the same time, and, therefore, the diet breadth is restricted to some degree due to scheduling conflicts. The advantage of this system is that the resources are relatively easy to harvest and process, but there is a limited harvest time.

Numic speakers also participated in brown phase procurement. To speed the procurement process and ensure access to the maximum number of patches during a limited time, they developed a number of specialized tools. The most common of these is the Numic twined seed beater and winnowing trays, which are distinctly absent in pre-Numic times (Adovasio and Pedler 1995; Bettinger 1995; Bettinger and Baumhoff 1982; Fig. 5.9). These items of basketry are not only new to the material culture record in Numic times but are constructed in totally different ways in terms of wall construction, twining and coiling patterns, weave methods, and elements of decoration (Adovasio and Pedler 1995). The styles go

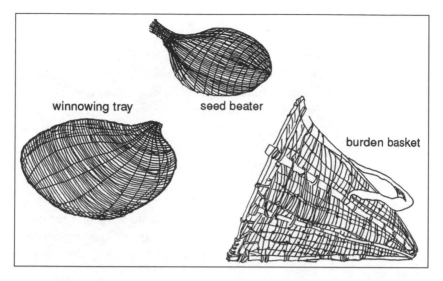

Figure 5.9 Charicteristic Numic baskets.

beyond functional shifts and represent differences in concepts of isochrestic patterns, as defined by Sackett (1990). Fremont and Archaic Great Basin–style basketry and sandals are absent in Numic sites.

In addition to the brown phase, *green phase procurement* is evident at Numic sites but absent from pre-Numic sites (Bettinger 1995). Green phase procurement occurs before the seed or nut is fully ripe, resulting in increased harvest time and decreased scheduling conflicts for seed-intensive collecting. However, processing time increases considerably. Piñon cones must be roasted and then beaten with a stick and anvil to loosen the nuts. Grass seeds must be dried, threshed, and winnowed. Winnowing floors, anvils, and other ground stone processing implements are common at Numic sites but absent in pre-Numic sites.

Projectile Points

Projectile points found at Numic sites are not new to the Great Basin, with Desert side-notched and Cottonwood triangular points the most diagnostic (Reed 1995; see Fig. 5.7). Both of these existed during Fremont times, though rarely together. Conversely, they are often found in associated context in Numic sites.

More indicative of the differences between Numic and pre-Numic peoples, however, is the distribution of these projectile points across the landscape. During pre-Numic times (Archaic, Fremont, and post-Fremont), projectile points are most often found at small hunting stations far from the base camps, as well as at the camps themselves (Bettinger and Baumhoff 1993). These hunting stations include upland warm-season camps and lowland cold-weather camps positioned in relationship to the seasonal round of the most common game, mountain sheep.

Numic period points are found only at base camps, usually containing large amounts of milling equipment and bedrock mortars. Specialized hunting camps are rare or absent, and projectile point distribution is determined by plant resource distribution and availability for Numic speakers, rather than seasonal movement of large game (Bettinger 1995; Bettinger and Baumhoff 1982). Even when Numic sites are found at higher elevations, the faunal assemblage is often dominated by smaller mammals (like marmots) rather than those producing more meat, such as deer or mountain sheep.

Settlement Pattern

On one hand, Numic speakers have low residential mobility, are at base camps for longer periods due to processing requirements, and have larger groups to facilitate labor organization. Pre-Numic groups on the other hand, are more mobile, less sedentary, and are organized into smaller social groups. This contrast is evident when the settlement patterns of both groups are examined.

Pre-Numic, post-Fremont sites are represented by small, ephemeral artifact scatters, indicating high mobility and small groups. Also, large base camps are rare (Reed 1995).

In contrast, Numic settlement patterns consist of base camps surrounded by close-in limited activity sites, which indicates that the populations are tethered to the base camp. The camps often contain large numbers of storage pits and round brush dwellings anchored by stones similar to historic wickiups (Bettinger 1995).

Rock Art

Pre-Numic rock art shows a great deal of stylistic and ideological continuity between the Archaic, Fremont, and post-Fremont periods. The rock art is often positioned on game trails and commonly depicts mountain sheep, hunting weapons, and trapezoidal anthropomorphic figures (see Fig. 5.2).

The iconography involved in this rock art is generally interpreted as representing concepts of wild resource fertility and hunting magic (Bettinger and Baumhoff 1982).

Modern Numic groups claim that this rock art is not theirs, that they do not know its meaning, and hunting magic is not important to them (Bettinger and Baumhoff 1982). Instead, historic Numic rock art is limited and concentrates on geometric patterns, especially concentric circles and geometric scratches on rock faces.

Pre-Numic rock art sites are almost always located away from residential sites and near preferential hunting areas. The segregation of both ritual and economic space in this way may have occurred to avoid scaring away the game. Numic rock art sites, however, are near residential areas (often extended base camps) in which seed processing is important (Bettinger and Baumhoff 1982).

Sometimes Numic patterns are superimposed on the earlier designs. In fact in several cases Fremont-style rock art appears to have been scratched out by Numic speakers, whereas pre-Numic rock art is never superimposed over Numic, although there are numerous instances where they do not occur together.

Bettinger and Baumhoff (1982) suggest that the destruction of pre-Numic rock art by later Numic inhabitants may be from attempts to either neutralize or purify potentially malevolent magic associated with pre-Numic designs. This ritual activity would permit safe site use and disrupt the activities of pre-Numic groups still using them as hunting locations during Numic expansion into an area.

CONCLUSIONS

Like other areas of the state, the northwest region witnessed a number of different adaptations and at least two separate occupations during the Holocene. During the Archaic period, hunting-and-gathering strategies dominated the subsistence economy whereas during the Fremont period corn agriculture is undertaken to varying degrees. Finally, the original inhabitants of the northwestern portion of the state abandoned both agriculture and the region in the early 1200s, to be replaced by Numic speakers.

CHAPTER 6

The Mountain Region

The high-elevation regions of the state contain a rich and long history of occupation. Although early researchers viewed this area as inhospitable, used only as a refuge during periods of drought at lower elevations, we now know that the region was continuously occupied from Paleoindian times through the Post-Archaic period (Benedict 1992b; Benedict 1979, 1981; Black 1991; Jodry and Stanford 1992). Additionally, demographic studies show no evidence for increased migrations into the mountain regions at any time other than the initial peopling of the area during the Paleoindian period, when peoples from the Great Basin expanded into the region, and during the protohistoric era when Numic speakers arrived (Black 1991; Guthrie, et al. 1984; Pitblado 1993; Reed 1995; see Chapter 5).

Scholars have argued that the mountain regions were exploited seasonally by peoples from the surrounding areas, but the most recent data suggest that the mountain zones were occupied year-round by an indigenous group throughout the Archaic and Post-Archaic periods (Bender and Wright 1988; Benedict 1992; Black 1986, 1991; Kent, et al. 1993; Metcalf and Black 1991). The nature of the settlement pattern and cultural adaptation of the inhabitants of the mountain region are not fully understood. The biggest hindrance to our knowledge of the area is the lack of absolute dates (Guthrie, et al. 1984). The result is that culture histories of adjacent areas are often applied, implying that similar adaptive patterns are present (Cassells 1983; Gunnerson 1987). More recently, however, data have been summarized and synthesized for the mountains themselves, and a new view has emerged.

This chapter summarizes the recent reexamination and current synthesis for the Mountain tradition. As defined by Black (1991), the area encompassed in the Mountain tradition is upland settings in the southern Rocky Mountains of central Colorado, south-central Wyoming, and north-central New Mexico. Included in this zone are the upland parks and peaks along the Continental Divide as well as the Front Range and eastern foothills (including the Hogback Valley west of Denver) and the western slope and high mesa regions to the west, including the Uncompaghre Plateau.

Regarding culture traits, Black (1991) argues that there are six factors generally separating the Mountain tradition from those to the east and west: 1. settlement patterns concentrating on upland locations; 2. the use of split cobble rather than bifacial core reduction; 3. the use of microtools, but not microblades; 4. projectile points with stylistic similarities to those found in the Great Basin; 5. use of short-term camps with structures in high-elevation settings; and 6. Great Basin–style rock art. Within these characteristics of the settlement pattern, environmental exploitation, and lithic technology vary through time.

CHRONOLOGY

The chronology of the mountain zone is problematic. Sites in both high and low elevations are often multicomponent, and the number of absolute dates for the region is limited. Using the dates that are available, along with the stratigraphic placement of diagnostic projectile points, we can establish a broad-based chronology, which represents changes in projectile point style with little or no apparent variation in behavior. From the beginning of the Archaic to the Post-Archaic periods, the mobility and settlement patterns, as well as the regional economic system, were remarkably stable and resilient (Anderson, et al. 1994; Benedict 1992a; Zier 1989). This is reinforced by the continued reuse of both campsites and game-drive systems through time, as well as long-term use of sacred shrines (Benedict 1995, 1996). The temporal breaks are based on stylistic changes in the projectile points, though changing behaviors argued for elsewhere in the state are often assumed to occur in this region as well (Anderson, et al. 1994; Cassells 1983; Gooding 1981; Hand 1991; Jepson and Hand 1994; Zier and Kalaz 1991). As such, Michlovic's (1986) call to abandon meaning-laden terms such as Early, Middle, and Late Archaic seems justified for the mountain region (see Chapter 3). However, because these terms are entrenched in the archaeological literature of the region, they are destined to remain in use.

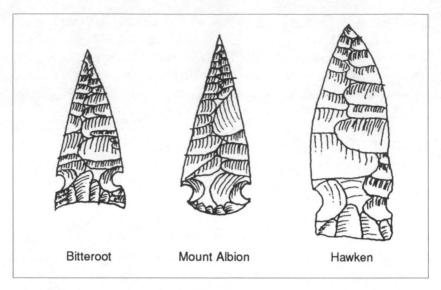

Figure 6.1 Early Archaic period projectile points of the Mountain region.

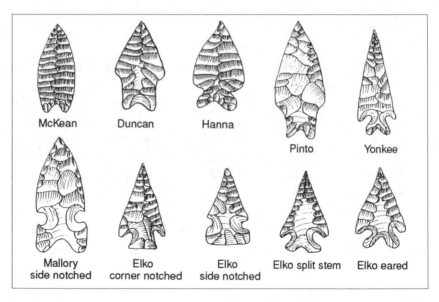

Figure 6.2 Middle Archaic period projectile points of the Mountain region.

The Early Archaic is dated between 5500 and 3000 B.C. and is characterized by the presence of a variety of side-notched projectile point types including Hawken, Bitterroot, and Mount Albion (Fig. 6.1). Locally the early part of this period is sometimes referred to as the Mount Albion

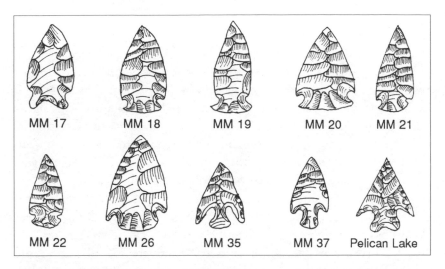

Figure 6.3 Late Archaic period projectile points of the Mountain region.

phase, whereas the later portion is known as the Magic Mountain phase. The Middle Archaic, dated between 3000 and 1000 B.C., is locally referred to as the Apex or McKean period. The McKean, Duncan, and Hanna points characterize the material culture of this period, but we also see Pinto, Mallory, Yonkee, and Elko points in small numbers (Fig. 6.2). The Late Archaic is dated between 1000 B.C. and A.D. 500, during which Pelican Lake and the Magic Mountain series dominate the points (Fig. 6.3).

The Post-Archaic period begins at approximately A.D. 500, but its ending date is unclear. It appears that local mountain populations are either replaced or absorbed by Numic speakers from the west shortly after A.D. 1300, possibly earlier (Reed 1995). The nature of the transition between these groups and the ultimate fate of the indigenous population are still unclear.

ARCHAIC AND POST-ARCHAIC ADAPTATIONS

Mountain occupation in the Archaic and Post-Archaic periods involves a seasonal round that makes use of elevational and seasonal changes. Although this elevationally based seasonal round appears to characterize most, if not all, of the southern Rocky Mountain region, its manifestation in the Front Range and the interior mountains is our focus here (Benedict 1992; Black 1986; Gleichman, Gleichman, and Karhu 1995; Metcalf and Black 1991).

Front Range

Based on seasonal availability and lithic source materials, Benedict (1992a) argues for a seasonal round for the Front Range that is anchored in the winter by base camps in the eastern foothills, particularly the Hogback Valley, and in the late summer and early fall by game drives along the Continental Divide (Fig. 6.4). There is some variability through time on the extent of north–south movement, but the east–west movement encompassing these zones is constant throughout the occupation of the region. Additionally, sites in both areas were frequently reused, though probably not yearly, for 7,000 to 8,000 years (Anderson, et al. 1994; Benedict 1985, 1996; Benedict and Olson 1978; Gooding 1981; Irwin and Irwin 1959; Irwin-Williams and Irwin 1966; Jepson and Hand 1994; Zier 1989; Zier and Kalaz 1991). Whereas sites between these two extremes are not well known, sites in the Hogback Valley and in the high elevations of the Front Range have been extensively studied.

The Hogback Valley. The Hogback Valley constitutes the far eastern edge of the Front Range and lies just west of the Denver basin (see Fig. 6.4). It is bordered on the east by a series of uptilted sandstone formations (hogbacks) and on the west by the sharply rising slopes of the Front Range. As such, it is in a protected location during the winter and affords easy access to a number of different environmental zones. The valley itself is included in the lower elevations of the Piñon-Juniper zone and contains large stands of Gambel oak. Prehistorically, large mammals wintering in the area include pronghorn, mule deer, and elk. Bison were common in the Denver basin and apparently exploited by the inhabitants of the Hogback Valley. Faunal assemblages from archaeological sites indicate a variety of small mammals, and birds were exploited prehistorically (Anderson, et al. 1994; Gleichman, Gleichman, and Karhu 1995; Irwin and Irwin 1959; Jepson and Hand 1994; Zier 1989).

In proximity are numerous outcroppings of raw materials. On the plains, petrified wood is common and cobbles of quartzite can be found in arroyo cuts. Additionally, chert and chalcedony nodules can be found in stream cuts through the hogback. These same raw materials are in highly curated and exhausted tools in high-elevation sites, leading Benedict (1992a) to argue that the two areas are connected in a seasonal round. The presence of lithic material from high-elevation sources in sites in the Hogback Valley, as well as the stylistic similarities in projectile

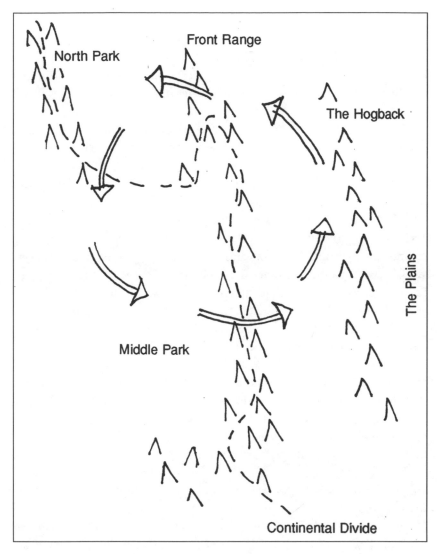

Figure 6.4 Areas of the Mountain region contained in Benedict's (1992a) model of seasonal movement.

points between the two areas, further support this model (Gleichman, Gleichman, and Karhu 1995).

Although systematic survey is not extensive here, numerous sites have been investigated, most of which are in shallow rock shelters or against rock walls near permanent water, all facing south or southwest. These locations allow maximum solar radiation to warm the sites in winter while protecting them from northern winds (Benedict 1992a). Most sites have extremely deep deposits and are multicomponent (Gleichman, Gleichman, and Karhu 1995; Irwin and Irwin 1959; Irwin-Williams and Irwin 1966). Recon John Shelter is one of the best understood of these (Zier 1989; Zier and Kalaz 1991). Comparison with other sites in the region indicates that it is fairly representative (Anderson et al. 1994; Jepson and Hand 1994).

Recon John Shelter is located on the Fort Carson Military Reservation, northwest of Pueblo. It lies in a shallow, west-facing rock shelter overlooking Turkey Creek. Its 2.5 meters (8 feet) of deposit and eleven hearths range from the Middle Archaic through the Early Ceramic periods. Specimens represent 30 plant and 32 animal taxa, as well as 4,159 chipped and ground stone artifacts. Comparisons of the items recovered from the three time periods represented indicate no significant differences in the economic, technological, or mobility strategies. For all three periods, resources were available within a short distance from the site. Combined these data suggest Recon John Shelter was a frequently reoccupied base camp. Throughout the occupation of Recon John Shelter, the prehistoric inhabitants participated in a broad-spectrum hunting-and-gathering strategy exploiting local resources with no evidence of nonlocal lithic or food resources.

High-Elevation Occupation. Two different kinds of sites are found at, and slightly above, the tree line in the Front Range: game-drive systems and base camps (Benedict 1984, 1985a, 1990, 1992a, 1996; Benedict and Olson 1978; Hutchinson 1989). Absolute dates and diagnostic artifacts indicate that both sites generally represent multicomponent occupations, though single component sites occasionally are present. Like sites in the Hogback Valley, high-elevation sites were reoccupied periodically throughout the Archaic and Post-Archaic period. These sites are tied to those in the Hogback by their lithic assemblages, which are dominated by raw materials from the lower elevations of the Front Range. Projectile point types are similar in style and manufacturing technique.

Game-drive sites consist of long walls or wall-and-cairn combinations (Benedict 1985, 1996; Benedict and Olson 1978; Hutchinson 1989). The game drives were not designed for mass kills by running the animals over a topographic feature. Instead mule deer, elk, and bighorn sheep were funneled from grazing lands into a constricted area where they could be ambushed by waiting hunters. These game-drive systems are often several miles long and focused on the natural movement of the animals rather than acting as barriers through which the animals were stampeded.

Seasonality is difficult to determine at high-elevation game-drive sites from archaeological data alone. However, given the periods when the area is impassable due to snow, and when the animals migrate into the higher elevations, late summer and early fall are the most likely times (Benedict 1992a). It should be noted that these game drives also are occasionally conducted at lower elevations, though they are rare (Southwell 1995). Game drives at lower elevations could be used later in the seasonal round. Small bison herds may also have been exploited at these sites, in addition to deer and elk.

Benedict (1992a) argues that high-elevation game drives would require cooperative activity to construct and may represent periods in which humans aggregated. However, small groups could have used these structures too because once constructed, little maintenance is required. Additionally, the hunting system relied on the natural movement of the animals through the game drive and therefore large numbers of people were not necessary. Therefore, rather than a seasonal aggregation, numerous small groups with fluid principles of group membership may have been more common. The social mechanism of the exchange of goods and marriage partners could have occurred through the fluidity of group membership resulting in extensive and far-flung social networks.

Data on group size from the high-elevation base camps is somewhat equivocal. However, relatively few hearths are evident in any one occupation level, giving credence to the presence of small groups. Base camps are located in protected locations in the subalpine forest near a permanent water source. Additionally, they are generally close to a number of different ecozones including the alpine tundra, mountain meadows, and marshes (Benedict 1985; Benedict and Olson 1978; Gooding 1981). This location allows the inhabitants to exploit not only forest products but also stands of bistort, bitterroot, and berries (see Chapter 1 and Appendices 1, 2, and 3).

Lithic materials at sites above the tree line of the Front Range are dominated by sources located in the lower elevations of the Front Range and Hogback Valley, though chert quarries in the upland parks also may have been used (Benedict 1985). The high degree of curation is due largely to the lack of high-quality stone above the timberline. Benedict (1992a) argues that lithic raw material is conserved while at the high-elevation sites in late summer and replenished during winter, when groups move back to lower-elevation camps.

This same pattern is evident throughout the Archaic and Post-Archaic periods in the Front Range. High-elevation sites along the western slope are not as well known, but the similarity in mobility patterns and lithic technology argues that they are similar. The amount of contact between mountain groups east and west of the Continental Divide is unknown at this point and in need of considerably more study. What is evident is that the adaptive strategy used during the prehistoric occupation of the Front Range is highly stable and resilient.

Intermountain Model

Data from the interior of the mountain ranges suggest a much smaller territorial round was used, though seasonal use of elevational differences remains important. Data from the Cottonwood Pass and the North Park areas have been used by Kevin Black and Michael Metcalf to reconstruct the following model (Black 1986; Metcalf and Black 1991).

They argue that the seasonal round in the interior mountain regions took advantage of elevational differences but was restricted in linear distance. Their estimates suggest that small groups of collectors used a broad-spectrum economy that encompassed between 500 and 1,000 square kilometers (310 to 621 square miles) (Metcalf and Black 1991). This restriction in territory can be seen as a continuation of the trends in the territorial restriction of the Paleoindian period in the mountain and plateau regions of the state (Pitblado 1993; see Chapter 3).

Site location and storage differentiate the settlement pattern of the interior mountains from the Front Range. Metcalf and Black (1991; Black 1986) argue that the prehistoric inhabitants of the interior mountains used long-term winter base camps where they relied on stored goods and hunting. In the summer, a series of base camps were used at higher elevations (Fig. 6.5).

Winter base camps were established in river basins and parklands, though not at the lowest elevations in these areas. They were in areas that minimized problems with cold air drainage while maximizing solar radiation, access to animals' winter ranges, and lithic raw material outcrops (Black 1986; Metcalf and Black 1991). They occur in open locations, where pit houses were used, and in rock shelters. Both site types feature extensive storage facilities with evidence at several locations of the reuse of sites in favored areas over long periods (Pool 1997).

While at the winter base camps inhabitants relied on stored goods and fresh meat. As such these camps are often surrounded by limited activity areas, particularly hunting blinds.

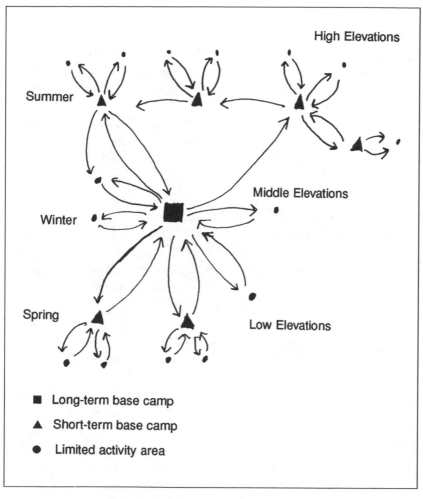

Figure 6.5 Idealized seasonal round proposed by Metcalf and Black (1991) for the interior mountains.

In the early spring, hunting-and-gathering expeditions to lower elevations centered on resources that were coming into fruition at lower elevations. With more resources came longer expeditions, necessitating short-term base camps that were surrounded by smaller limited activity areas (e.g., gathering stations and hunting blinds).

As summer approached and snowmelt occurred in higher elevations, the Mountain Forest and Tundra zones were used. Hunting-and-gathering in these areas was logistically organized with limited activity areas (gathering stations, game drives, and butchering sites) tied to a series of sequentially used base camps. Toward the end of summer and in early fall, intensive hunting-and-gathering built up stores for the winter, which were transported back to the winter base camps. This hunting-and-gathering occurred at higher elevations until the snows began, after which it intensified closer to the winter base camps (Metcalf and Black 1991).

This pattern is evident in the interior mountains during the Archaic and Post-Archaic periods. The long period of stability in the subsistence system combined with the long-term reuse of winter sites indicate a highly resilient system.

SACRED SHRINE SITES

The landscape contained not only resources to be exploited for economic reasons but also sacred spaces, which were often marked or surrounded by shrines that were used over long periods. Old Man Mountain in Estes Park is one example that represents a vision quest site used for over 3,000 years, including the historic period (Benedict 1985b).

Old Man Mountain is an isolated rock formation with a 360-degree view of the surrounding area from the summit and steep drop-offs on all sides. Several distinct artifact clusters are present, each containing a number of rare artifacts including obsidian flakes and a steatite bowl. Also present are ceramics, numerous projectile points, and burned bone, materials that are consistent with those cited in the archaeological record as offerings made by pilgrims to the site. Further supporting the interpretation of ritual activities are numerous river cobbles and boulders from the creeks at the base of the mountain. In some areas these are arranged in patterns similar to those for the construction of sweat lodges, in others the rocks are randomly scattered across the landscape. Benedict's (1985b) review of the ethnographic literature indicates it was common for pilgrims visiting vision quest sites to prove their worthiness and dedication through physical hardship such as transporting heavy materials to the shrine site.

In short, Benedict (1985b) argues that the location of the site and the artifact inventory are consistent with those from the ethnographic record and indicate the fasting, self-mutilation, and acts of purification and dedication of vision quests. Further, based on the findings at Old Man Mountain, he argues that there are numerous similar sites throughout the mountain region.

SCARRED TREE SITES

By A.D. 1300 a new group appeared in the mountain regions of Colorado, the Numic speakers (see Chapter 5). During the historic period, a new type of site is found in the mountain regions associated with the Numic presence—the scarred tree site (Martorano 1981, 1988).

In spring, when ponderosa pines begin their yearly growth, new plant material is generated between the outer bark and the outer ring of the tree. This material is easily removed by scraping once the outer bark has been removed and produces a large amount of highly nutritious material rich in protein, fat, carbohydrates, and numerous minerals (Martorano 1988). This was an important food source for many ethnographic groups.

The peeling process results in a scarred tree, leaving an area without outer bark. The date at which the peeling occurred can be determined by examining dendrochronological samples for the missing ring fragments. Marilyn Martorano (1988) has compiled data regarding the distribution and dates of forty sites containing scarred ponderosa pines—all date after 1790, with most between 1815 and 1875. These sites were found throughout the mountain region and represent one part of the diverse subsistence regimen used by Numic peoples in the 1800s.

CONCLUSIONS

The mountain ranges of Colorado have been occupied from Paleoindian times on. The adaptive strategies used during this time are highly resilient and very stable. It relies on seasonal movement of groups to exploit resources at various elevations.

When and why this pattern stopped being used is unclear. What is clear is that by the A.D. 1300s, a new group, Numic speakers, entered the area from the west. This group originated in the Great Basin (see Chapter 7) and changed its pattern of adaptation slightly and added new food sources as it moved into the higher elevation, across the Continental Divide and into the Front Range and western high Plains region. These patterns of adaptation are discussed in the next chapter.

CHAPTER 7

Epilogue:
The Ethnographic Groups

By the late prehistoric period, much of Colorado had been abandoned by indigenous groups. The southwestern portion of the state was abandoned by the early 1300s. The Fremont adaptation ended between A.D. 950 and 1250 in the northwest and disappeared throughout the Great Basin cultural zone by the mid-1200s. Indigenous Plains peoples withdrew from eastern Colorado by the mid-1400s, probably moving to the east and south. These local abandonments were followed by reoccupation of the state by various groups. Numic-speaking peoples came from the west as part of the Numic spread (see Chapter 5). Eventually, Ute groups occupied most of western Colorado, the Mountain region, and the Front Range and at one time the Comanche dominated eastern Colorado. The Plains were initially reoccupied by Apache groups in the mid-1500s. Plains Apache adaptation peaked in northeastern Colorado with the Dismal River complex along the Republican River from 1640 to 1700, and Plains Apache sites are found throughout the southeastern part of the state during the 1600s. The Plains Apache adaptation ended with the entrance of the Comanche (Numic speakers from the northwest) onto the Plains, an event that effectively displaced Plains Apache groups to the south (see Chapter 3). Following the Apache, the plains witnessed a number of migrations including the Comanche from the west and Athapaskan and Algonquin groups from the north (Fig. 7.1).

All of the historic groups interacted frequently and all were affected by encroaching western expansion. This period was dynamic in terms of group structure, especially changes in subsistence, mobility, and economy related to introduction of the horse and gun (Table 7.1).

TABLE 7.1

Time Line of Events Affecting Indigenous Groups of the Historic Period

Numic Groups

Northwestern Colorado abandoned	950–1250
Southwestern Colorado abandoned	1250–1375
First Numic sites	1350
Comanche/Shoshoni in eastern Rockies in Wyoming	late 1600s
Pueblo revolt in New Mexio	1680s
Comanche obtain the horse	1705
Mexican Records of Comanche raids on Rio Grande	1706

Algonkian Groups

Eastern Colorado abandoned	1400–1450
Plains Apache in Colorado	mid-1500s
Dismal River complex	1640–1700
Arapahoe on Red River, Minnesota	1600
Cheyenne at the mouth of the Wisconsin River	1673
Cheyenne in Minnesota	1684–1688
Cheyenne in a single village on the Sheyenne River, with mixed economy	1700–1770/1790
Cheyenne adopt horse	1750–1770
Close alliance between Cheyenne and Arapaho solidified	1776
Sheyenne River village destroyed by Chippewa	1770/1790
Cheyenne on the Missouri River, ranging to the Black Hills for bison hunting	1794–1795
Cheyenne on the North Platte River	1812
Cheyenne throughout the central plains	1830
Bent's Fort built on the Arkansas River	1833–1834
First wagon train across the Oregon Trail	1841
Pike's Peak gold find	1858
50,000 Americans come to Denver in Gold Rush	1859
Increased warfare with Americans	1857–1879
Sand Creek massacre	1864
Reservations founded	1878

Compiled from Berthrong 1963; Callaway et al., 1986; Hoebel 1960; Noyes 1993; Trenholm 1970; Weist 1977.

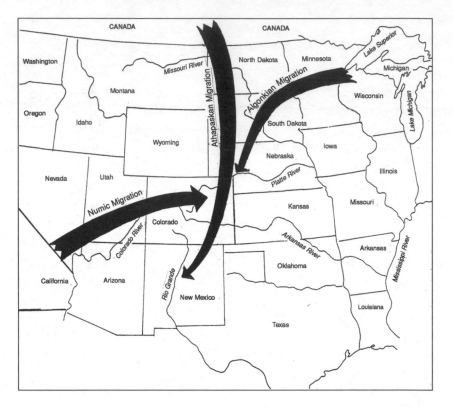

Figure 7.1 Historic migrations of indigenous peoples into Colorado.

NUMIC SPEAKERS

Numic speakers came to the northern Colorado Plateau from the Great Basin relatively recently (see Chapter 6). In Colorado the Numic groups are represented by the Ute and Comanche while the Shoshoni inhabited Wyoming. Because the areas they inhabited and the economic and social organizations they followed were so different, the Ute and Comanche are discussed separately.

Ute

Ute groups in the Great Basin and northern Colorado Plateau are generally divided into eleven bands, six of which inhabited Colorado (Callaway, et al. 1986). The historic location of these groups is as follows: the Mauche Ute

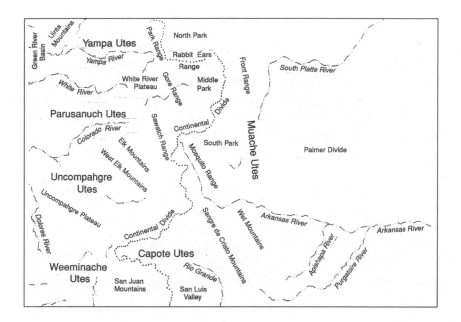

Figure 7.2 Distribution of Ute bands in the 1600s.

occupied the southeastern edge of Ute territory along the Front Range from Trinidad north to Denver (Fig. 7.2). To the west were the Capote Ute, who occupied the area along the Continental Divide south to Conejos County and east to the Rio Grande. The San Luis Valley south to Chama was the major area of occupation, although the higher elevations were also exploited. The Weeminache Ute occupied the area to the west of the Continental Divide in southern Colorado and northern New Mexico. Their territory extended west to the Blue Mountains of Utah. The Uncompahgre Plateau was inhabited by Uncompahgre Ute, who ranged as far east as South Park and as far north as Grand Junction. The higher elevations of the Elk Mountains were also exploited by the Uncompahgre Ute. The Parusanuch and Yampa Ute were found on the White and Yampa Rivers, respectively, but their territories ranged east into the mountains as well. The Parusanuch Ute exploited territories as far east as Middle Park whereas the Yampa Ute territory extended east to North Park.

Bands consisted of a group of related extended families that inhabited an area. Although it was rare for an entire band to aggregate, smaller portions of it did so, seasonally. Generally speaking, the basic economic unit was the extended family, which moved across the landscape either alone or in the company of another family in a seasonal round of hunting-and-gathering for most of the year, using elevational differences to schedule collection times and short-term storage in the winter (Leitch 1979). Multiple families (20 to 30 families or 50 to 100 people) would aggregate in sheltered areas in the winter and separate in the spring (Leitch 1979). Which families traveled together in the smaller groups and which aggregated varied, as alliances were highly fluid (Callaway, et al. 1986).

Comanche

Comanche are a branch of the eastern Shoshoni, who migrated to the eastern slope through the low passes on the Colorado–Wyoming border and spread up and down the Front Range during the last decades of the 1600s (Leitch 1979; Noyes 1993). From this position they successfully exploited both western plains and eastern mountain resources in a foraging pattern similar to their Ute cousins. The southern branch of the eastern Shoshoni spent increasing amounts of time on the Plains, exploiting Plains resources, eventually becoming the Comanche. When they ventured onto the Plains, they were dog nomads; however, in 1705 they obtained the horse and quickly expanded their territories to the south and east.

The Comanche accepted and quickly became dependent on horse nomadism. One reason the horse may have been so attractive is that it significantly lessened the number of people required to take a large number of bison. Given the relatively small size of Shoshoni/Comanche groupings at this time, this would have significantly improved their ability to exploit the Central High Plains.

Horses first became available to the Comanche when the Spanish released many after the Pueblo Revolt of 1680, when the southwestern Pueblos temporarily expelled the Spanish from the northern Rio Grande. However, even after the Spanish returned, the Southwest, especially Spanish settlements, remained a major source of horses through either trade or raids. Comanche raiding activities on Spanish settlements are recorded as early as 1706 (Noyes 1993).

The Comanche were one of the first groups to fully adopt horse nomadism on the central and southern Plains and were known for their expert horsemanship and massive herds. As the horse became more important in the economy of Plains groups, increasing pressure was put on the Comanche as a source of horses (Noyes 1993). In addition to raiding Spanish and American settlements for horse in New Mexico and Texas, the

Comanche themselves were raided by the Cheyenne and Arapaho. The Cheyenne and Arapaho were so successful in their raids that they gradually pushed the Comanche south as they entered Colorado in the early 1800s.

The Cheyenne and Arapaho possessed neither more people nor more firearms, as the Comanche were well supplied through their own trade relations with the Caddoan villagers on the southeastern Plains. Cheyenne and Arapaho success over the Comanche appears to be largely political. They were successful in raids and active warfare against the Comanche, essentially pushing them south of the Arkansas River by 1830, because of their decision-making procedures. The Cheyenne and Arapaho had a series of warrior societies in which decisions about raiding and warfare were centralized. The Comanche lacked these societies and were therefore at an organizational disadvantage (Bamforth 1988). The result is that while eastern Colorado was dominated by the Comanche in the 1700s, it was dominated by the Cheyenne and Arapaho in the 1800s.

ALGONQUIN SPEAKERS

Algonquin groups in Colorado include the Arapaho and Cheyenne, both of which originated in the Great Lakes area and migrated into Colorado in the 1800s, displacing the Comanche. Of the two, the Cheyenne are better known, primarily because they had greater contact with American, British, and French fur traders beginning in the 1600s. The Cheyenne and Arapaho had close trading alliances during the mid-1700s and 1800s and probably earlier. These alliances included calls for mutual aid and a mutalistic economic arrangement in which the Cheyenne often acted as middlemen for the Arapaho in trade relations with other groups (Jablow 1994). Because the Cheyenne are so much better documented in historic records, most of the detailed information relates to them.

The Arapaho were generally on the southwestern or western edge of Cheyenne territory, and similar shifts in economy, mobility, and territoriality occurred in both groups, though at slightly earlier dates for the Arapaho. As recently as A.D. 1600, the Arapaho were living along the Red River of Minnesota (Trenholm 1970). Similarly, French traders record the Cheyenne as a small group living at the mouth of the Wisconsin River in the 1600s (Berthrong 1963; Jablow 1994). Both groups were woodland foragers, exploiting small game, stands of wild rice, and other wild resources. However, the mid-1600s saw competition between northeastern groups due to the rising importance of the European (predominantly French and British) fur trade in native economies and over access to beaver pelts. This was heightened by the competition between French and English traders attempting to establish monopolies in the area (Jablow 1994).

Because of the small size of the Arapaho and Cheyenne groups, they were at a distinct disadvantage. The domination of the area by Cree, Assiniboin, Chippewa, and Sioux resulted in the Arapaho and Cheyenne being pushed west in the late 1600s. By 1700 the Cheyenne had settled in one village on the Sheyenne River in North Dakota and were pursuing a mixed forager/horticultural economy. The Arapaho continued their hunting-and-gathering lifestyles ranging from the Sheyenne River to the Black Hills as dog nomads (Berthrong 1963; Hoebel 1960; Jablow 1994; Weist 1977).

At this time, both groups began to exploit plains products, bison in particular. Neither group possessed the horse or gun, so bison hunting was by individually stalking lone animals or, more commonly, through communal hunts using surrounds. The entire community participated. Women, children, and older men directed the herd into either a natural or artificially created corral where they would be dispatched by hunters with bow and arrow. The animals were then skinned, butchered, and transported by dog-pulled travois back to the village (Weist 1977).

Because the entire community was involved, the Cheyenne would temporarily abandon their village during the summer, after the crops were planted, to mount hunting expeditions. While on the hunt, small conical structures covered with skins (tepees) were used as temporary structures, which became the dominant structure for the Arapaho. Tepees associated with dog nomads are smaller than those of horse nomads, because of the dog's carrying capacity.

Structure size and hunting techniques changed dramatically after 1750, when the Cheyenne obtained the horse. Because the horse was capable of carrying or dragging considerably more weight, the structures became larger. Also, because the bison could now be hunted from horseback with bow and arrow, surrounds were no longer needed to obtain large amounts of meat. As a result, the entire village no longer left the settlement to hunt, and smaller parties ventured out from this time on. After 1750 some Cheyenne migrated farther west, to the Missouri River valley, to find larger herds. The excess meat and hides of these herds allowed the Cheyenne to trade for European goods, especially horses. The remainder of the Cheyenne joined this group on the Missouri River sometime between 1770 and 1790 when their village was destroyed by a group of Chippewa during a raid (Hoebel 1960; Weist 1977).

When they moved to the Missouri River, Cheyenne demand for European goods increased, particularly guns, ammunition, and metal knives needed for defense and bison hunting. Two hindrances to obtaining these goods had to be overcome, which dramatically changed their way of life.

First, the horticultural groups already living on the Missouri River (the Mandan, Hidatsa, and Arikara) had a monopoly on European trade goods in the area and greatly discouraged the traders from making contact with other groups (Jablow 1994). As a result, the Arapaho and Cheyenne had to go through a middleman, specifically the Arikara, rather than trade with the Europeans directly. This meant that the Cheyenne and Arapaho had to produce something that the Arikara did not, to exchange for the European goods. Because the Arikara were horticulturalist, corn was not an option. But the Cheyenne and Arapaho did have horses and bison robes and meat, which were in demand by the Arikara, the French, the British, and, increasingly, American traders. Therefore, while the Cheyenne maintained settled villages on the Missouri River where they participated in horticultural activities, farming was deemphasized as bison hunting became increasingly important (Berthrong 1963; Jablow 1994). This led the Cheyenne to spend more time each year on the Plains, ranging the full length of the Missouri River, west to the Black Hills and south to the Platte River. By 1780 the Arikara were wintering in the Black Hills and returning to the Missouri River villages for trade (Weist 1977). The Arapaho wintered in the Black Hills, south to the headwaters of the Platte River, and eventually the Arkansas River, venturing onto the Plains in the warmer months (Leitch 1979; Trenholm 1970).

The second hindrance was their relationship with the area's nomadic Sioux groups, who had been in competition with each other dating from when the Cheyenne and Arapaho were still in the Great Lakes region. Competition between them increased in the late 1700s as they began to trade in agricultural goods with the Arikara. The Arikara produced excess agricultural goods for trade with Plains groups. The Cheyenne traded horses and plains products for these goods, and the Sioux traded guns and ammunition they had obtained from the east. Jablow (1994) argues that the Sioux attempted to limit Cheyenne contact with the Arikara so they could have exclusive access to Arikara agricultural products and to prevent guns from being traded from the Arikara to their traditional enemies. Because the Sioux were larger in number and had an independent source of firearms, they had the advantage over the Cheyenne. To better their position, the Cheyenne formed alliances with the Arapaho, which equalized the demographic imbalance and increased the supply of horses and bison products available to the Cheyenne for trade with the Arikara (Berthrong 1963). The Cheyenne, in effect, became middlemen between the Arapaho and the Arikara (Jablow 1994; Weist 1977). This arrangement not only strengthened the Cheyenne and Arapaho position relative to the Sioux but also opened up a trade network anchored by Europeans on both ends that stretched across the entire Plains.

The primary source of horses, both wild and tame, was in the Spanish/Mexican settlements of the Southwest. The horses came to the Plains in different ways. First, after the Pueblo Revolt of 1680 the horses that the fleeing Spanish left behind were dispersed onto the Plains through trade, raids, and in wild herds. The Comanche capitalized on this and soon managed large herds. They increased their herd size by further capturing or raiding later Spanish/Mexican settlements.

These herds became the source of horses for the Arapaho, Cheyenne, and other groups in the central and northern Plains. The Arapaho and Cheyenne obtained horses from the wild herds or from trading or raiding Comanche herds. These horses were then traded north where they were in shortage. In contrast, firearms were not available from Southwestern sources because it was specifically outlawed for Spanish to trade guns to the indigenous population (Bamforth 1988). French and British traders in the Northeast had no such prohibition and traded guns and ammunition, along with a variety of other goods, for furs. Therefore, firearms entered the Plains from the northeast and horses from the southwest. This geographic distribution reinforced the alliances between the Arapaho and Cheyenne, as each had better access to a different source. Plains groups, such as the Arapaho and Cheyenne, were instrumental in moving goods from one end of the Plains to the other, with firearms and horses quickly becoming the medium of trade on the plains, and bison meat and robes at the ends of the trade network.

Cheyenne and Arapaho settlement patterns and organization changed, along with their mobility patterns, as the importance of bison increased. Although the Cheyenne lived in a single village on the Sheyenne River, seasonal fissioning of the community became the norm on the Plains. Both the Cheyenne and the Arapaho aggregated into large groups during the spring and summer when the bison herds were gathered and then dispersed into bands in the fall and winter to the eastern Rockies, where they wintered.

The tepee, which had served as a temporary shelter on hunting trips, was now the main structure. Tepees consist of several long poles that come together to form a cone with a point at the top. A covering of hides that have been stitched together and sealed is placed over the poles, leaving a hole at the top for smoke to escape and an entrance near the ground. The poles and edges of the tepee are weighted down with stones. Archaeologically, tepee locations are evident from the remaining rock rings (Brasser 1982). Tepees are easily transported by horse; the poles were used as a frame for the travois and the hide covering was stretched between them to hold belongings.

When a new camp was set up, ceremonies were performed before and during tepee construction (Leitch 1979). These rituals were found in many Plains groups and center around the tepee as a symbolic demarcator, reconstructing the symbolic landscape. Unfortunately, the symbolism associated with Cheyenne and Arapaho tepees and their internal organization are not well understood (Wilson 1995).

The basic habitation, economic, and social unit for the Cheyenne and Arapaho is the extended family. Whereas descent is traced bilaterally, residence tends to be matrilocal, as extended families occupy a cluster of tepees within the site. Several extended families joined together to form a band of 300 to 500 people. The Cheyenne had ten bands, the Arapaho, four. In the winter camps, each band had its favorite spot along the eastern edge of the Rockies. In spring and summer all the bands aggregated, each inhabiting one portion of the camp (Leitch 1979; Trenholm 1970; Weist 1977). During these aggregations cylindric ceremonies were performed, communal hunts were undertaken, and marriages were arranged.

The bands were united not only by common ritual and intermarriage but also by a political structure. Cross-cutting matrilocal family residences, and often, therefore, bands, were a series of men's sodalities, often called warrior societies, although they also had social and civic functions. Membership in these societies was voluntary, and men joined the society of their fathers (Moore 1974). Because of the matrilocal residence pattern, societies cross-cut the bands as well as the extended families, thus uniting the tribe (Hoebel 1960; Leitch 1979; Weist 1977).

The Council of 44, a political body that oversaw and united all the bands, was crucial to the political stability of the Cheyenne (Leitch 1979). Four representatives from each band, as well as four ritual leaders from the tribe as a whole, were chosen. Each representative was a headman in the band and served a ten-year term, after which he selected his successor (Hoebel 1960). The Council of 44 met during the summer gatherings to discuss issues affecting all Cheyenne, and their decisions were carried out by the warrior societies (Weist 1977).

During the 1800s the Cheyenne and Arapaho dominated the area between the Platte and the Arkansas Rivers in eastern Colorado and frequently traveled to the Missouri villages to trade (Hoebel 1960; Leitch 1979). Their position in this trade network was strengthened by a series of alliances with their neighbors and by the construction of Bent's Fort on the Arkansas River in eastern Colorado in 1833–34 (Berthrong 1963; Weist 1977). After its construction, Bent's Fort became a major southern trading post. In many ways it truncated the southern end of the previous trade network because it provided all the goods available from the Spanish/Mexican settlements of the Southwest, including firearms. With the construction of Bent's Fort and the marriage of William Bent to the Cheyenne leader's daughter in 1835, the Cheyenne controlled the entire area between the northern and southern ends of the Plains network, even though the Sioux were eroding their position between the Black Hills and the Missouri villages (Jablow 1994). As a result, different bands of the Cheyenne concentrated on each end of the network, resulting in a division between the Northern and Southern Cheyenne. The Arapaho, on the southwestern edge of the Cheyenne territory, allied with the southern branch.

Unfortunately the Cheyenne's and Arapaho's strength was relatively short-lived. In 1841 the first wagon train crossed the Oregon Trail, and although the pioneers did not settle on the Plains, they brought with them epidemics that decimated the Plains tribes. In addition, in 1858 gold was discovered in Colorado, and within the next year 50,000 Americans swept into the Denver basin, disrupting the bison herd along with the traditional trade networks and alliances (Weist 1977). With American settlement in eastern Colorado came increasing conflict, and by 1878 the Cheyenne and Arapaho were forced to resettle on reservations (Hoebel 1960).

HISTORIC TRADE NETWORK ON THE PLAINS

During the 1800s, the trade network that encompassed the Plains drew the indigenous peoples into the world system. Although the details of the Plains trade network of the 1800s have long been known, there was no explanation for the internal dynamics of formed alliances. Patricia Albers (1993) has developed a model that integrates ritual and economic organization, territoriality, alliances, warfare, and trade and explains how the system operated

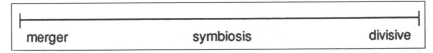

| merger | symbiosis | divisive |

Figure 7.3 Albers's (1993) tripartite division of forms of interdependence.

and why it fell apart in the mid-1800s. As mentioned, British, French, and American guns, ammunition, and metal knives from the Northeast, and Spanish and Mexican horses from the Southwest were traded for bison robes. Plains groups acted as producers and middlemen to move the goods in both directions. All of the parties in this network became interdependent, and a change in the supply or demand for goods in any one sector affected the entire system.

Albers argues that, as a heuristic model, trade relationships that organize ethnically diverse groups into regionally integrated alliances are a tripartite division of a continuum of ethnic interaction and contrasting forms of interdependence (Fig 7.3). Groups moved back and forth along this continuum as trade networks formed and then broke. It is important to realize that Albers views this tripartite division as points on a continuum and that the relationship between two groups can and did vary through time.

Merger relationships are characterized by cooperation and shared resources (the Cheyenne and Arapaho had this type of relationship). Symbiotic relationships are based on mutual need, each group providing a good or service that was desired by another group, such as the relationship between the Arikara and the Cheyenne in the 1700s. Divisive relationships are those in which cooperation is absent and competition, often manifested in raiding and warfare, is prevalent. The Cheyenne had divisive relationships with both the Sioux and the Comanche.

In cooperative social relations, members of different ethnic groups—Arapaho and Cheyenne, for example—could claim affiliation, despite their ethnic differences, by reference to similar sodalities or pan-tribal ritual concepts. These various relationship types were used and manipulated by individuals to foster trade and recruit for cooperative labor or raiding activities, or wage war, depending on whether their relationship was merger, symbiosis, or divisive.

With the introduction of guns and horses, and their increasing importance, the nature and intensity of the trade relations changed on the Plains, as some groups began to specialize in goods their neighbors wanted. Other groups became middlemen who moved goods between ethnic groups. Some groups moved from symbiotic relationships to merger relationships, such as the Cheyenne and Arapaho, whereas others changed from mutualistic to increasingly divisive, such as the Cheyenne and Comanche. By the end of the 1700s there was a well-established pattern of competitive trade networks running parallel to each other from southwest to northeast across the entire length of the Plains. Even though individuals on the ends of the networks were not in direct contact, they became increasingly interdependent because of the networks, particularly for their supply of guns and horses. For example, even though the Arikara and the Comanche were not in direct contact, they quickly became interdependent as the Arikara passed guns south to get horses, usually from Comanche sources. The Cheyenne and Arapaho were in the middle and facilitated this exchange with bison meat and robes as well as guns and horses.

During the late 1800s these relationships broke down. As a result, more and more relationships between the indigenous peoples shifted to the divisive side of the continuum as competition increased with westward expansion. Because of increasing numbers of trading posts supplying European and American goods throughout the networks, the various groups began to jockey for positions on what was left of the trade routes. Bent's Fort was the first of these incursions in Colorado, and it was quickly followed by the establishment of Denver and mining towns to the west. Since the railroads, and therefore the supply of European and American trade goods, traveled from east to west, alliances between these groups formed while there was increasing competition along the north and south axis. The result was a series of intertribal wars, as well as increasing conflict between settlers and Plains groups.

CONCLUSION

The late prehistoric and early historic period witnessed considerable movement of both indigenous and European populations through Colorado. As a result, political and economic alliances were in a constant flux as competition for access to trade goods heightened. The position of a group in the trade network at any one point in time varied depending on the relative strength of their neighbors in terms of demography and organizational principles.

Plants of Colorado

These plants are found in the various environmental zones of Colorado. Plants with asterisks before their names are known to have been used by ethnographic groups as part of their subsistence system; those with a plus sign were part of the medicinal system. Zone designations are as follows: zone 1 = Plains Grasslands; zone 2 = Upland Grasslands; zone 3 = Lowland Riparian; zone 4 = Upland Riparian; zone 5 = Semidesert Shrubland; zone 6 = Sagebrush Shrubland; zone 7 = Mountain Shrubland; zone 8 = Piñon-Juniper Forest; zone 9 = Ponderosa Pine Forest; zone 10 = Douglas Fir Forest; zone 11 = Aspen Forest; zone 12 = Lodgepole Pine Forest; zone 13 = Limber and Bristlecone Pine Woodland; zone 14 = Engelmann Spruce–Subalpine Fir Forest; zone 15 = Alpine Tundra. (Compiled from Armstrong [1972], Fowler [1986], Grinnell [1962], Johnston [1987], Mutel and Emerick [1992] and Trenholm and Carley [1964].)

Plant	Zones
Forbs, Grasses, and Herbaceous Plants	
common alum-root (*Heuchera parvifolia*)	13
*amaranth (*Amaranthus arenicola*)	1
giant angelica (*Angelica ampla*)	4
broad-leaved arnica (*Arnica latifolia*)	14
heart-leaved arnica (*Arnica cordifolia*)	10, 12, 14
*arrowhead (*Sagittaria latifolia*)	3
golden aster (*Heterotheca villosa*)	7, 8

smooth aster (*Symphyotrichum laeve*)	10
alpine avens (*Acomastylis rosii*)	15
mountain avens (*Dryas octopetala*)	15
baby-blue-eyes (*Collinsia parviflora*)	10
*arrowleaf balsamroot (*Balsamorhiza sagittata*)	6, 7
*foxtail barly (*Critesion jubatum*)	1, 2, 3, 5, 6, 7
fragrant bedstraw (*Galium triflorum*)	11
Rocky Mountain bee plant (*Cleome serrulata*)	1
*alpine bistort (*Bistorta vivipara*)	15
*American bistort (*Bistorta bistortoides*)	15
bitter-cress (*Cardamine cordifolia*)	4
pygmy bitterroot (*Lewisia pygmaea*)	15
black-eyed Susan (*Rudbeckia hirta*)	2
mountain bladderpod (*Lesquerella montana*)	1, 9
blanket flower (*Gaillardia aristata*)	6, 7, 9
blue-eyed grass (*Sisyrinchium montanum*)	2
bluegrass (*Poa* spp.)	11
alpine bluegrass (*Poa alpina*)	15
Canada bluegrass (*Poa compressa*)	2
Kentucky bluegrass (*Poa pratensis*)	1
big bluestem (*Andropogon gerardii*)	1
little bluestem (*Schizachyrium scoparium*)	1
sand bluestem (*Andropogon hallii*)	1
green bog orchid (*Coeloglossum viride*)	10
northern bog orchid (*Limnorchis hyperborea*)	4
buffalograss (*Buchloe dactyloides*)	1
bulrush (*Schoenoplectus lacustris*)	3, 4
bur-reed (*Sparganium angustifolium*)	4
snow buttercup (*Ranunculus adoneus*)	15
mountain candytuft (*Noccaea montana*)	13
*broad-leaved cattail (*Typha latifolia*)	3, 4
white checker mallow (*Sidalcea candida*)	4
cheatgrass (*Anisantha tectorum*)	1, 2, 6, 7, 8
chiming bells (*Mertensia ciliata*)	4
sticky cinquefoil (*Drymocallis arguta*)	2
dwarf clover (*Trifolium nanum*)	15
Parry's clover (*Trifolium parryi*)	15

Plant	Zones
+prairie clover (*Dalea candida*)	1
whiproot clover (*Trifolium dasyphyllum*)	15
prairie cord-grass (*Spartina pectinata*)	3
Colorado blue columbine (*Aquilegia caerulea*)	11, 14
red columbine (*Aquilegia elegantula*)	14
*cow parsnip (*Heracleum sphondylium*)	4, 11
black-headed daisy (*Erigeron melanocephalus*)	15
Easter daisy (*Townsendia hookeri*)	9
one-headed daisy (*Erigeron simplex*)	15
showy daisy (*Erigeron speciosus*)	2, 11
common dandelion (*Taraxacum officinale*)	2
timber danthonia (*Danthonia intermedia*)	2
*prairie dropseed (*Sporobolus heterolepis*)	1, 3
*sand dropseed (*Sporobolus cryptandrus*)	1, 8
elephantella (*Pedicularis groenlandica*)	15
bushy eriogonum (*Eriogonum effusum*)	5, 6
nodding eriogonum (*Eriogonum cernuum*)	5
prairie evening primrose (*Oenothera albicaulis*)	1
white stemless evening primrose (*Oenothera caespitosa*)	1
fairy slipper (*Calypso bulbosa*)	10, 14
New Mexican feathergrass (*Stipa neomexicana*)	8
bracken fern (*Pteridium aquilinum*)	11
Arizona fescue (*Festuca arizonica*)	6, 7
Idaho fescue (*Festuca idahoensis*)	2, 6, 7
spike fescue (*Leucopoa kingii*)	9
Thurber's fescue (*Festuca thurberii*)	2, 11
alpine forget-me-not (*Eritrichum aretioides*)	15
four o'clock (*Mirabillis multiflora*)	8
*galletagrass (*Hilaria jamesii*)	5, 8
+Kansas gayfeather (*Liatris punctata*)	1
arctic gentian (*Gentianodes algida*)	15
blue gentian (*Pneumonanthe affinis*)	14
star gentian (*Swertia perennis*)	4
+common wild geranium (*Geranium caespitosum*)	9
white geranium (*Geranium richardsonii*)	2, 11
scarlet gilia (*Ipomopsis aggregata*)	6, 7
golden banner (*Thermopsis divaricarpa*)	2, 11

Plant	Zones
goldenrod (*Solidago* spp.)	6, 7
smooth goldenrod (*Solidago missouriensis*)	1
*wild gourd (*Cucurbita foetidissima*)	1
blue grama (*Chondrosum gracile*)	1, 2, 5, 6, 7, 8, 9
side-oats grama (*Bouteloua curtipendula*)	1, 7, 8, 9
Oregon grape (*Manonia repens*)	9
blowout grass (*Redfieldia flexuosa*)	1
+gumweed (*Grindelia squarrosa*)	8, 9
*tufted hairgrass (*Deschampsia caespitosa*)	2, 15
common harebell (*Campanula rotundifolia*)	2
slender hawkweed (*Chlorocrepis tristis*)	10
heliotrope (*Euploca convolvulacea*)	1
field horsetail (*Equisetum arvense*)	4
Indiangrass (*Sorghastrum avenaceum*)	1
wild Iris (*Iris missouriensis*)	2
Junegrass (*Koeleria macrantha*)	1, 2, 6, 7, 8, 9, 11, 13
Jacob's ladder (*Polemonium pulcherrimum*)	14
king's crown (*Rhodiola integrifolia*)	15
kobresia (*Kobresia myosuroides*)	15
kochia (*Kochia sieversiana*)	3, 5, 6, 7
koenigia (*Koenigia islandica*)	15
Nelson larkspur (*Delphinium nuttallianum*)	9
+wild licorice (*Glycyrrhiza lepidota*)	3
alp lily (*Lloydia serotina*)	15
*Mariposa lily (*Calochortus gunnisonii*)	6, 7, 11
sand lily (*Leucocrinum montanum*)	9
+Colorado locoweed (*Oxytropis lambertii*)	6, 7
+drop-pod locoweed (*Oxytropis delexa*)	12
Rocky Mountain locoweed (*Oxytropis sericea*)	2, 6, 7, 13
curled lousewort (*Pedicularis racemosa*)	14
Gray's lousewort (*Pedicularis procera*)	11
Porter's lovage (*Ligusticum porteri*)	11
common lupine (*Lupinus argenteus*)	6, 7, 11
copper mallow (*Sphaeralcea coccinea*)	5, 6, 7, 8
*manna grass (*Glyceria* spp.)	4
mare's-tail (*Hippuris vulgaris*)	4
marsh elder (*Iva axillaris*)	5

Plant	Zones
marsh marigold (*Psychorophila leptosepala*)	15
Fendler meadowrue (*Thalictrum fendleri*)	11
green mertensia (*Mertensia lanceolata*)	15
miner's candle (*Oreocarya virgata*)	9
dwarf mistletoe (*Arceuthobium vaginatum*)	9, 12
*common yellow monkey flower (*Mimulus guttatus*)	4
pink moss (*Silene acaulis*)	15
mountain muhly (*Muhlenbergia montana*)	2, 7, 9, 13
sandhill muhly (*Muhlenbergia pungens*)	1
mule-ears (*Wyethia amplexicaulis*)	6, 7
*tansy mustard (*Descurainia pinnata*)	8
muttongrass (*Poa fendleriana*)	6, 7, 8, 13, 14
nailwort (*Paronychia pulvinata*)	15
needle-and-thread (*Stipa comata*)	1, 2, 7, 8, 9
green needlegrass (*Stipa viridula*)	1
Letterman needlegrass (*Stipa lettermanii*)	14
old-man-on-the-mountain (*Rydbergia grandiflora*)	15
purple oniongrass (*Bromelica spectabilis*)	11
alpine paintbrush (*Castilleja puberula*)	15
Indian paintbrush (*Castilleja* spp.)	6, 7
scarlet paintbrush (*Castilleja miniata*)	2
Wyoming paintbrush (*Castilleja linarifolia*)	12
yellow mountain parsley (*Pseudocymopterus montanus*)	11
wiskbroom parsley (*Harbouria trachypleura*)	9
+pasqueflower (*Pulsatilla patens*)	9
alpine penstemon (*Penstemon glabere*)	13
greenleaf penstemon (*Penstemon virens*)	9
one-sided penstemon (*Penstemon secundiflorus*)	9
Whipple's penstemon (*Penstemon whippleanus*)	13
alpine phlox (*Phlox pulvinata*)	15
*rough pigweed (*Amaranthus retroflexus*)	1
pinedrops (*Pterospora andromedea*)	12
pisissewa (*Chimaphila umbellata*)	10, 14
poison ivy (*Toxicodendron rydbergii*)	3
yellow pond lily (*Nuphar luteum*)	4
pondweed (*Potamogeton* spp.)	3, 4
*prince's plum (*Stanleya pinnata*)	5

Plant	Zones
mountain pussytoes (*Antennaria parvifolia*)	2
western ragweed (*Ambrosia psilostachya*)	1
Canadian reedgrass (*Calamagrostis canadensis*)	2, 4
*Indian ricegrass (*Stipa hymenoides*)	5, 6, 7, 8
Drummond rockcress (*Boechera drummondii*)	13
rose crown (*Clementsia rhodantha*)	15
Colorado rubber plant (*Picradenia richardsonii*)	2
Drummond's rush (*Juncus drummondii*)	15
subalpine rush (*Juncus mertensianus*)	4
*alkali sacaton (*Sporobolus airoides*)	5
pasture sage (*Artemisia frigida*)	1, 2
prairie sage (*Artemisia ludoviciana*)	2
saltgrass (*Distichlis stricta*)	3, 5
*scratchgrass (*Muhlenbergia asperifolia*)	5
spike-rush (*Eleocharis palustris*)	2
alpine sandwort (*Lidia obtusiloba*)	15
elk sedge (*Carex geyeri*)	4, 14
Pyrennian sedge (*Carex crandallii*)	4, 15
Rocky Mountain sedge (*Carex scopulorum*)	4, 15
sun sedge (*Carex heliophila*)	4, 9
rock selaginella (*Selaginella densa*)	15
arrowleaf senecio (*Senecio triangularis*)	4
Wooton senecio (*Senecio wootonii*)	14
shooting star (*Dodecatheon pulchellum*)	4
sibbaldia (*Sibbaldia procumbens*)	15
sky pilot (*Polemonium viscosum*)	15
broom snakeweed (*Gutierrezia sarothrae*)	1
orange sneezeweed (*Dugaldia hoopesii*)	11, 14
snow-on-the-mountain (*Agaloma marginata*)	1
snowball saxifrage (*Micranthes rhomboidea*)	15
false Solomon's seal (*Maianthemum* spp.)	10
alpine sorrel (*Oxyria digyna*)	15
spiderwort (*Tradescantia occidentalis*)	9
*spike-rush (*Eleocharis* spp.)	4
squirrel tail (*Elymus longifolius*)	1, 8
stonecrop (*Sedum lanceolatum*)	2, 13, 15
*wild strawberry (*Fragaria virginiana*)	2, 11

Plant	Zones

sulphur flower (*Eriogonum umbellatum*) — 9
*sunflower (*Helianthus nuttallii*) — 3
*common sunflower (*Helianthus annuus*) — 1
*prairie sunflower (*Helianthus petiolaris*) — 8
switchgrass (*Panuum virgatum*) — 1
Hooker thistle (*Cirsium scopulorum*) — 13
Russian thistle (*Salsola australis*) — 1, 8
red three-awn (*Aristida purpurea*) — 1, 8
timothy (*Phleum pratense*) — 2
alpine timothy (*Phleum commutatum*) — 15
spike trisetum (*Trisetum spicatum*) — 15
tumblegrass (*Schedonnardus paniculatus*) — 1
twin-flower (*Linnaea borealis*) — 14
twisted stalk (*Streptopus fassettii*) — 10
*American vetch (*Vicia americana*) — 11
*milk vetch (*Astragalus missouriensis*) — 1, 5
alpine wallflower (*Erysimum capitatum*) — 15
western wallflower (*Erysimum capitatum*) — 9
water-plantain (*Alisma plantagoaquatica*) — 3
*slender wheatgrass (*Elymus trachycaulus*) — 2, 5, 6, 7, 11
spreading wheatgrass (*Elymus scribneri*) — 15
western wheatgrass (*Pascopyrum smithii*) — 1, 3, 7
whiteweed (*Cardaria* spp.) — 5
whitlow-wort (*Draba* spp.) — 13
blue wild-rye (*Elymus glaucus*) — 11
lesser wintergreen (*Pyrola minor*) — 14
one-sided wintergreen (*Orthilia secunda*) — 12
wood nymph (*Moneses uniflora*) — 14
spike woodrush (*Lazula spicata*) — 15
yarrow (*Achillea lanulosa*) — 2
⁺yucca (*Yucca glauca*) — 1
wild zinnia (*Zinnia grandiflora*) — 8

Cacti

candelabra cactus (*Cylindropuntia imbricata*) — 1, 8
*pincushion cactus (*Coryphantha vivipara*) — 1
*prickly pear cactus (*Opuntia polyacantha*) — 1, 8

Shrubs

alder (*Alnus incana*)   4

*Apache plume (*Fallugia paradoxa*)   8

+baneberry (*Actaea rubra*)   10

barrenground (*Salix brachycarpa*)   15

bitterbrush (*Purshia tridentata*)   6, 7, 8, 9

blackbrush (*Coleogyne ramosissima*)   5

blueberry (*Vaccinium myrtillus*)   12, 14

bog birch (*Betula glandulosa*)   2, 4

buckbrush (*Ceanothus fendleri*)   7, 9

*buffaloberry (*Shepherdia canadensis*)   12, 13

*chokecherry (*Padus virginiana*)   4, 7, 10, 11

shrubby cinquefoil (*Pentaphylloides floribunda*)   2, 4, 13, 14

cliffrose (*Purshia stansburiana*)   7

*high-bush cranberry (*Viburnum edule*)   14

*Colorado currant (*Ribes coloradense*)   14

*wax currant (*Ribes cereum*)   2, 3, 9

red-osier dogwood (*Swida sericea*)   4

red-berried elder (*Sambucus microbotrys*)   12, 14

common gooseberry (*Ribes inerme*)   4, 11

*greasewood (*Sarcobatus vermiculatus*)   5

*hawthorn (*Crataegus* spp.)   3, 4, 7

beaked hazelnut (*Corylus cornuta*)   4

bush honeysuckle (*Distegia involucrata*)   4, 11

broom huckleberry (*Vaccinium scoparium*)   12, 13, 14

common juniper (*Juniperus communis*)   9, 10, 11, 12, 13

*kinnikinick (*Arctostaphylos uva-ursi*)   9, 10, 11, 12, 13

*New Mexico locust (*Robinia neomexicana*)   4

mountain ash (*Sorbus scopulina*)   10

mountain lover (*Paxistima myrsinites*)   10, 14

mountain mahogany (*Cercocarpus montanus*)   7, 8, 9

mountain maple (*Acer glabrum*)   4, 10, 11

Mormon tea (*Epuedra* spp.)   5, 8

ninebark (*Physocarpus monogynus*)   7, 10

*Gambel oak (*Quercus gambelii*)   7, 8, 9

*gray oak (*Quercus grisea*)   7

Plant	Zones
planeleaf (*Salix planifolia*)	15
wild plum (*Prunus americana*)	3, 4, 7
rabbitbrush (*Chrysothamnus nauseosus*)	1, 5, 6, 7, 8
*wild rasberry (*Rubus idaeus*)	10, 13
wild rose (*Rosa woodsii*)	2, 3
Wood's rose (*Rosa woodsii*)	6, 7, 10, 11, 12, 13, 14
Great Basin big sagebrush (*Seriphidium tridentatum*)	5, 6,8
mountain big sagebrush (*Seriphidium vaseyanum*)	6
sand sagebrush (*Oligosporus filifolius*)	1
*four-winged saltbush (*Atriplex canescens*)	1, 5, 8
*serviceberry (*Amelanchier* spp.)	6, 7, 8, 11, 13
*shadescale (*Atriplex confertifolia*)	5, 8
skunkbrush (*Rhus aromatica*)	7, 8
snakeweed (*Gutierrezia* spp.)	5
snow (*Salix reticulata* ssp. *nivalis*)	15
*snowberry (*Symphoricarpos occidentalis*)	3, 6, 7, 8, 11
moutain spray (*Holodiscus dumosus*)	7
sticky-laurel (*Ceanothus velutinus*)	12, 13
*thimbleberry (*Rubacer parviflorus*)	10
waxflower (*Jamesia americana*)	10
arctic willow (*Salix arctica*)	15
sandbar willow (*Salix exigua*)	3, 4
shrub willow (*Salix* spp.)	2, 4
winterfat (*Krascheninnikovia lanata*)	1, 5, 6, 7

Trees

Plant	Zones
quaking aspen (*Populus tremuloides*)	4, 11
green ash (*Fraxinus pennsylvanica*)	3
*box elder (*Negundo aceroides*)	3
plains cottonwood (*Populus deltoidea* ssp. *occidentalis*)	3
lanceleaf cottonwood (*Populus x acuminata*)	4
narrowleaf cottonwood (*Populus angustifolia*)	4
valley cottonwood (*Populus deltoidea* ssp. *Wislizenii*)	3
corkbark fir (*Abies arizonica*)	14
+Douglas fir (*Pseudotsuga menziesii*)	10
+subalpine fir (*Abies bifolia*)	14

Plant	Zones
*white fir (*Abies concolor*)	4
hackberry (*Celtis reticulata*)	3
one-seed juniper (*Sabina monosperma*)	8
+Rocky Mountain juniper (*Sabina scopulorum*)	8, 9, 10
Utah juniper (*Sabina osteosperma*)	8
bristlecone pine (*Pinus aristata*)	13
*limber pine (*Pinus flexilis*)	13
lodgepole pine (*Pinus contorta*)	12
*ponderosa pine (*Pinus ponderosa*)	9
*Colorado piñon pine (*Pinus edulis*)	8
balsam poplar (*Populus balsamifera*)	4
Engelmann spruce (*Picea engelmannii*)	14
Colorado blue spruce (*Picea pungens*)	4
peach-leaved willow (*Salix amygdaloides*)	3

Terrestrial Animals of Colorado

These animals, including seasonal occupants, are found in the various environmental zones of Colorado. Zone 1 = Plains Grasslands; zone 2 = Upland Grasslands; zone 3 = Lowland Riparian; zone 4 = Upland Riparian; zone 5 = Semidesert Shrubland; zone 6 = Sagebrush Shrubland; zone 7 = Mountain Shrubland; zone 8 = Piñon-Juniper Forest; zone 9 = Ponderosa Pine Forest; zone 10 = Douglas Fir Forest; zone 11 = Aspen Forest; zone 12 = Lodgepole Pine Forest; zone 13 = Limber and Bristlecone Pine Woodland; zone 14 = Engelmann Spruce–Subalpine Fir Forest; zone 15 = Alpine Tundra. (Compiled from Armstrong 1972; Mutel and Emerick 1992.)

Animals	Zones
Amphibians and Reptiles	
bullfrog (*Rana catesbeiana*)	3
bull snake (*Pituophis melanoleucus*)	1, 3, 7, 8, 9
coachwhip (*Masticophis flagellum*)	1
boreal chorus frog (*Pseudacris triseriata*)	2, 15
northern leopard frog (*Rana pipiens*)	2, 4
plains leopard frog (*Rana blairi*)	3
striped chorus frog (*Pseudacris triseriata*)	3, 4
wood frog (*Rana sylvatica*)	4
collared lizard (*Crotaphytus collaris*)	8
eastern fence lizard (*Sceloporus undulatus*)	5, 6, 7, 8, 9
lesser earless lizard (*Holbrookia maculata*)	1

Animal	Zones
many-lined skink lizard (*Eumeces multivirgatus*)	9
northern sagebush lizard (*Sceloporus graciosus*)	9
northern side-blotched lizard (*Uta stansburiana*)	5, 6, 7, 8
northern tree lizard (*Urosaurus ornatus*)	5, 6, 7, 8, 9
sagebrush lizard (*Sceloporus graciosus*)	5, 6, 8
short-horned lizard (*Phrynosoma douglasii*)	1, 5, 6, 7, 8, 9
six-lined race-runner lizard (*Cnemidophorus sexlineatus*)	3
plateau striped whiptail lizard (*Cnemidophorus veloy*)	8
western whiptail lizard (*Cnemidophorus tigris*)	5, 6, 8
massasauga (*Sistrurus catenatus*)	1
western rattlesnake (*Crotalus viridis*)	1, 5, 6, 7, 8, 9
tiger salamander (*Ambystoma tigrinum*)	2, 3, 4
plains garter snake (*Thamnophis radix*)	1, 3
red-sided garter snake (*Thamnophis sirtalis*)	3
wandering garter snake (*Thamnophis elegans*)	2, 4
Great Basin gopher snake (*Pituophis melanoleucus deserticola*)	5, 6, 7, 8
smooth green snake (*Opherdrys vernalis*)	4
milk snake (*Lampropeltis triangulum*)	9
northern water snake (*Nerodia sipedon*)	3
boreal toad (*Bufo boseas*)	2, 4, 15
Great Plains toad (*Bufo cognatus*)	3
plains spadefoot toad (*Scaphiopus bombifrons*)	1
Woodhouse toad (*Bufo woodhousii*)	3, 9
painted turtle (*Chrysemys picta*)	3
snapping turtle (*Chelydra serpentina*)	3
western box turtle (*Terrapene ornata*)	1
yellow mud turtle (*Kinosternon flavescens*)	3
striped whipsnake (*Masticophis taeniatus*)	5, 8

Birds

Bird	Zones
Brewer's blackbird (*Euphagus cyanocephalus*)	2
red-winged blackbird (*Agelaius phoeniceus*)	3
mountain bluebird (*Sialia currucoides*)	2, 8, 9, 11
western bluebird (*Sialia mexicana*)	9
northern bobwhite (*Colinus virginianus*)	3
indigo bunting (*Passerina cyanea*)	7

lazuli bunting (*Passerina amoena*)	7
bushtit (*Psaltriparus minimus*)	8
black-capped chickadee (*Parus atricapillus*)	3, 4, 11
mountain chickadee (*Parus gambeli*)	4, 8, 9, 10, 11, 12, 13, 14
American coot (*Fulica americana*)	3
brown creeper (*Certhia americana*)	9, 10, 12, 14
red crossbill (*Loxia curvirostra*)	9, 10, 12, 13, 14
American crow (*Corvus brachyrhynchos*)	9
yellow-billed cuckoo (*Coccyzus erythropthalmus*)	3
long-billed curlew (*Numenius americanus*)	1
American dipper (*Cinclus mexicanus*)	4
mourning dove (*Zenaida macroura*)	8, 9
golden eagle (*Aquila chrysaetos*)	1, 8, 9
snowy egret (*Egretta thula*)	3
prairie falcon (*Falco mexicanus*)	1, 2, 8, 15
Cassin's finch (*Carpodacus cassinii*)	9, 10, 12, 13, 14
rosy finch (*Leucosticte arctoa*)	15
northern flicker (*Colaptes auratus*)	3, 9, 10, 11
ash-throated flycatcher (*Myiarchus cinerascens*)	3, 8
cordilleran flycatcher (*Empidonax difficilis*)	4, 8, 11
dusky flycatcher (*Empidonax wrightii*)	6, 8
olive-sided flycatcher (*Contopus borealis*)	9, 14
willow flycatcher (*Empidonax traillii*)	4
blue-gray gnatcatcher (*Polioptila caerulea*)	7, 8
American goldfinch (*Carduelis tristis*)	4
Canada goose (*Branta canadensis*)	3
northern goshawk (*Accipiter gentilis*)	9, 10, 14
western grebe (*Aechmophorus occidentalis*)	3
black-headed grosbeak (*Pheucticus melanocephalus*)	3, 7
evening grosbeak (*Coccothraustes vespertinus*)	9, 10, 12, 13, 14
pine grosbeak (*Pinicola enucleator*)	14
blue grouse (*Dendragapus obscurus*)	10, 12, 14
sage grouse (*Centrocercus urophasianus*)	6
northern harrier (*Circus cyaneus*)	1, 2, 5
Cooper's hawk (*Accipiter cooperii*)	4, 9, 10, 11
ferruginous hawk (*Buteo regalis*)	1, 2, 3, 8, 9
red-tailed hawk (*Buteo jamaicensis*)	1, 5

Swainson's hawk (*Buteo swainsoni*)	1, 5
black-crowned night-heron (*Nycticorax nycticorax*)	3
great blue heron (*Ardea herodias*)	3
broad-tailed hummingbird (*Selasphorus platycercus*)	2, 9, 10, 11, 12
blue jay (*Cyanocitta cristat*)	3
gray jay (*Perisoreus canadensis*)	12, 13, 14
pinyon jay (*Gymnorhinus cyanocephalus*)	8
scrub jay (*Aphelocoma coerulescens*)	7, 8
Steller's jay (*Cyanocitta stelleri*)	8, 9, 10, 12, 13, 14
dark-eyed junco (*Junco hyemalis*)	9, 10, 11, 12, 13, 14
American kestrel (*Falco sparverius*)	1, 2, 8
killdeer (*Charadrius vociferus*)	4
eastern kingbird (*Tyrannus tyrannus*)	3
western kingbird (*Tyrannus verticalis*)	3
belted kingfisher (*Ceryle alcyon*)	3, 4
golden-crowned kinglet (*Regulus satrapa*)	10, 13, 14
ruby-crowned kinglet (*Regulus calendula*)	10, 12, 14
lark bunting (*Calamospiza melanocorys*)	1
horned lark (*Eremophila alpestris*)	1, 2, 15
chestnut-collared longspur (*Calcarius ornatus*)	1
McCown's longspur (*Calcarius mccownii*)	1
black-billed magpie (*Pica pica*)	3, 4, 8, 9
mallard (*Anas platyrhynchos*)	3, 4
western meadowlark (*Sturnella neglecta*)	1, 2
northern mockingbird (*Mimus polyglottos*)	3
common nighthawk (*Chordeiles minor*)	1, 2, 8, 9
Clark's nutcracker (*Nucifraga columbiana*)	10, 12, 13, 14
pygmy nuthatch (*Sitta pygmaea*)	9
red-breasted nuthatch (*Sitta canadensis*)	11, 14
white-breasted nuthatch (*Sitta carolinensis*)	9, 10, 11, 12, 13, 14
northern oriole (*Icterus galbula*)	3
orchard oriole (*Icterus spurius*)	3
boreal owl (*Aegolius funerius*)	14
burrowing owl (*Athene cunicularia*)	1
barn owl (*Tyto alba*)	3
flammulated owl (*Otus flammeolus*)	9
great horned owl (*Bubo virginianus*)	3, 4, 8, 9, 10

northern pygmy-owl (*Glaucidium gnoma*)	11
northern saw-whet owl (*Aegolius acadicus*)	8, 9
ring-necked pheasant (*Phasianus colchicus*)	1
northern pintail (*Anas acuta*)	3
American pipit (*Anthus rubescens*)	15
mountain plover (*Charadrius montanus*)	1
common poorwill (*Phalaenoptilus nuttallii*)	8, 9
greater prairie-chicken (*Tympanuchus cupido*)	1
lesser prairie-chicken (*Tympanuchus pallidicinctus*)	1
white-tailed ptarmigan (*Lagopus leucurus*)	15
Gambel's quail (*Callipepla gambelii*)	5, 6
scaled quail (*Callipepla squamata*)	6
Virginia rail (*Rallus limicola*)	3
common raven (*Corvus corax*)	9, 10, 12, 13, 14, 15
American robin (*Turdus migratorius*)	3, 4, 9, 11
greater roadrunner (*Geococcyx californianus*)	6
spotted sandpiper (*Actitis macularia*)	4
upland sandpiper (*Bartramia longicauda*)	1
Williamson's sapsucker (*Sphyrapicus thyroideus*)	9, 11, 12, 14
red-naped sapsucker (*Sphyrapicus nuchalis*)	11
eastern screech-owl (*Otus asio*)	3
western screech-owl (*Otus kennicottii*)	3, 4
pine siskin (*Carduelis pinus*)	9, 10, 12, 13, 14
common snipe (*Gallinago gallinago*)	4
Townsend's solitaire (*Myadestes townsendi*)	9, 10, 14
black-throated sparrow (*Amphispiza bilineata*)	5
Brewer's sparrow (*Spizella breweri*)	6
chipping sparrow (*Spizella passerina*)	8, 9
Cassin's sparrow (*Aimophila cassinii*)	1
fox sparrow (*Passerella iliaca*)	4
grasshopper sparrow (*Ammodramus savannarum*)	1
lark sparrow (*Chondestes grammacas*)	1, 3, 8
Lincoln's sparrow (*Melospiza lincolnii*)	2, 4
sage sparrow (*Amphispiza belli*)	6
savannah sparrow (*Passerculus sandwichensis*)	2
song sparrow (*Melospiza melodia*)	3, 4
vesper sparrow (*Pooecetes gramineus*)	1, 2

Animals	Zones
white-crowned sparrow (*Zonotrichia leucophrys*)	4, 15
barn swallow (*Hirundo rustica*)	3
cliff swallow (*Hirundo pyrrhonota*)	3
northern rough-winged swallow (*Stelgidopteryx serripennis*)	3
tree swallow (*Tachycineta bicolor*)	4, 11
violet-green swallow (*Tachycineta thalassina*)	4, 9, 11
western tanager (*Piranga ludoviciana*)	9
green-winged teal (*Anas crecca*)	4
black tern (*Chlidonias niger*)	3
Forster's tern (*Sterna forsteri*)	3
brown thrasher (*Toxostoma rufum*)	3
sage thrasher (*Orcoscoptes montanus*)	6
hermit thrush (*Catharus guttatus*)	10, 12, 13, 14
Swainson's thrush (*Catharus ustulatus*)	4, 14
plain titmouse (*Parus inornatus*)	8
canyon towhee (*Pipilo fuscus*)	5, 6, 8
green-tailed towhee (*Pipilo chlorurus*)	6, 7
rufous-sided towhee (*Pipilo erythrophthalmus*)	6, 7
wild turkey (*Meleagris gallopavo*)	8, 9
gray vireo (*Vireo vicinior*)	8
solitary vireo (*Vireo solitarius*)	8, 9
warbling vireo (*Vireo gilvus*)	4, 11
black-throated gray warbler (*Dendroica nigrescens*)	8
Grace's warbler (*Dendroica graciae*)	9
MacGillivray's warbler (*Oporornis tolmiei*)	4
orange-crowned warbler (*Vermivora celata*)	11
Virginia's warbler (*Vermivora virginiae*)	7
Wilson's warbler (*Wilsonia pusilla*)	4
yellow warbler (*Dendroica petechia*)	3, 4
yellow-rumped warbler (*Dendroica coronata*)	9, 10, 12, 13, 14
downy woodpecker (*Picoides pubescens*)	3, 4, 8, 9, 10, 11
hairy woodpecker (*Picoides villosus*)	4, 9, 10, 11, 12, 13, 14
Lewis' woodpecker (*Melanerpes lewis*)	3
red-headed woodpecker (*Melanerpes erythrocephalus*)	3
three-toed woodpecker (*Picoides tridactylus*)	14
western wood-pewee (*Contopus sordidulus*)	3, 4, 9, 11, 12
Bewick's wren (*Thryomanes bewickii*)	3, 8

house wren (*Troglodytes aedon*)	3, 4, 9, 10, 11, 12
marsh wren (*Cistothorus palustris*)	3
rock wren (*Salpinctes obsoletus*)	15

Mammals

badger (*Taxidea taxus*)	1, 2, 5, 6, 7, 8, 15
big brown bat (*Eptesicus fuscus*)	3
hoary bat (*Lasiurus cinereus*)	9, 12, 14
pallid bat (*Antrozous pallidus*)	8
silver-haired bat (*Lasionycteris noctivagans*)	11
Townsend's big-eared bat (*Plecotus townsendii*)	7, 9
black bear (*Ursus americanus*)	4, 9, 10, 11, 12, 13, 14
beaver (*Castor canadensis*)	3, 4
bison (*Bison bison*)	1
bobcat (*Felis rufus*)	4, 5, 6, 7, 8, 9, 10, 12, 13, 14, 15
Colorado chipmunk (*Tamias guadrivittatus*)	2, 7, 8, 9, 10
Hopi chipmunk (*Tamias rufus*)	8
least chipmunk (*Tamias minimus*)	2, 4, 5, 6, 7, 8, 9, 10, 11, 12, 13, 14, 15
Uinta chipmunk (*Tamias umbrinus*)	2, 10, 12, 14
desert cottontail (*Sylvilagus audubonii*)	1, 5, 6, 7, 8
eastern cottontail (*Sylvilagus floridanus*)	3
Nuttall's cottontail (*Sylvilagus nuttallii*)	2, 4, 6, 7, 8, 9, 10, 11, 12, 13, 14
coyote (*Canis latrans*)	1, 2, 3, 4, 5, 6, 7, 8, 9, 10, 11, 12, 13, 14, 15
mule deer (*Odocoileus hemionus*)	1, 2, 3, 4, 5, 6, 7, 8, 9, 10, 11, 12, 13, 14, 15
white-tailed deer (*Odocoileus virginianus*)	3
elk (*Cervus elaphus*)	1, 2, 8, 9, 10, 11, 14, 15
ermine (*Mustela erminea*)	10, 11, 12, 13, 14, 15
black-footed ferret (*Mustela nigripes*)	1
gray fox (*Urocyon cinereoargenteus*)	5, 7, 8, 9
kit fox (*Vulpes macrotis*)	8
red fox (*Vulpes vulpes*)	3, 15
swift fox (*Vulpes velox*)	1
golden-mantled ground squirrel (*Spermophilus lateralis*)	2, 6, 7, 8, 9, 10, 11, 12, 13, 14, 15
thirteen-lined ground squirrel (*Spermophilus tridecemlineatus*)	1
Wyoming ground squirrel (*Spermophilus elegans*)	2, 9

Animals	Zones
snowshoe hare (*Lepus americanus*)	10, 11, 12, 13, 14, 15
black-tailed jackrabbit (*Lepus californicus*)	1, 5, 7, 8
white-tailed jackrabbit (*Lepustownsendii*)	2, 6, 7, 8, 9, 10, 12, 13, 14, 15
Ord's kangaroo rat (*Dipodomys ordii*)	1, 5, 6
mountain lion (*Felis concolor*)	4, 5, 6, 7, 8, 9, 10, 12, 13, 14, 15
lynx (*Felis lynx*)	10, 11, 12, 14
yellow-bellied marmot (*Marmota flaviventris*)	2, 7, 9, 10, 11, 12, 14, 15
marten (*Martes americana*)	10, 12, 13, 14, 15
mink (*Mustela vison*)	3, 4
brush mouse (*Peromyscus boylii*)	7
canyon mouse (*Peromyscus crinitus*)	8
deer mouse (*Peromyscus maniculatus*)	1, 2, 3, 4, 5, 6, 7, 8, 9, 10, 11, 12, 13, 14, 15
hispid pocket mouse (*Chaetodipus hispidus*)	1
northern grasshopper mouse (*Onychomys leucogaster*)	1, 5, 6
piñon mouse (*Peromyscus truei*)	8
plains harvest mouse (*Reithrodontomys montanus*)	1
rock mouse (*Peromyscus difficuilis*)	7, 8, 9
silky pocket mouse (*Perognathus flavus*)	1
western jumping mouse (*Zapus princeps*)	4, 10, 11, 12, 14, 15
western harvest mouse (*Reithrodontomys megalotis*)	1, 3
white-footed mouse (*Peromyscus leucopus*)	3
muskrat (*Ondatra zibethicus*)	3, 4
little brown myotis (*Myotis lucifufus*)	3
long-legged myotis (*Myotis volans*)	8, 9, 11, 14
western small-footed myotis (*Myotis cilioabrum*)	2, 3, 7
Virginia opossum (*Didelphis virginiana*)	3
pika (*Ochotona princeps*)	15
northern pocket gopher (*Thomomys talpoides*)	2, 11, 15
plains pocket gopher (*Geomys bursarius*)	1
porcupine (*Erethizon dorsatum*)	8, 9, 10, 11, 12, 13, 14
black-tailed prairie dog (*Cynomys ludovicianus*)	1
Gunnison's prairie dog (*Cynomys gunnisoni*)	5, 7
white-tailed prairie dog (*Cynomys leucurus*)	5, 6
pronghorn (*Antilocapra americana*)	1, 5, 6
raccoon (*Procyon lotor*)	3, 4
hispid cotton rat (*Sigmodon hispidus*)	3

Animals	Zones
ringtail (*Bassariscus astutus*)	8
bighorn sheep (*Ovis canadensis*)	2, 9, 15
dwarf shrew (*Sorex nanus*)	7, 15
masked shrew (*Sorex cinereus*)	2, 3, 4, 10, 11, 12, 13, 14, 15
Merriam's shrew (*Sorex merriami*)	6, 7, 8, 9
montane shrew (*Sorex monticolus*)	2, 4, 10, 11, 12, 13, 14, 15
water shrew (*Sorex palustris*)	4, 14
striped skunk (*Mephitis mephitis*)	2, 3, 4, 5, 6, 7, 8, 9, 10, 11, 12
western spotted skunk (*Spilogale gracilis*)	3, 5, 7, 8
Abert's squirrel (*Sciurus aberti*)	9
fox squirrel (*Sciurus niger*)	3
pine squirrel (*Tamiasciurus hudsonicus*)	10, 12, 13, 14
rock squirrel (*Spermophilus variegatus*)	7, 8, 9
white-tailed antelope squirrel (*Ammospermophilus leucurus*)	5, 7
heather vole (*Phenacomys intermedius*)	10, 12, 14
long-tailed vole (*Microtus longicaudus*)	2, 4, 6, 9, 10, 11, 12, 14, 15
meadow vole (*Microtus pennsylvanicus*)	2, 3, 4, 11
montane vole (*Microtus montanus*)	4, 10, 11, 12, 14, 15
prairie vole (*Microtus ochrogaster*)	3
southern red-backed vole (*Clethrionomys gapperi*)	10, 12, 13, 14
long-tailed weasel (*Mustela frenata*)	2, 3, 4, 8, 9, 10, 11, 12, 13, 14, 15
gray wolf (*Canis lupus*)	1
wolverine (*Gulo gulo*)	10, 12
bushy-tailed woodrat (*Neotoma cinerea*)	8, 9, 10, 12, 13, 14, 15
desert woodrat (*Neotoma lepida*)	8
eastern woodrat (*Neotoma floridana*)	3
Mexican woodrat (*Neotoma mexicana*)	7, 8, 9
white-throated woodrat (*Neotoma albigulu*)	8

Fish and Shellfish of Colorado

Location designations indicate elevation restriction: zone 1 = lowlands; zone 2 = uplands. (From Mutel and Emerick 1992).

Species	Zone
Shellfish	
clams (*Mollusca, Pelecypoda* spp.)	1
crayfish (*Arthropoda, Crustacea*)	1
snails (*Mollusca, Gastropoda*)	1
Fish	
largemouth bass (*Micropterus salmoides*)	1
smallmouth bass (*Micropterus dolomieui*)	1
bluegill (*Lepomis macrochirus*)	1
black bullhead (*Ictalurus melas*)	1
carp (*Cyprinus carpio*)	1
channel catfish (*Ictalurus punctatus*)	1
bonytail chub (*Gila elegans*)	1
creek chub (*Semotilus atromaculatus*)	1
humpback chub (*Gila cypha*)	1
roundtail chub (*Gila robusta*)	1
black crappie (*Pomoxis nigromaculatus*)	1
longnose dace (*Rhinichthys cataractae*)	1

speckeled dace (*Rhinichthys osculus*)	1
johnny darter (*Etheostoma nigrum*)	2
plains killfish (*Fundulus zebrinus*)	1
fathead minnow (*Pimephales promelas*)	1, 2
yellow perch (*Perca flavescens*)	1
kokanee salmon (*Oncorhynchus nerka*)	2
mottled sculpin (*Cottus bairdi*)	2
rainbow smelt (*Osmerus mordax*)	1
brook stickleback (*Culaea inconstans*)	1
Colorado squawfish (*Ptychocheilus lucius*)	1
bluehead sucker (*Catostomus discobolus*)	1
longnose sucker (*Catostomus catostomus*)	1, 2
white sucker (*Catostomus commersoni*)	1, 2
green sunfish (*Lepomis cyanellus*)	1
orange-spotted sunfish (*Lepomis humilis*)	1
pumpkinseed sunfish (*Lepomis gibbosus*)	1
brook trout (*Salvelinus fontinalis*)	2
brown trout (*Salmo trutta*)	2
cutthroat trout (*Oncorhynchus clarki*)	2
lake trout (*Salvelinus namaycush*)	2
rainbow trout (*Oncorhynchus mykiss*)	2
mountain whitefish (*Posopium williamsoni*)	1

GLOSSARY

activity areas: areas in which specific activities (food processing, tool production, hide processing, etc.) are carried out to the exclusion of other activities.

alibates flint: high-quality chert from quarries in the Texas Panhandle.

archaeomagnetic: method of dating that is based on the principle that the earth's magnetic pole is not stable. Clays used to line hearths with high iron content can be analyzed to determine the location of the magnetic pole at the time of use. This location is then compared to a master magnetic curve for an area to determine the date of a site.

articulated: bones are still in the position they would have been when muscle and tendons held them in place.

atlatl: spear-throwing device.

Beringia: the land bridge formed between Siberia and Alaska during the Ice Age.

biface: a chipped stone tool in which flakes have been removed from both faces, or sides.

blade: a flake that is at least twice as long as it is wide.

B.P.: date before present.

burin: a chipped stone tool that has been flaked to produce a chiseled edge.

calcareous: soils with high calcium carbonate content.

chronometric data: a series of highly accurate, absolute dating techniques.

coprolite: preserved human feces that can be analyzed for plant parts that have passed through the digestive system thus indicating the last meal of the individual.

core: the source material from which flakes are removed to produce chipped stone artifacts.

cryptocrystalline: very high quality lithic raw material with favorable flaking qualities. Materials in Colorado in this category include chert, chalcedony, petrified wood, agates, and jaspers.

curated tools: tools that are kept for some time and frequently resharpened to lengthen their use life.

debitage: waste material produced during chipped stone production that is not used. The most common type of debitage is unused flakes and shatter.

dendrochronology: tree ring dating.

dendroclimatological: climatic reconstructions of precipitation rates based on the size of growth rings in trees.

denticulates: chipped stone tool with deeply serrated edges.

disarticulated: bones that have moved from the positions they would have been in during life.

ecozone: specific environmental niche.

ethnogenesis: the process of the formation of ethnic groups.

flake: the most common shaped artifact produced during the chipped stone production. Flakes may remain unused or may be used to create a variety of tools.

fleshers: artifacts that are used to remove flesh from hides during the hide-processing procedure.

formalization: the process in which relationships become more formal and institutionalized.

geomorphology: the study of soil deposits to understand the geological process that produced them.

glottochronology: the process of dating the split between two or more language groups based on the number of differences present. The assumption is, the more similar two languages are the more recently they had a common root. Conversely, the more diverse they are, the longer they have been separate languages.

gorget: large ornament worn on the chest, usually suspended by a string around the neck. They are commonly made of shell.

gravers: a chipped stone tool used for engraving.

ground stone: a large class of tools used to process plant foods by grinding them. Alternatively, ground stone tools may be tools formed by grinding during the production process.

hafted: a method of connecting a chipped stone tool to a shaft to form a spear or arrow.

hammerstone: the stone used during chipped stone production to remove flakes from a core.

holocene: the modern geological era.

iconography: the symbolic representation of an idea, organization, or supernatural being.

isochrestic: a type of style that is passive in nature. Isochrestic style is the way of making or decorating an item due to historical tradition without a conscious attempt by the makers to make a statement about their identity.

jacal: an architectural form that has a wood or brush center covered on both sides by mud.

kiva/Great Kiva: ceremonial structure used by Pueblo peoples. It is semi-subterranean in nature. Great Kivas are very large kivas, generally larger than 20 meters (66 feet) in diameter.

knapping: the process of flaking stone to make chipped stone tools.

lithic: chipped stone artifacts.

macrobotanical: preserved plant materials that are large enough to see with the naked eye, though complete identification may require the use of a microscope.

mano: a ground stone artifact used in connection with a metate. Manos are the hand stone used to grind grains against a base stone, or metate.

matrilocal: a postmarital residence pattern in which the married couple lives with the wife's family.

metate: a ground stone artifact used in connection with a mano. Metates are the base stones used to grind grains with a hand stone, or mano.

microblade: a very small blade used as part of a composite tool.

microband/macroband phenomena: the social process in which hunter-gatherer groups break apart into small social groups at some time and join together into large multifamily groups at others.

microcores: very small cores.

microwear: the use wear evident on artifacts, usually lithics that is not visible to the naked eye. Microwear can be examined microscopically to determine what the tool was used for.

midden: a trash pile.

obsidian: a very high quality lithic raw material formed during volcanic activity. Obsidian is volcanic glass and usually black to gray in color, although it can be green.

orthoquartzites: a series of quartzite materials found in the mountains of Colorado with poor knapping qualities.

ossuary: a mortuary feature in which the bodies of numerous individuals are buried together. Ossuaries usually contain disarticulate skeletons in which the bones of multiple individuals have been mixed, suggesting the bodies have been buried or stored elsewhere prior to final interment in the ossuary.

paleoecology: the ecology of past environments.

palynological: the study of ancient pollen to determine the plant communities present at a site.

parallel convergent flaking pattern: a flaking pattern on the face of an artifact in which the flakes are parallel to each other and converge in the center of the artifact.

pit house: a semisubterranean habitation structure with a brush or wood superstructure.

playa: a shallow basin that fills with water seasonally and was probably a lake during the Pleistocene.

Pleistocene: the geological and climatic era prior to the current one in which glaciers covered large portions of the earth.

pressure flake: a small flake removed from the edge of a tool to resharpen it.

protohistoric: the archaeological time period at the end of prehistory, immediately before written records exist for an area.

retouch: resharpening activities on chipped stone tools.

scrapers: a chipped stone tool that is used to scrape, usually hides, or as planes. Scrapers are usually unifaces.

sodality: a voluntary social, ceremonial, or religious group that cross-cuts family ties.

steatite: a rock that is soft and easily carved to form jewelry and stone bowls.

step fracture: a type of fracture encountered during chipped stone production in which the force traveling through the rock is suddenly stopped and diverted 90 degrees due to an imperfection in the stone. The result is a flake termination that forms a right angle.

subsistence system: the system a group uses to procure foodstuffs.

taphonomic: the natural process of postmortem bone deterioration and movement.

temper: aplastic inclusions added to clay during ceramic production to lessen the structural stresses involved in the contraction of the clay body during the drying and firing process.

use wear: small changes to the surface of an artifact that are the result of the use.

utilized flake: a flake that has been used as a tool but not resharpened.

BIBLIOGRAPHY

Adair, Mary J.
1988   *Prehistoric Agriculture in the Central Plains.* Publications in Anthropology No. 16, University of Kansas, Lawrence.

Adler, Michael A.
1992   The Upland Survey. In *The Sand Canyon Archaeological Project, a Progress Report,* edited by W. D. Lipe, pp. 1–11. Occasional Paper No. 2, Crown Canyon Archaeological Center, Cortez, Colo.

Adler, Michael A. and Richard H. Wilshusen
1990   Large-Scale Integrative Facilities in Tribal Societies: Cross-Cultural and Southwestern Examples. *World Archaeology* 22:133–145.

Adovasio, James
1980   Yes, Virginia, It Really Is That Old: A Reply to Haynes and Mead. *American Antiquity* 45:588–595.

Adovasio, James, J. Konahue, and R. Stuckenrath
1990   The Meadowcroft Rockshelter Radiocarbon Chronology 1975–1990. *American Antiquity* 55:348–354.

Adovasio, J. M. and David R. Pedler
1995   A Tisket, a Tasket: Looking at the Numic Speakers Through the "Lens" of a Basket. In *Across the West, Human Population Movement and the Expansion of the Numa,* edited by D. B. Madsen and D. Rhode, pp. 114–123. University of Utah Press, Salt Lake City.

Aikens, C. Melvin.
1995   Adaptive Strategies and Environmental Change in the Great Basin and Its Peripheries as Determinants in the Migrations of Numic-Speaking Peoples. In *Across the West, Human Population Movement and the Expansion of the Numa,* edited by D. B. Madsen and D. Rhode, pp. 35–43. University of Utah Press, Salt Lake City.

Aikens, C. Melvin and David B. Madsen
1986   Prehistory of the Eastern Area. In *Handbook of North American Indians: Vol. 11, Great Basin,* edited by W. L. D'Azevedo, pp. 149–160. Smithsonian Institution, Washington, D.C.

Albers, Patricia C.
1993   Symbiosis, Merger, and War: Contrasting Forms of Intertribal Relationship Among Historic Plains Indians. In *The Political Economy of North American Indians,* edited by J. H. Moore, pp. 94–133. University of Oklahoma Press, Norman.

Anderson, Jane L., Lawrence C. Todd, Galen R. Burgett, and David Rapson
1994   *Archaeological Investigations at the Massey Draw Site (5JF339).* Archaeological Research Series No. 3, Colorado Department of Transportation, Denver.

Armstrong, David M.
1972   *Distribution of Mammals in Colorado.* Monograph No. 3, Museum of Natural History, University of Kansas, Lawrence.

Bamforth, Douglas B.
1988   *Ecology and Human Organization on the Great Plains.* Plenum Press, New York.

Baugh, Timothy G.
1994   Holocene Adaptations in the Southern High Plains. In *Plains Indians, A.D. 500–1500,* edited by K. H. Schlesier, pp. 264–289. University of Oklahoma Press, Norman.

Bell, Robert E.
1984   *Prehistory of Oklahoma.* Academic Press, Orlando, Fla.

Bender, S. J. and G. A. Wright
1988   High-Altitude Occupations, Cultural Process, and High Plains Prehistory. *American Anthropologist* 90(3):619–639.

Benedict, James B.
1979   Getting Away From It All: A Study of Man, Mountains and the Two Drought Altithermal. *Southwestern Lore* 45(3):1–12.

1981   *The Fourth of July Valley.* Research Report No. 2, Center for Mountain Archaeology, Ward, Colo.

1985a   *Arapaho Pass: Glacial Geology and Archaeology at the Crest of the Colorado Front Range.* Research Report No. 3, Center for Mountain Archaeology, Ward, Colo.

1985b   *Old Man Mountain: A Vision Quest Site in the Colorado High Country.* Research Report 4, Center for Mountain Archaeology, Ward, Colo.

1990   *Archaeology of the Coney Creek Valley.* Research Report 5, Center for Mountain Archaeology, Ward, Colo.

1992a   Footprints in the Snow: High-Altitude Cultural Ecology of the Colorado Front Range, U.S.A. *Arctic and Alpine Research* 24(1):1–16.

1992b   Along the Great Divide: Paleoindian Archaeology of the High Colorado Front Range. In *Ice Age Hunters of the Rockies,* edited by D. J. Stanford and J. S. Day, pp. 343–360. University of Colorado Press, Niwot.

1996   *The Game Drives of Rocky Mountain National Park.* Research Report No. 7, Center for Mountain Archaeology, Ward, Colo.

Benedict, James B. and Byron L. Olson
1978   *The Mount Albion Complex.* Research Report No. 1. Center for Mountain Archaeology, Ward, Colo.

Berthrong, Donald J.
1963   *The Southern Cheyenne.* University of Oklahoma Press, Norman.

Bettinger, Rogert L.
1995   How, When, and Why Numic Spread. In *Across the West, Human Population Movement and the Expansion of the Numa,* edited by D. B. Madsen and D. Rhode, pp. 44–55. University of Utah Press, Salt Lake City.

Bettinger, Robert L. and Martin A. Baumhoff
1982   The Numic Spread: Great Basin Cultures in Competition. *American Antiquity* 47(3):485–503.

Binford, Lewis R.
1980   Willow Smoke and Dogs' Tails. *American Antiquity* 45:4–20.

Black, Kevin D.

1986   *Mitigative Archaeological Excavations at Two Sites for the Cottonwood Pass Project, Chaffee and Gunnison Counties, Colorado.* Metcalf Archaeological Consultants, Eagle, Colo.

1991   Archaic Continuity in the Colorado Rockies: The Mountain Tradition. *Plains Anthropologist* 36(133):1–29.

Bradley, Bruce A.

1992   Excavations at Sand Canyon Pueblo. In *The Sand Canyon Archaeological Project, a Progress Report*, edited by W. D. Lipe, pp. 79–98. Occasional Paper No. 2, Crown Canyon Archaeological Center, Cortez, Colo.

Brasser, Ted J.

1982   The Tipi as an Element in the Emergence of Historic Plains Indian Nomadism. *Plains Anthropologist* 27(98):309–322.

Braun, David

1979   Illinois Hopewell Burial Practices and Social Organization: A Reexamination of the Klunk-Gibson Mound Group. In *Hopewell Archaeology*, edited by D. Brose and N. Greber, pp. 66–79. Kent State University, Kent, Ohio.

1986   Midwestern, Hopwellian Exchange and Supralocal Interaction. In *Peer Polity Interaction and Socio-Political Change*, edited by C. Renfrew and J. F. Cherry, pp. 117–126. Cambridge University Press, United Kingdom.

Brunswig, Robert H. Jr.

1992   Paleoindian Environments and Paleoclimates in the High Plains and Central Rocky Mountains. *Southwestern Lore* 58(4)5–23.

Butler, William

1986   *Taxonomy in Northeastern Colorado Prehistory.* Ph.D. dissertation, Department of Anthropology, University of Missouri, Columbia.

1988   The Woodland Period in Northeastern Colorado. *Plains Anthropologist* 33(122):449–465.

1990   Reinterpreting the Magic Mountain Site. *Southwestern Lore* 56(6):8–21.

1992   Bison Presence and Absence in Colorado. *Southwestern Lore* 58(3):1–14.

Butzer, Karl W.

1991   An Old World Perspective on Potential Mid-Wisconsinan Settlement of the Americas. In *The First Americans: Search and Research*, edited by R. D. Dillehay and D. J. Meltzer, pp. 137–156. CRC Press, Boca Raton, Fla.

Callaway, Donald G., Joel C. Janetski, Omer C. Stewart

1986   Ute. In *Handbook of North American Indians, Great Basin, Vol. 11*, edited by W. L. D'Azevedo, pp. 336–367. Smithsonian Institution, Washington, D.C.

Cameron, Catherine M.

1993   The Collapse of the Chacoan System: Fragmentation and Social Reorganization in the American Southwest. Paper presented at the 58th Annual Meeting of the Society for American Archaeology, St. Louis.

1994   Migration and the Movement of Southwestern Peoples. Paper presented at the 1994 Southwest Symposium, Tempe, Ariz.

Cassells, E. Steve

1983   *The Archaeology of Colorado.* Johnson Books, Boulder.

1992   A History of Colorado Archaeology I. In *The State of Colorado Archaeology*, edited by P. Duke and G. Matlock, pp. 4–34. Colorado Archaeological Society, Denver.

Charles, Douglas K. and Jane E. Buikstra
1983   Archaic Mortuary Sites in the Central Mississippi Drainage: Distribution, Structures and Behavioral Implications. In *Archaic Hunters and Gatherers in the American Midwest*, edited by J. Phillips and J. Brown, pp. 117–145. Academic Press, New York.

Chronic, Halka
1980   *Roadside Geology of Colorado*. Mountain Press Publishing, Missoula, Mont.

Collins, Susan
1992   Governmental Involvement in Colorado Archaeology and the Art of the State. In *The State of Colorado Archaeology*, edited by P. Duke and G. Matlock, pp. 95–108. Colorado Archaeological Society, Denver.

Cordell, Linda S.
1984   *Prehistory of the Southwest*. Academic Press, San Diego.
1989   Northern and Central Rio Grande. In *Dynamics of Southwest Prehistory*, edited by L. S. Cordell and G. J. Gumerman, pp. 293–336. Smithsonian Institution, Washington, D.C.

Cordell, Linda S. and George J. Gumerman
1989   Cultural Interaction in the Prehistoric Southwest. In *Dynamics of Southwest Prehistory*, edited by L. S. Cordell and G. J. Gumerman, pp. 1–18. Smithsonian Institution, Washington, D.C.

Dillehay, Tom D.
1974   Late Quaternary Bison Population Changes of the Southern Plains. *Plains Anthropologist* 19(65):180–96.

Dillehay, Tom and David Meltzer
1991   Finale: Processes and Prospects. In *The First Americans: Search and Research*, edited by T. Dillehay and D. Meltzer, pp. 287–294. CRC Press, Boca Raton, Fla.

Eighmy, Jeffrey L.
1994   The Central High Plains: A Cultural Historical Summary. In *Plains Indians A.D. 500–1500*, edited by Karl H. Schlesier, pp. 224–239. University of Oklahoma, Norman.

Ellwood, Priscilla B.
1995   Pottery of Eastern Colorado's Early and Middle Ceramic Periods. In *Archaeoogical Pottery of Colorado*, edited by R. H. Brunswig, B. Bradley, and S. M. Chandler, pp. 129–161. Occasional Papers No. 2, Colorado Council of Professional Archaeologists, Denver.

Fisher, John W. Jr.
1992   Observations on the Late Pleistocene Bone Assemblage from the Lamb Spring Site, Colorado. In *Ice Age Hunters of the Rockies*, edited by D. J. Stanford and J. S. Day, pp. 51–82. University Press of Colorado, Niwot.

Ford, Richard I.
1981   Gardening and Farming Before A.D. 1000: Patterns of Prehistoric Cultivation North of Mexico. *Journal of Ethnobiology* 1:6–27.
1984   Ecological Consequences of Early Agriculture in the Southwest. In *Papers on the Archaeology of Black Mesa*, edited by S. Plog and S. Powell, pp. 127–138. Southern Illinois University, Carbondale.

Fowler, Catherine S.
1986   Subsistence. In *Great Basin*, edited by W. L. D'Alzevedo, pp. 64–97. Handbook of North American Indians, Vol. 11. Smithsonian Institution, Washington, D.C.

Frison, George C.
1991   *Prehistoric Hunters of the High Plains* (2nd ed.). Academic Press, San Diego.
1992   The Foothills-Mountains and the Open Plains: The Dichotomy in Paleoindian Subsistence Strategies Between Two Ecosystems. In *Ice Age Hunters of the Rockies*, edited by D. J. Stanford and J. S. Day, pp. 323–342. University of Colorado, Niwot.

Frison, G. C. and D. C. Grey
1980   Pryor Stemmed: A Specialized Late Paleo-Indian Ecological Adaptation. *Plains Anthropologist* 25(87):27–46.

Frison, G. C. and Dennis Stanford
1982   *The Agate Basin Site.* Academic Press, New York.

Gilman, Patricia A.
1987   Architecture as Artifact: Pit Structures and Pueblos in the American Southwest. *American Antiquity* 52:538–564.

Glassow, Michael
1980   *Prehistoric Agricultural Development in the Northern Southwest.* Anthropological Paper No. 16, Ballena Press, Menlo Park, Calif.

Gleichman, Peter J., Carol L. Gleichman, and Sandra L. Karhu
1995   *Excavations at the Rock Creek Site: 1990–1993.* Native Cultural Services, Boulder, Colo.

Goebel, Ted, Roger Powers, and Nancy Bigelow
1991   The Nenana Complex of Alaska and Clovis Origins. In *Clovis: Origins and Adaptations*, edited by R. Bonnichsen and K. L. Turnmire, pp. 49–80. Center for the Sudy of the First Americans, Oregon State University, Corvallis.

Gooding, John D.
1981   *The Archaeology of Vail Pass Camp.* Highway Salvage Report No. 35. Colorado Department of Highways, Boulder.

Grayson, Donald K.
1993   *The Desert's Past, a Natural Prehistory of the Great Basin.* Smithsonian Institution Press, Washington, D.C.

Greenberg, Joseph H., Christy G. Turner II, and Stephen L. Zegura
1986   The Settlement of the Americas: A Comparison of Linguistic, Dental and Genetic Evidence. *Current Anthropology* 27(5):477–497.

Greiser, Sally Thompson
1985   Predictive Models of Hunter-Gatherer Subsistence and Settlement Strategies on the Central High Plains. Memoir 20, *Plains Anthropologist* 30(110), part 2.

Griffiths, Mel and Lynnell Rubright
1983   *Colorado, a Geography.* Westview Press, Boulder, Colo.

Grinnell, George Bird
1962   *The Cheyenne Indians, Their History and Ways of Life.* Cooper Square Publishers, New York.

Gunnerson, James H.
1987   *Archaeology of the High Plains.* Cultural Resource Series No. 19, Bureau of Land Management-Colorado, Denver.
1989   Apishapa Canyon Archaeology: Excavations at the Cramer, Snake Blakeslee and Nearby Sites. Reprints in Anthropology, Vol. 41. J. and L. Reprint Company, Lincoln.

Gustafson, Alice

1994   *The Duncan Ranch Site 1: Evidence for Late Woodland-Incipient Antelope Creek Phase Development.* Unpublished M.A. thesis, Department of Anthropology, University of Colorado at Denver.

Guthrie, Mark R., Powys Gadd, Renee Johnson, and Joseph J. Lischka

1984   *Colorado Mountains Prehistoric Context.* Colorado Historical Society, Denver.

Hand, O. D.

1991   *Salvage Excavations at Sites 5CF554 and 5CF555, Chaffee County, Colorado.* Colorado Department of Transportation, Denver.

Hayden, Bryan

1981   Interaction Parameters and the Demise of Paleo-Indian Craftsmanship. *Plains Anthropologist* 27(96):109–124.

Haynes, C. Vance, Roelf P. Beukens, A. J. T. Jull and Owen K. Davis

1992   New Radiocarbon Dates for Some Old Folsom Sites: Accelerator Technology. In *Ice Age Hunters of the Rockies,* edited by D. J. Stanford and J. S. Day, pp. 83–100. University Press of Colorado, Niwot, Colo.

Hegmon, Michelle

1989   Social Integration and Architecture. In *The Architecture of Social Integration in Prehistoric Pueblos,* edited by W. D. Lipe and M. Hegmon, pp. 5–14. Occasional Paper No. 1, Crow Canyon Archaeological Center, Cortez, Colo.

Hoebel, E. Adamson

1960   *The Cheyennes.* Holt, Rinehart, and Winston, New York.

Hoffecker, John F, W. Roger Powers, and Ted Goebel

1993   The Colonization of Beringia and the Peopling of the New World. *Science* 259:46–53.

Holden, Preston

1970   *The Hoe and the Horse on the Plains.* University of Nebraska, Lincoln.

Hopkins, David M.

1982   Aspects of the Paleogeography of Beringia During the Late Pleistocene. In *Paleoecology of Beringia,* edited by D. M. Hopkins, J. V. Matthews Jr., C. E. Schweger, and S. B. Young, pp. 3–28. Academic Press, Orlando, Fla.

Howard, Calvan D.

1990   The Clovis Point: Characteristics and Type Descriptions. *Plains Anthropologist* 35(129):255–262.

Huber, Thomas P.

1993   *Colorado: The Place of Nature, the Nature of Place.* University of Colorado Press, Niwot.

Hurst, Winston B. and Christy G. Turner II

1993   Rediscovering the "Great Discovery": Wetherill's First Cave 7 and Its Record of Basketmaker Violence. In *Anasazi Basketmaker: Papers from the 1990 Wetherill–Grand Gulch Symposium,* edited by V. M. Atkins, pp. 143–192. Cultural Resource Series No. 24. Bureau of Land Management, Salt Lake City.

Hutchinson, Lewis A.

1989   *Archaeological Investigations of High Altitude Sites Near Monarch Pass, Colorado.* Unpublished M.A. thesis, Department of Anthropology, Colorado State University, Fort Collins.

Irwin, Henry J. and Cynthia C. Irwin
1959   *Excavations at the LoDaisKa Site in the Denver, Colorado, Area.* Proceedings No. 8, Denver Musem of Natural History, Denver.

Irwin, H. T. and H. M. Wormington
1970   Paleo-Indian Tool Types in the Great Plains. *American Antiquity* 35:24–34.

Irwin-Williams, Cynthia
1973   *The Oshara Tradition: Origins of Anasazi Culture.* Contributions in Anthropology, Vol. 5, No. 1. Eastern New Mexico University, Portales.

Irwin-Williams, Cynthia and Henry J. Irwin.
1966   *Excavations at Magic Mountain: a Diachronic Study of Plains-Southwest Relations.* Proceedings No. 12, Denver Museum of Natural History, Denver.

Jablow, Joseph
1994   *The Cheyenne in the Plains Indian Trade Relations 1795–1840* (2nd ed.). University of Nebraska Press, Lincoln.

Janetski, Joel C.
1993   The Archaic to Formative Transition North of the Anasazi: Basketmaker Perspective. In *Anasazi Basketmaker: Papers from the 1990 Wetherill-Grand Gulch Symposium,* edited by V. M. Atkins, pp. 223–242. Cultural Resource Series No. 24. Bureau of Land Management, Salt Lake City.

Jennings, Jesse D.
1978   Prehistory of Utah and the Eastern Great Basin. Anthropological Papers No. 98, University of Utah, Salt Lake City.

Jepson, Daniel A. and O. D. Hand
1994   *Archaeological Excavations at a Portion of the Dutch Creek Site (5JF463).* Archaeological Research Series No. 4, Colorado Department of Transportation, Denver.

Jodry, Margaret A.
1987   *Stewart's Cattle Guard Site: A Folsom Site in Southern Colorado, a Report of the 1981 and 1983 Field Seasons.* Unpublished M.A. Thesis, Department of Anthropology, University of Texas, Austin.

Jodry, Margaret A. and Dennis J. Stanford
1992   Stewart's Cattle Guard Site: An Analysis of Bison Remains in a Folsom Kill-Butchery Campsite. In *Ice Age Hunters of the Rockies,* edited by D. J. Stanford and J. S. Day, pp. 101–168. University of Colorado Press, Niwot.

Johnson, Alfred E. and W. Raymond Wood
1980   Prehistoric Studies on the Plains. In *Anthropology on the Great Plains,* edited by W. R. Wood and M. Liberty. University of Nebraska Press, Lincoln.

Johnston, Alex
1987   *Plants and the Blackfoot.* Occasional Paper No. 15. Lethbridge Historical Society, Lethbridge, Alberta.

Judge, W. James
1989   Chaco Canyon–San Juan Basin. In *Dynamics of Southwest Prehistory,* edited by L. S. Cordell and G. J. Gumerman, pp. 209–262. Smithsonian Institution, Washington, D.C.

1991   Chaco: Current Views of Prehistory and the Regional System. In *Chaco and Hohokam,* edited by P. L. Crown and W. J. Judge, pp. 11–30. School of American Research, Santa Fe.

1993   Resource Distribution and the Chaco Phenomenon. In *The Chimney Rock Archaeological Symposium*, edited by J. M. Malville and G. Matlock, pp. 35–36. General Technical Report RM-227, USDA Forest Service, Rocky Mountain Forest and Range Experiment Station, Fort Collins, Colo.

Kane, Allen E.

1986   Prehistory of the Dolores River Valley. In *Dolores Archaeological Program: Final Synthetic Report*, edited by D. A. Breternitz, C. K. Robinson, and G. T. Gross, pp. 353–435. Bureau of Reclamation, Department of the Interior, Denver.

1993   Settlement Analogues for Chimney Rock: A Model of 11th and 12th Century Northern Anasazi Society. In *The Chimney Rock Archaeological Symposium*, edited by J. M. Malville and G. Matlock, pp. 43–60. General Technical Report RM-227, USDA Forest Service, Rocky Mountain Forest and Range Experiment Station, Fort Collins, Colo.

Kelly, Robert L.

1988   The Three Sides of a Biface. *American Antiquity* 53:717–734.

Kelly, Robert L. and Lawrence C. Todd

1988   Coming into the Country: Early Paleoindian Hunting and Mobility. *American Antiquity* 53:231–244.

Kent, Jo, James Kirk, and Kimberly Lovett

1994   Settlement Patterns in the Middle Archaic Period. Paper presented at the 59th Annual Meeting of the Society for American Archaeology, Anaheim, Calif.

Kingsbury, Lawrence A. and Lorna H. Gabel

1983   Eastern Apache Camp Sites in Southeastern Colorado: A Hypothesis. *Plains Anthropologist* 28 (102, part 2): 319–326.

Kohler, Timothy A.

1992   Fieldhouses, Villages, and the Tragedy of the Commons in the Early Northern Anasazi Southwest. *American Antiquity* 57:617–635.

1993   News from the Northern American Southwest: Prehistory on the Edge of Chaos. *Journal of Archaeological Research* 1:267–321.

Krause, Richard A.

1995   Great Plains Mound Building: a Post-Processual View. In *Beyond Subsistence: Plains Archaeology and the Post-Processual Critique*, edited by P. Duke and M. C. Willson, pp. 129–142. University of Alabama, Tuscaloosa.

La Point, Halcyon

1987   *An Overview of Prehistoric Cultural Resources, Little Snake Resource Area, Northwestern Colorado*. Cultural Resources Series, No 20. Bureau of Land Management Colorado, Denver.

Lamb, Sydney

1958   Linguistic Prehistory in the Great Basin. *International Journal of American Linguistics* 24(2):95–100.

Lauglin, W. S.

1986   Comment. *Current Anthropology* 27:489–490.

Leitch, Barbara A.

1979   *A Concise Dictionary of Indian Tribes of North America*. Reference Publications, Algonac, Mich.

Lekson, Stephen H.

1988   The Idea of the Kiva in Anasazi Archaeology. *Kiva* 53:213–234.

1989   Kivas? In *The Architecture of Social Integration in Prehistoric Pueblos*, edited by W. D. Lipe and M. Hegmon, pp. 161–168. Occasional Paper No. 1, Crow Canyon Archaeological Center, Cortez, Colo.

1991   Settlement Patterns and the Chaco Region. In *Chaco and Hohokam*, edited by P. L. Crown and W. J. Judge, pp. 31–56. School of American Research, Santa Fe.

Lekson, Stephen H. and Catherine M. Cameron

1995   The Abandonment of Chaco Canyon, the Mesa Verde Migrations, and the Reorganization of the Pueblo World. *Journal of Anthropological Archaeology* 14: 184–202.

Lightfoot, Ricky

1993   Abandonment Processes in Prehistoric Pueblos. In *Abandonment of Settlements and Regions*, edited by C. M. Cameron and S. A. Tomka, pp. 165–177. Cambridge University, United Kingdom.

Lindsay, La Mar W.

1986   Fremont Fragmentation. In *Anthropology of the Desert West*, edited by C. J. Condie and D. D. Fowler, pp. 229–252. Anthropological Paper No. 110, University of Utah, Salt Lake City.

Lintz, Christopher L.

1986   *Architecture and Community Variability within the Antelope Creek Phase of the Texas Panhandle*. Studies in Oklahoma's Past No. 14, Oklahoma Archaeological Survey, Norman.

Lipe, William D.

1992   Summary and Concluding Comments. In *The Sand Canyon Archaeological Project: A Progress Report*, edited by W. D. Lipe, pp. 121–134. Occasional Paper No. 2, Crow Canyon Archaeological Center, Cortez, Colo.

1993   The Basketmaker II Period in the Four Corners Area. In *Anasazi Basketmaker: Papers from the 1990 Wetherill–Grand Gulch Symposium*, edited by V. M. Atkins, pp. 1–12. Cultural Resource Series No. 24. Bureau of Land Management, Salt Lake City.

Madsen, David B. and Michael S. Berry

1975   A Reassessment of Northeastern Great Basin Prehistory. *American Antiquity* 40:391–405.

Madsen, David B. and David Rhode

1995   *Across the West, Human Population Movement and the Expansion of the Numa*. University of Utah Press, Salt Lake City.

Martorano, Marilyn A.

1981   *Scarred Ponderosa Trees Reflecting Cultural Utilization of Bark*. Unpublished M.A. thesis, Department of Anthropology, Colorado State University, Fort Collins.

1988   Culturally Peeled Trees and Ute Indians in Colorado. In *Archaeology of the Eastern Ute: A Symposium*, edited by P. R. Nickens, pp. 5–21. Occasional Papers No. 1, Colorado Council of Professional Archaeologists, Denver.

Marwitt, John P.

1986   Fremont Cultures. In *Handbook of North American Indians: Vol. 11, Great Basin*, edited by W. L. D'Azevedo, pp. 161–172. Smithsonian Institution, Washington, D.C.

Matlock, Gary

1993   Introduction. In *The Chimney Rock Archaeological Symposium*, edited by J. M. Malville and G. Matlock, pp. 1–5. General Technical Report RM-227, USDA

Forest Service, Rocky Mountain Forest and Range Experiment Station, Fort Collins, Colo.

Matlock, Gary and Philip Duke

1992 The State of the State: A Critical Review. In *The State of Colorado Archaeology*, edited by P. Duke and G. Matlock, pp. 173–205. Colorado Archaeological Society, Denver.

Matson, R. G.

1994 *The Origins of Southwestern Agriculture*. The University of Arizona Press, Tucson.

Matson, R. G. and Gary Coupland

1995 *The Prehistory of the Northwest Coast*. Academic Press, New York.

McQuire, Randall H. and Michael B. Schiffer

1983 A Theory of Architectural Design. *Journal of Anthropological Archaeology* 3:277–303.

Metcalf, Michael D. and Kevin D. Black

1991 *Archaeological Excavations at the Yarmony Pit House Site, Eagle County, Colorado*. Colorado Bureau of Land Management, Denver.

Michlovic, Michael G.

1986 Cultural Evolutionism and Plains Archaeology. *Plains Anthropologist* 31(113):207–218.

Milanich, Jerald T. and Charles H. Fairbanks.

1980 *Florida Archaeology*. Academic Press, New York.

Minnis, Paul E.

1989 Prehistoric Diet in the Northern Southwest: Macroplant Remains from Four Corners Feces. *American Antiquity* 54:543–563.

Mitchell, Mark

1996 *The Upper Purgatorie Complex in Regional Perspective: An Examination of Prehistoric Frontiers in Southeastern Colorado*. Paper presented at the 61st annual meeting of the Society for American Archaeology, New Orleans.

Mobley-Tanaka, Jeannette L.

1993 Intracommunity Interactions at Chimney Rock: The Inside View of the Outlier Problem. In *The Chimney Rock Archaeological Symposium*, edited by J. M. Malville and G. Matlock, pp. 37–42. General Technical Report RM-227, USDA Forest Service, Rocky Mountain Forest and Range Experiment Station, Fort Collins, Colo.

1997 Gender and Ritual Space During the Pithouse to Pueblo Transition: Subterranean Mealing Rooms in the Northern American Southwest. *American Antiquity* 62:437–448.

Moore, John H.

1974 Cheyenne Political History 1820–1894. *Ethnohistory* 21:329–360.

Morris, Elizabeth A., Daniel Mao, Richard C. Blakeslee, and Patrick W. Bower.

1983 Current Perspectives on Stone Ring Structures in Northeastern Colorado. *Plains Anthropologist* 28 (102, part 2):45–58.

Morse, Dan F. and Phyllis A. Morse

1982 *Archaeology of the Central Mississippi Valley*. Academic Press, New York.

Muller, Jon

1986 *Archaeology of the Lower Ohio River Valley*. Academic Press, Orlando, Fla.

Mutel, Cornelia Fleischer and John C. Emerick

1992 *From Grassland to Glacier* (2nd ed.). Johnson Printing, Boulder, Colo.

Noyes, Stanley

1993 *Los Comanches, The Horse People 1751–1845*. University of New Mexico Press, Albuquerque.

Parry, William J. and F. E. Smiley

1990 Hunter-Gatherer Archaeology in Northeastern Arizona and Southeastern Utah. In *Perspectives on Southwestern Prehistory*, edited by P. E. Minnis and C. L. Redman, pp. 47–56. Westview Press, Boulder, Colo.

Petersen, Kenneth Lee

1988 *Climate and the Dolores River Anasazi*. Anthropological Papers No. 113, University of Utah, Salt Lake City.

Pitblado, Bonnie

1993 *Paleoindian Occupation of Southwest Colorado*. Unpublished M.A. thesis, Department of Anthropology, University of Arizona, Tucson.

Plog, Stephen

1990 Sociopolitical Implications of Southwestern Stylistic Variation. In *The Use of Style in Archaeology*, edited by M. Conkey and C. Hastorf, pp. 61–72. Cambridge University, United Kingdom.

1989 Ritual, Exchange, and the Development of Regional Systems. In *The Architecture of Social Integration in Prehistoric Pueblos*, edited by W. D. Lipe and M. Hegmon, pp. 125–142. Occasional Paper No. 1, Crow Canyon Archaeological Center, Cortez, Colo.

Pool, Kelly J.

1997 *The Red Army Rockshelter (5RT345)*. Metcalf Archaeological Consultants, Eagle, Colo.

Powers, William R. and John F. Hoffeker

1989 Late Pleistocene Settlement in the Nenana Valley, Central Alaska. *American Antiquity* 54:263–287.

Preucel, Robert W.

1990 *Seasonal Agricultural Circulation and Residential Mobility: A Prehistoric Example from the Parajito Plateau, New Mexico*. Garland Press, New York.

Rancier, James, Gary Haynes, and Dennis Stanford

1982 1981 Investigations of Lamb Spring. *Southwestern Lore* 48(2):1–17.

Rayne, Angela

1995 *The CRADDLE Project, or How to Get a Date in Colorado*. Paper presented at the 59th annual Plains Conference, Laramie, Wyo.

Reed, Alan D.

1995 The Numic Occupation of Western Colorado and Eastern Utah During the Late Prehistoric and Protohistoric Periods. In *Across the West, Human Population Movement and the Expansion of the Numa*, pp. 188–199. University of Utah Press, Salt Lake City.

Roberts, Frank H. H. Jr.

1938 The Folsom Problem in American Archaeology. *Annual Report of the Smithsonian Institution*, pp. 531–546. U.S. Government Printing Office, Washington, D.C.

Rohn, Arthur H.

1989   Northern San Juan Prehistory. In *Dynamics of Southwest Prehistory*, edited by
        L. S. Cordell and G. J. Gumerman, pp. 149–178. Smithsonian Institution,
        Washington, D.C.

Roper, Donna C.

1995   Spatial Dynamics and Historical Processes in the Central Plains Tradition.
        Plains Anthropologist 40(153):203–221.

Rothschild, Nan A., Barbara J. Mills, T. J. Ferguson, and Susan Dublin

1993   Abandonment at Zuni Farming Villages. In *Abandonment of Settlements and
        Regions*, edited by C. M. Cameron and S. A. Tomka, pp. 123–137. Cambridge
        University Press, United Kingdom.

Sackett, James

1990   Style and Ethnicity in Archaeology: The Case for Isochrestism. In *The Uses of
        Style in Archaeology*, edited by M. W. Conkey and C. A. Hastorf, pp. 32–43.
        Cambridge University Press, United Kingdom.

Saitta, Dean

1991   Room Use and Community Organization at the Pettit Site, West-Central New
        Mexico. *Kiva* 56:383–409.

Saxe, Arthur A.

1970   *Social Dimensions of Mortuary Practices*. Ph.D. dissertation, Department of
        Anthropology, University of Michigan, Ann Arbor.

Schlanger, Sarah H.

1986   Population Studies. In *Dolores Archaeological Program: Final Synthetic Report*,
        edited by D. A. Breternitz, C. K. Robinson, and G. T. Gross, pp. 493–524. Bureau
        of Reclamation, Department of the Interior, Denver.

1988   Patterns of Population Movement and Long-Term Population Growth in
        Southwestern Colorado. *American Antiquity* 53:773–793.

Schlesier, Karl H.

1994   Commentary: A History of Ethnic Groups in the Great Plains A.D. 150–1550. In
        Plains Indians, A.D. 500–1500, edited by K. H. Schlesier, pp. 308–381. University
        of Oklahoma, Norman.

Schroeder, Albert H.

1994   Development in the Southwest and Relations with the Plains. In *Plains Indians,
        A.D. 500–1500*, edited by K. H. Schlessier, pp. 290–-307. University of Oklahoma
        Press, Norman.

Schroedl, Alan

1976   *The Archaic of the Northern Colorado Plateau*. Unpublished Ph.D. dissertation,
        Department of Anthropology, University of Utah, Salt Lake City.

Schweger, Charles E., J. V. Matthews Jr., David M. Hopkins, and Steven B. Young

1982   Paleoecology of Beringia—A Synthesis In *Paleoecology of Beringia*, edited by D.
        M. Hopkins, J. V. Matthews Jr., C. E. Schweger, and S. B. Young, pp. 424–444.
        Academic Press, Orlando, Fla.

Sebastian, Lynne

1991   Sociopolitical Complexity and the Chaco System. In *Chaco and Hohokam*,
        edited by P. L. Crown and W. J. Judge, pp. 109–134. School of American
        Research, Santa Fe.

Shelly, Phillip H., and George Agongion

1983   Agate Basin technology: An Insight. *Plains Anthropologist* 28(100): 113–118.

Siemer, Eugene G.

1977   *Colorado Climate.* Colorado Experiment Station, Colorado State University, Fort Collins.

Smiley, Francis E.

1994   The Agricultural Transition in the Northern Southwest: Patterns in the Current Chronometric Data. *Kiva* 60:165–190.

Smith, Jack

1992   A History of Colorado Archaeology II. In *The State of Colorado Archaeology*, edited by P. Duke and G. Matlock, pp. 35–60. Colorado Archaeological Society, Denver.

Snow, Dean

1980   *The Archaeology of New England.* Academic Press, New York.

Southwell, Carey

1996   Colorado Game Drive Systems: A Comparative Analysis. Paper presented at the 61st annual meeting of the Society for American Archaeology, New Orleans.

Speth, John D. and Katherine A. Spielmann

1983   Energy Source, Protein Metabolism, and Hunter-Gatherer Subsistence Strategies. *Journal of Anthropological Archaeology* 2:1–31.

Spielmann, Katherine A.

1983   Late Prehistoric Exchange Between the Southwest and Southern Plains. *Plains Anthropologist* 28(102):257–272.

Stanford, Dennis

1983   Pre-Clovis Occupation South of the Ice Sheets. In *Early Man in the New World*, edited by R. Shutler, pp. 65–72. Sage Publications, Beverly Hills.

Stanford, Dennis, Waldo R. Wedel, and Glenn R. Scott

1981   Archaeological Investigations of the Lamb Spring Site. *Southwestern Lore* 47(1):14–27.

Stone, Tammy

1994a   The Impact of Raw-Material Scarcity on Ground-Stone Manufacture and Use: An Example from the Phoenix Basin Hohokam. *American Antiquity* 59:680–694.

1994b   The Process of Aggregation in the Zuni Region: Reasons and Implications. In *Exploring Social, Political and Economic Organization in the Zuni Region*, edited by T. L. Howell and T. Stone, pp. 9–24. Anthropological Research Papers No. 46, Arizona State University, Tempe.

Stone, Tammy and Todd L. Howell

1994   Contemporary Theory in the Study of Socio-Political Organization. In *Exploring Social, Political and Economic Organization in the Zuni Region*, edited by T. L. Howell and T. Stone, pp. 103–110. Anthropological Research Papers No. 46, Arizona State University, Tempe.

Stuart, David and Rory Gauthier

1984   *Prehistoric New Mexico: Background for Survey.* New Mexico Historic Preservation Bureau, Santa Fe.

Tankersley, Kenneth B.

1994   The Effects of Stone and Technology on Fluted-Point Morphometry. *American Antiquity* 59:498–510.

Taylor, Andrew M.
1982   *Guide Book to the Geology of Red Rocks Park and Vicinity.* Cataract Lode Mining Company, Golden, Colo.

Toll, H. Wolcott
1991   Material Distributions and Exchange in the Chaco System. In *Chaco and Hohokam*, edited by P. L. Crown and W. J. Judge, pp. 77–108. School of American Research, Santa Fe.

Toll, Mollie S. and Anne C. Cully
1994   Archaic Subsistence and Seasonal Population Flow in Northwest New Mexico. In *Archaic Hunter-Gatherer Archaeology in the American Southwest*, edited by B. J. Vierra, pp. 103–120. Contributions in Anthropology, Vol 13. Eastern New Mexico University, Portales.

Toth, Nicholas
1991   The Material Record. In *The First Americans: Search and Research*, edited by R. D. Dillehay and D. J. Meltzer, pp. 53–76. CRC Press, Boca Raton, Fla.

Tucker, Gordon C. Jr.
1993   Chimney Rock and Chaco Canyon: A Critical Reexamination of the Outlier Concept. In *The Chimney Rocky Archaeological Symposium*, edited by J. Malville and G. Matlock, pp. 65–71. General Technical Report RM-227, USDA Forest Service, Rocky Mountain Forest and Range Experiment Station, Fort Collins, Colo.

Trenhom, Virginia Cole
1970   *The Arapahoes, Our People.* University of Oklahoma Press, Norman.

Trenholm, Virgina C. and Maurine Carley
1964   *The Shoshonis.* University of Oklahoma, Norman.

Trimble, M. K.
1988   Chronology of Epidemics Among Plains Village Horticulturalist 1738–1838. *Southwestern Lore* 54:4–31.

Turner, Christy G. II
1983   Dental Evidence for the Peopling of the Americas. In *Early Man in the New World*, edited by R. Shutler Jr., pp. 147–157. Sage Publications, Beverly Hills.
1992   New World Origins: New Research from the Americas and the Soviet Union. In *Ice Age Hunters of the Rockies*, edited by D. J. Stanford and J. S. Day, pp. 7–50. University Press of Colorado, Niwot.

Van West, Carla R.
1990   *Modeling Prehistoric Climatic Variability and Agricultural Production in Southwestern Colorado: A G.I.S. Approach.* Unpublished Ph.D. dissertation, Department of Anthropology, Washington State University, Pullman.

Van West, Carla R. and William D. Lipe
1992   Modeling Prehistoric Climate and Agriculture in Southwestern Colorado. In *The Sand Canyon Archaeological Project: A Progress Report*, edited by W. D. Lipe, pp. 105–120. Occasional Paper No. 2, Crow Canyon Archaeological Center, Cortez, Colo.

Varien, Mark D. and Ricky R. Lightfoot
1989   Ritual and Nonritual Activities in Mesa Verde Region Pit Structures. In *The Architecture of Social Integration in Prehistoric Pueblos*, edited by W. D. Lipe and M. Hegmon, pp. 73–88. Occasional Paper No. 1, Crow Canyon Archaeological Center, Cortez, Colo.

Varien, Mark D., William D. Lipe, Michael A. Adler, Ian M. Thompson, and Bruce A. Bradley

1996   Southwestern Colorado and Southeastern Utah Settlement Patterns A.D. 1100–1300. in *The Prehistoric Pueblo World, A.D. 1150–1350*, edited by M. A. Adler, pp. 86–113. University of Arizona, Tucson.

Vehik, Susan C.

1994   Cultural Continuity and Discontinuity in the Southern Prairies and Cross Timbers. In *Plains Indians, A.D. 500–1500*, edited by K. H. Schlessier, pp. 239–263. University of Oklahoma Press, Norman.

Vierra, Bradley J.

1990   Archaic Hunter-Gatherer Archaeology in Northwestern New Mexico. In *Perspectives on Southwestern Prehistory*, edited by P. E. Minnis and C. L. Redman, pp. 57–67. Westview Press, Boulder.

1994a   Introduction. In *Archaic Hunter-Gatherer Archaeology in the American Southwest*, edited by B. J. Vierra, pp. 5–61. Contributions in Anthropology, Vol. 13. Eastern New Mexico University, Portales.

1994b   Archaic Hunter-Gatherer Mobility Strategies in Northwestern New Mexico. In *Archaic Hunter-Gatherer Archaeology in the American Southwest*, edited by B. J. Vierra, pp. 121–154. Contributions in Anthropology, Vol. 13. Eastern New Mexico University, Portales.

Vierra, Bradley J. and William H. Doleman

1994   The Organization of Archaic Settlement-Subsistence Systems in the Northern Southwest. In *Archaic Hunter-Gatherer Archaeology in the American Southwest*, edited by B. J. Vierra, pp. 76–102. Contributions in Anthropology, Vol. 13. Eastern New Mexico University, Portales.

Vivian, R. Gwinn

1991   Chacoan Subsistence. In *Chaco and Hohokam*, edited by P. L. Crown and W. J. Judge, pp. 57–76. School of American Research, Santa Fe.

Warburton, Miranda and Philip Duke

1995   Projectile Points as Cultural Symbols: Ethnography and Archaeology. In *Beyond Subsistence: Plains Archaeology and the Postprocessual Critique*, edited by P. Duke and M. C. Wilson, pp. 211–229. University of Alabama Press, Tuscaloosa.

Weist, Tom

1977   *A History of the Cheyenne People*. Montana Council for Indian Education, Billings.

Wedel, Waldo R.

1986   *Central Plains Prehistory*. University of Nebraska, Lincoln.

Wendland, Wayne

1978   Holocene Man in North America: The Ecological Setting and Climatic Background. *Plains Anthropologist* 23(82): 273–287.

West, F. H.

1967   The Donnelly Ridge Site and the Definition of an Early Core and Blade Complex in Central Alaska. *American Antiquity* 32:360–382.

Wheat, Joe Ben

1972   The Olsen-Chubbuck Site. *SAA Memoir 26*.

1978   Olsen-Chubbuck and Jurgens Sites: Four Aspects of Paleo-Indian Bison Economy. *Plains Anthropologist* 23(82):84–89.

1979   The Jurgens Site. *Plains Anthropogist Memoir 15*.

Wiessner, Polly

1988   Is There a Unity of Style? In *The Use of Style in Archaeology*, edited by M. Conkey and C. Hastorf, pp. 105–112. Cambridge University, United Kingdom.

Wilcox, David R.

1981   The Entry of Athapaskans into the North American Southwest: The Problem Today. In *The Protohistoric Period in the North American Southwest A.D. 1450–1700*, edited by D. R. Wilcox and W. B. Massee, pp. 213–256. Anthropological Research Paper No. 24, Arizona State University, Tempe.

1993   The Evolution of the Chacoan Polity. In *The Chimney Rock Archaeological Symposium*, edited by J. M. Malville and G. Matlock, pp. 76–90. General Technical Report RM-227, USDA Forest Service, Rocky Mountain Forest and Range Experiment Station, Fort Collins, Colo.

Wills, W. H.

1988   *Early Prehistoric Agriculture in the American Southwest*. School of American Research, Santa Fe.

Wilmsen, Edwin N.

1970   *Lithic Analysis and Cultural Inference: A Paleo-Indian Case*. Anthropological Paper No. 16, University of Arizona, Tucson.

Wilmsen, Edwin N. and Frank H. H. Roberts Jr.

1978   *Lindenmeier, 1934–1974: Concluding Report on Investigations*. Contributions to Anthropology Number 24. Smithsonian Institution, Washington, D.C.

Wilshusen, Richard H.

1989a   Unstuffing the Estufa: Ritual Floor Features in Anasazi Pit Structures and Pueblo Kivas. In *The Architecture of Social Integration in Prehistoric Pueblos*, edited by W. D. Lipe and M. Hegmon, pp. 89–112. Occasional Papers No. 1, Crow Canyon Archaeological Center, Cortez, Colo.

1989b   Architecture as Artifact—Part II: A Comment on Gilman. *American Antiquity* 54:826–833.

1991   *Early Villages in the American Southwest: Cross-Cultural and Archaeological Perspectives*. Unpublished Ph.D. dissertation, Department of Anthropology, University of Colorado, Boulder.

Wilson, C. Dean and Eric Blinman

1995   Ceramic Types of the Mesa Verde Region. In *Archaeological Pottery of Colorado*, edited by R. H. Brunswig, B. Bradley, and S. Chandler, pp. 33–88. Occasional Papers No. 2. Colorado Council of Professional Archaeologists, Denver.

Wilson, Michael C.

1995   Archaeological Implications for Plains Stone Circle Sites. In *Beyond Subsistence: Plains Archaeology and the Postprocessual Critique*, edited by P. Duke and M. C. Wilson, pp. 169–192. The University of Alabama Press, Tuscaloosa.

Wright, H. E. Jr.

1991   Environmental Conditions for Paleoindian Immigration. In *The First Americans: Search and Research*. Edited by T. D. Dillehay and D. J. Meltzer, CRC Press, Boca Raton, Fla.

Zier, Christian J.

1989   *Archaeological Excavation of Recon John Shelter (5PE648) on the Fort Carson
        Military Reservation, Pueblo County, Colorado.* Centennial Archaeology, Fort
        Collins, Colo.

Zier, Christian J. and Stephen M. Kalasz

1991   Recon Jon Shelter and the Archaic-Woodland Transition in Southeastern
        Colorado. *Plains Anthropologist* 36(135):111–138.

INDEX

Note: page numbers printed in *italic* type refer to tables or figures.

Archaeomagnetic dates, 81

Archaic period: and adaptation in Mountain region, 139–46; on Central High Plains, 56–63; in northwestern Colorado, 112–17; in southwestern Colorado and Four Corners, 86–91. *See also* Early Archaic period; Late Archaic period; Middle Archaic period

Architecture: Antelope Creek complex of Middle Ceramic period, 79; Dismal River sites of Late Ceramic period, 84; Graneros complex of Early Ceramic period, 70; Great Salt Lake branch of Fremont period, 124–25; and Pueblo I period, 95, 97; and Pueblo II period, 100, 103–104; Sopris complex of Middle Ceramic period, 80; Upper Republican complex of Middle Ceramic period, 75. *See also* Masonry construction; Pit houses

Arikara, 155–56, 160

Arizona, rock shelters in Mogollan highlands of, 89, 91

Arkansas River drainage, and geography of Colorado, 4–5

Aspen Forest zone, 12–13

Assiniboin, 154

Athapaskan linguistic groups, 24, 148

Atlantic period, in eastern Colorado, 16–17

Atlatl hooks, and eastern complex of Plano period, 44

B

Base camps: and intermountain model of adaptation, 144–45, 146; and Numic settlement patterns, 134. *See also* Seasonal rounds; Winter sites

Basketmaker II period, in southwestern Colorado, 91–93

Basketmaker III period, in southwestern Colorado, 93–95

Basketry, and characteristic Numic forms, 132, *133*

Bat Cave (New Mexico), 89, 90

Baugh, Timothy G., 80

Baumhoff, Martin, 128, 129–31, 135

Beans, and early agriculture in Southwest, 89, 90

Bear River phase, 125

Benedict, James B., 57, 140, *141*, 143, 146

Bent, William, 158

Bent's Fort (Arkansas River), 158, 160

Beringia, and Late Wisconsin Glacial period, 25–27

Bettinger, Robert, 128, 129–31, 132, 135

Binford, Lewis R., 58

Biotic zones, and vegetation and animal communities of Colorado, 8–14

Birds, species found in Colorado, 172–77

Bison: and Arapaho and Cheyenne in historic period, 154, 156; Folsom period and *Bison antiquus*, 35–36; and Middle Ceramic period on Central High Plains, 72; modern *Bison bison* compared to *Bison antiquus*, 16; and Plano period, 50–54; and Sub-Atlantic period, 17

Black, Kevin D., 57, 137, 144

Black Knoll phase, 113–14

Black Rock period (Utah), 114

Bone tools: and Great Salt Lake branch of Fremont period, 124; and Sevier branch of Fremont period, 123; and sites with early C14 dates, 27, 28. *See also* Tool complexes

Boreal forest, and late Glacial period in eastern Colorado, 15–16

Boutellier interval, of Late Wisconsin Glacial period, 26

Bow and arrow, and Dirty Devil phase, 115

Brown phase procurement, and Numic sites, 132

Buick complex, 77–78

Burials. *See* Mortuary practices

Butchering sites: Clovis period, 34; Folsom period, 35–36; Plano period, 52. *See also* Hunting; Kill sites

Butler, William, 60, 62, 63

C

Cacti, species found in Colorado, 167

Caddoan speakers: and Dismal River sites of Late Ceramic period, 84–85; and Middle Ceramic period on Central

High Plains, 72, 78, 83; and trade with Comanches in historic period, 153

Cameron, Catherine M., 109

Capote Ute, 151

Cassells, E. Steve, 65

Castle Valley phase, 114–15

Central High Plains (Colorado): Archaic period in, 56–63; dating of different cultural periods in, 55–56, 57; Early Ceramic period of Post-Archaic era, 63–71; eastern and western sections of, 55; Late Ceramic period of Post-Archaic era, 84–85; major topographic features of, 15; map of, 56; Middle Ceramic period of Post-Archaic era, 72–83; overview of Post-Archaic period in, 63–64

Ceramics: and Basketmaker III period, 94; Chimney Rock site of Pueblo II period and Chacoan, 104–105; Early Ceramic period of Post-Archaic era, 64, 67, 70–71; end of Archaic period and introduction of, 56; and Great Salt Lake branch of Fremont period, 124; and Middle Ceramic period of Post-Archaic era, 73, 80, 83; and Parowan branch of Fremont period, 121; and San Rafael branch of Fremont period, 126; and Sevier branch of Fremont period, 123; typology for eastern Colorado, 64; and Uinta branch of Fremont period, 125

Chaco Canyon cultures: and Pueblo II period in Colorado, 100–105; and trade with Middle Ceramic cultures of Central High Plains, 81

Chalcedony nodules, 140

Chapalote corn, 89

Chert nodules, 4, 140, 143

Chetro Ketl (Pueblo II town), 101

Cheyenne, 153–58, 159, 160

Chimney Rock site, 100, 101–105

Chippewa, 154, 155

Chronologies: of Archaic cultures of Central High Plains, 57; and indigenous groups of historic period, 149; and mountain zone, 137–39; Pecos

designations for cultures of southwestern Colorado, 87

Cienega Creek, 90, 91

Climate, of Colorado: and Clovis period, 31; factors affecting modern, 6–8; and landforms, 3; and Middle Ceramic period of Post-Archaic era on Central High Plains, 72; paleoenvironmental reconstructions of, 14–22; and reoccupation of eastern Colorado after 1500, 83. See also Droughts; Precipitation

Clovis period: and early Paleoindian adaptation, 31–34; and Nenana complex, 30

Cody complex, 46, 51

Colorado: American settlement in eastern and conflict with indigenous groups, 158; cultural diversity of indigenous peoples, 2; history of archaeological research in, 1; local abandonments and reoccupation by historic groups of indigenous peoples, 148; regional approach to prehistory of, 1–2; species of fish and shellfish found in, 180–81; species of plants found in, 161–70; species of terrestrial animals found in, 171–79; time line for indigenous groups of historic period, 149. See also Abandonment; Central High Plains; Eastern Colorado; Environment; Ethnography; Four Corners; Mountain region; Northwestern Colorado; Paleoindian era; Southwestern Colorado; Western Colorado

Colorado Plateau: geology and geography of Colorado, 6; as physiographic zone of Great Basin culture area, 111; and Semidesert Shrubland zone, 10; and traveler strategies of pre-Numic speakers, 130; and weather patterns, 3

Colorado River, and geography of Colorado, 5

Comanches, 84, 85, 148, 152–53, 156, 159, 160

Community clusters, and Pueblo II and Pueblo III periods, 107

Continental Divide: contact between mountain groups to east and west of, 144; and Mountain Shrubland zone, 11

Continental position, and climate, 6, 7

Cordell, Linda S., 89, 109

Corn: and Basketmaker II period, 93; and Basketmaker III period, 94; Early Ceramic period of Post-Archaic and introduction of to Central High Plains, 64; and Fremont period, 120; first evidence for in Southwest, 89, 90; Middle Ceramic period of Post-Archaic and drought-resistant species of, 74. *See also* Agriculture

Cottonwood Pass, 144

Council of 44 (Cheyenne), 157–58

Cree, 154

Cub Creek phase, 125

D

Death Valley, and Numic sites, 128, 132

Decoration, of ceramics during Basketmaker III period, 95

Denali complex (Alaska), 29, 30

Dendroclimatology and dendrochronology: and paleoenvironmental reconstructions, 17–18, 21; and Pueblo II period, 104; and scarred tree sites, 147

Dentition, Native American groups and patterns of, 24

Denver basin, geology of, 4

Dirty Devil phase, 115–17

Dismal River complex, 84–85, 148

Dog nomads, 154

Dolores River area: and Basketmaker III sites, 93; and Pueblo I sites, 97, 98, 99

Douglas Fir Forest zone, 12

Droughts: and abandonment of eastern Colorado by mid-1400s, 83; and abandonment of Four Corners area in thirteenth century, 82, 107–10; and Archaic period on Central High Plains, 56–57; and paleoenvironmental reconstructions in western Colorado, 20, 21–22; and Sub-Atlantic period in eastern Colorado, 17

Dutch Creek site, 59

Dutton site (Colorado), 28

Duvanny Yar interval, of Late Wisconsin Glacial period, 26

Dyukhtai tradition (Siberia), 30

E

Early Archaic period: chronology of, 58, 138–39; economy and organization of on Great Plains, 59–60; and tool technology, 61. *See also* Archaic period

Early Ceramic period, of Post-Archaic era on Central High Plains, 63–71

Earth lodges, and Upper Republican complex, 75–76

Eastern Colorado, and paleoenvironmental reconstructions, 14–17

Eastern (Plains) complexes, of Plano period, 42, 44–46, 48–54

Economy: Archaic period on Great Plains, 59–60; Archaic period in northwestern Colorado, 114; social and ecological environments of prehistoric populations in Colorado, 2. *See also* Adaptation; Subsistence

Eddy, Frank, 101

Elephants, behavior of as model for mammoth behavior, 33

Elevation: and climate, 7, 8; high-elevation occupation in Front Range, 142–44; and subsistence economy during Archaic period in northwestern Colorado, 114

Ellwood, Priscilla, 64

Emerick, John C., 8

Engelmann Spruce-Subalpine Fir Forest zone, 13

Environment, of Colorado: and early Paleoindian adaptation, 31; geology and geography, 3–6; and modern climate, 6–8; paleoenvironmental reconstructions of, 14–22; and physiographic zones of Great Basin culture area, 111; and species of fish and shellfish, 180–81; and species of plants, 161–70; and species of terrestrial animals, 170–79; vegetation and animal communities, 8–14

Epidemics, and Plains tribes in historic period, 158

Escalante site, 100

Ethnogenesis, and Middle Ceramic period of Post-Archaic era, 72

Ethnography, of Colorado: Algonquin speakers and historic groups in Colorado, 153–58; and distribution of Numic language groups in Great Basin culture area, *129*; migration of Numic speakers in historic period, 148, 150–53; and model for meat storage in Plano period, 54; and mortuary rituals, 91; overview of historic groups, 148; and scarred tree sites in Mountain region, 147; and stone circles, 77–78; time line for indigenous groups of historic period, *149*; trade network on Plains in historic period, 158–60; and vision quest sites in Mountain region, 146

F

Family, extended as basic social unit for Cheyenne and Arapaho, 157

Field houses, and Pueblo III period, 107

Figurines, and Fremont period, 119, 126–27

Firearms, and trade of indigenous groups with Europeans in historic period, 156, 159–60

Fish: and Athapaskan cultures, 84; species found in Colorado, 180–81

Folsom period: and Agate Basin points of Plano period, 45; and Lindenmeier site, 36–39; overview of, 34–36; and projectile points, *33*; and Stewart's Cattle Guard site, 35, 36, 40

Foothills-Mountain complex, 48, *49*

Fort Carson Military Reservation, 142

Four Corners (Colorado): Anasazi and Fremont cultures in, 120; and pit houses of Basketmaker II period, 92; population levels in Pueblo III period, 107–10; and Pueblo II period, 102

Fremont period, in northwestern Colorado: Great Salt Lake branch of, 124–25; overview of, 117–21; Parowan branch of, 121–23; San Rafael branch of, 126–27; Sevier branch of, 123; Uinta branch of, 125–26

Frison, George C., 32, 33, 34, 50, 53, 54

Front Range: adaptation in Archaic and Post-Archaic periods, 140–44; geology of, 5. *See also* Rocky Mountains

Fur trade, 153, 154

G

Gambel oak, 12

Game-drive sites, 142–43

Genetic surveys, of Native American groups, 24–25

Geography: of Beringia during Late Wisconsin Glacial period, 25; and climate of Colorado, 6–7; and geology of Colorado, 3–6

Geology: and geography of Colorado, 3–6; and lithic materials in Hogback Valley, 4, 140, 143

Glacial periods: and Beringia during Late Wisconsin, 25–27; and deglaciation in western Colorado, 18; and paleoenvironmental reconstructions in eastern Colorado, 15–16

Glottochronology, and evidence for three migration model, 28. *See also* Linguistics

Graneros complex, 70, 83

Grasses, species found in Colorado, 161–67

Grave goods: and Basketmaker II period, 92; and Upper Republican complex, 76

Gray-ware ceramics, 94–95

Grazing, and behavior of bison, 50–51

Great Basin: as culture area of northwestern Colorado, 111; ethnographic distribution of Numic language groups, *129*; and Fremont period, 118; physiographic zones of, 111, *112*; and traveler strategies of pre-Numic speakers, 130

Great Plains: and Archaic period, 59–60; geology and geography of Colorado, 6; historic groups as model for sociopolitical organization in Paleoindian period, 54; and historic trade networks, 158–60; late Glacial period, 15; Sub-Boreal period, 17; and weather patterns, 3

Great Salt Lake branch, of Fremont period, 118, *119*, 124–25

Greenberg, Joseph H., 24, 25

Green phase procurement, and Numic sites, 133

Green River basin: geology and geography of Colorado, 6; and weather patterns, 3

Green River phase, 115

Growing season: average temperatures and length of, *8*; and precipitation in western Colorado, 21

Gunnerson, James H., 44, 55, 62–63, 65, 74, 80, 82, 84

Guns. *See* Firearms

H

Hafting, socketed and split-stem in Plano period, 42, *43*, 48

Hamlets, and Pueblo III period, 104–105. *See also* Villages

Happy interval, of Wisconsin Glacial period, 26

Hayden, Brian, 43

Hell Gap projectile points, 46

Herbaceous plants, species found in Colorado, 161–67

Herd behavior, of bison, 50, 51

Hidatsa, 155

High-elevation occupation, and sites in Front Range, 142–44

Hoffecker, John F., 27

Hogback Valley: and adaptation in Archaic and Post-Archaic periods, 140–42; geological resources and lithic technology, 4, 140, 143

Holocene, and climate of eastern Colorado, 16

Hopewell cultures, 67, 68, 72

Horse: Comanche nomadism and acquisition of, 152, 156; impact of acquisition on Cheyenne economy, 154;

and trade relations on Plains in historic period, 159–60

Hovenweep district, 104–105

Hungo Pavi (Pueblo II town), 101

Hunting: Clovis techniques and mammoth behavior, 33–34; game drives in Mountain region, 143; Paleoindian period in northwestern Colorado, 113. *See also* Bison; Butchering sites; Kill sites

I

Iconography, of pre-Numic rock art, 135

Idaho, and Great Basin culture area, 111

Ida Jean site, 100

Inuit, 54

Intermountain model, of adaptation, 144–46

Irwin, H. T., 44

J

Jablow, Joseph, 155

Jack Wade Creek (Alaska), 27

Japan, Hokkaido Island of northern, 30

Jet stream, 7

Jurgens site, 52

K

Kane, Allen E., 102, 103, 104

Kansas: and Keith complex, 67–69; and Smoky Hill complex, 78; and Upper Republican complex, 74

Katchina cult, and Pueblo III period, 108

Kawaiisu language, 128

Keith complex, and Early Ceramic period of Post-Archaic, 67–69

Kelly, Robert L., 31

Kill sites: and Clovis period, 32, 33–34; and Folsom period, 35–36; and Plano period, 44, 50–54. *See also* Butchering sites; Hunting

Kivas: and Pueblo I period, 97, 98; and Pueblo II period, 100, 101; and Pueblo III period, 106

Knives, and Cody complex, 46

Kohler, Timothy A., 108

Krause, Richard A., 68, 76, 77

L

Lake Creek complex, 71

Lamb, Sydney, 128

Lamb Springs (Colorado), 28

Landscape, reuse of in Late Archaic and Early Ceramic periods on Central High Plains, 69

Language groups: migration of Athapaskan and Algonquin groups to Colorado, 148; Numic family of, 128, 129. *See also* Caddoan speakers; Linguistics; Numic speakers

La Point, Halcyon, 18

Late Archaic period: chronology of, 58, 139; economy and organization on Great Plains, 59–60; and lithic assemblages, 63. *See also* Archaic period

Late Ceramic period, and Post-Archaic era on Central High Plains, 84–85

Late Wisconsin Glacial period, 25–27

Latitude, and climate, 6, 7

Laughlin, W. S., 25

Leeve phase, 125

Lekson, Stephen H., 97

Limber and Bristlecone Pine Woodland zone, 13

Lindenmeier site, 36–39, 50, 54

Linguistics: diversity of indigenous languages, 24; and evidence for three migration model, 28. *See also* Glottochronology; Language groups

Lipe, William D., 87, 93

Lithic assemblages: Archaic and Post-Archaic periods in Front Range, 143; and Early Ceramic period of Post-Archaic, 64; eastern and western traditions of Plano period, 42–43; Folsom sites, 38–39, 40; Middle Ceramic period of Post-Archaic, 72–73; Nenana and Denali complexes compared, 29; raw materials in Hogback Valley, 4, 140, 143; trade in obsidian during Pueblo III period, 109. *See also* Projectile points; Tool complexes

Lodgepole Pine Forest zone, 13

Long houses, and Smoky Hill complex of Middle Ceramic period, 78

Lowland Riparian zone, 10

Lowry site, 100

M

Magic Mountain phase, 139

Mammals, species found in Colorado, 177–79. *See also* Bison; Mammoth

Mammoth, hunting of in Clovis period, 32, 33–34

Mandan, 155

Martorano, Marilyn, 147

Masonry construction: and Antelope Creek complex of Middle Ceramic, 79; and Apishapa complex of Middle Ceramic, 83

Massey Draw site, 59

Matrilocality, of Cheyenne and Arapaho families, 157

Mauche Ute, 150–51

McElmo Creek, and Pueblo II sites, 99

McKean period, 139

McKean Point complex, 61–63

McPhee village site, 97

Meadowcroft Shelter (Pennsylvania), 28

Megafauna, and late Glacial period in eastern Colorado, 15, 16. *See also* Bison; Mammoth

Mesa Verde black-on-white ceramics, 105

Metates, and Basketmaker II period, 93

Metcalf, Michael, 144

Michlovic, Michael G., 59–60, 137

Midden deposits, and Parowan branch of Fremont period, 121

Middle Archaic period: chronology of, 58, 139; economy and organization on Great Plains, 59–60; and McKean Point complex, 61–63. *See also* Archaic period

Middle Ceramic period, of Post-Archaic era on Central High Plains, 72–83

Middle Park, 5

Migration, and abandonment of Four Corners area during thirteenth century, 108–10. *See also* Abandonment

Minnis, Paul E., 94

Mississippian cultures, 76

Missouri River valley, and Cheyenne, 154–55

Pueblo peoples, and trade: and Antelope
    Creek complex, 79; and Lake Creek
    complex, 71
Pueblo Revolt of 1680, 152
Pueblo I period, in southwestern
    Colorado, 95–100
Pueblo II period, in southwestern
    Colorado, 100–105
Pueblo III period, in southwestern
    Colorado, 94, 106–10

R
Rabbit Ears Range, 5
Rayne, Angela, 41
Recon John Shelter, 142
Regional approach, to prehistory of
    Colorado, 1–2
Reptiles, species found in Colorado, 171–72
Resource processing areas, and
    Basketmaker III villages, 94. *See also*
    Butchering sites
Rio Grande River: and geography of
    Colorado, 5; and Pueblo III period in
    Four Corners area, 108–10
Rituals. *See* Kivas; Mortuary rituals
River systems, and geography of
    Colorado, 5
Roasting pits, and Dismal River sites, 84
Roberts, Frank H. H., 36–37
Rock art: and Basketmaker II period, 93;
    of Fremont period, 119, 120, 126; pre-
    Numic and Numic, 134–35
Rock rings. *See* Stone circles
Rock shelters: and adaptation in
    Mountain region, 141–42; in Mogollon
    highlands, 89
Rocky Mountains: and deglaciation, 18;
    geology of, 5; and weather patterns, 3,
    6–7. *See also* Front Range; Mountain
    region
Rohn, Arthur H., 87, 106

S
Sacred shrine sites, in Mountain region,
    146
Sagebrush Shrubland zone, 11
Saitta, Dean, 108

Sand Canyon ruin, 106
Sangre de Cristo Mountains, 6
San Juan basin, and Oshara variant of
    Southwestern Archaic tradition, 86
San Juan Mountains: and deglaciation, 18;
    geology and geography of Colorado, 5, 6
San Louis Valley: geology and geography
    of, 5–6; and Semidesert Shrubland
    zone, 11
San Rafael branch, of Fremont period,
    118, 119, 126–27
Schroeder, Albert H., 81
Schroedl, Alan, 113
Seasonal rounds: and adaptation in
    Mountain region, 140–44; and Archaic
    period in southwestern Colorado,
    88–89; and Great Salt Lake branch of
    Fremont period, 124. *See also* Base
    camps; Winter sites
Sediment cores: and climate of Beringia
    during Late Wisconsin Glacial period,
    27; and reconstruction of early
    paleoenvironment of western
    Colorado, 18
Seed harvesting and processing, and
    Numic sites, 132–33
Semidesert Shrubland zone, 10–11
Settlement patterns: and Middle Ceramic
    period of Post-Archaic, 79; of Numic
    speakers, 134. *See also* Hamlets; Towns;
    Villages
Sevier branch, of Fremont period, 118, 119,
    123
Shellfish, species found in Colorado, 180
Shoshoni and Shoshoni language, 128, 152
Shrubs, species found in Colorado, 168–69
Siberia, and evidence for three migration
    model, 29–30
Siemer, Eugene G., 8
Sioux, 154, 155–56, 158, 159
Site-specific approach, to prehistory of
    Colorado, 1–2
Smoky Hill complex, 78
Sociopolitical organization: Archaic
    period on Great Plains, 59–60; of
    Cheyenne and Arapaho in historic
    period, 157–58; Chimney Rock site and

THE PREHISTORY OF COLORADO

Pueblo II period, 101–105; and Paleoindian period in Colorado, 54. *See also* Aggregation

Sopris complex, of Middle Ceramic period, 79–82

South America, early C14 dates from sites in, 27

South Park, 5

South Platte River, and geography of Colorado, 5

Southwest (U.S.): Anasazi culture areas and landmarks of, *87*; first evidence for corn in, 89; influence on Early Ceramic cultures of Colorado, 70–71; and Sopris complex of Middle Ceramic period, 81

Southwest Archaeomagnetic Master Curve, 81

Southwestern Colorado: Archaic period in, 86–91; and Basketmaker II period, 91–93; and Basketmaker III period, 93–95; and Pueblo I period, 95–100; and Pueblo II period, 100–105; and Pueblo III period, 106–10

Spanish settlements, Comanche raids on, 152, 156

Spatial variability, and precipitation in western Colorado, 21

Spruce, and paleoenvironmental reconstruction in western Colorado, 18, 22

Squash, and early agriculture of Southwest, 89, 90

Stanford, Dennis, 53, 54

Stewart's Cattle Guard site, 35, 36, 40

Stone circles: Buick complex and ethnographic analogy, 77–78; and tepee locations, 157

Storage pits: and Basketmaker II period, 92; and bison hunters of Plano period, 53, 54; and Dismal River sites of Late Ceramic period, 85; and Parowan branch of Fremont period, 121

Sub-Atlantic period, in eastern Colorado, 17

Sub-Boreal period, in eastern Colorado, 17

Subsistence: and Archaic period in northwestern Colorado, 114; and eastern and western systems of Plano period, 41–42; traveler and processor strategies of Numic speakers, 129–31. *See also* Adaptation; Economy

Summit phase, of Parowan Fremont, 122

T

Temperature: establishment of modern ranges of in western Colorado, 20; length of growing season and average, *8*

Tepees, 154, 157

Texas: and Antelope Creek complex, 78; and Lake Creek complex, 71

Three Fir Shelter (Arizona), 89, 91

Three migration model, for initial occupation of New World by indigenous peoples, 24–31

Todd, Lawrence C., 31

Tool complexes: Archaic period on Central High Plains, 61; of Clovis period, 32; eastern and western assemblages of Plano period, 42–43. *See also* Bone tools; Lithic assemblages

Topography, of Colorado: and Central High Plains, *15*; and climate, 6–7; major features of, *4*

Towns, and Pueblo II period, 101. *See also* Villages

Trade: and Antelope Creek Complex of Middle Ceramic period, 79; and Basketmaker II period, 93; Comanche and Caddoan villages in historic period, 153; Great Salt Lake branch of Fremont period, 124; of indigenous groups with Europeans in historic period, 155–56, 158–60; and Lake Creek sites of Early Ceramic period, 71; patterns of in Middle Ceramic period on Central High Plains, 74, 83; and Pueblo II period, 101, 102–103, 105; and Pueblo III period, 109; San Rafael branch of Fremont period, 126; and Sopris complex of Middle Ceramic period, 81–82. *See also* Fur trade

Traveler strategies, and subsistence patterns of Numic speakers, 129–31

Trees: scarred tree sites in Mountain region, 147; species found in Colorado,

169–70. *See also* Gambel oak; Piñon pine; Spruce

Tribute payments, Chaco Canyon and trade during Pueblo II period, 101

Tularosa Cave, 90–91

Turner, Christy G., II, 24, 25, 29, 30

Twin Trees gray ceramics, 94–95

U

Uinta branch, of Fremont period, 118, *119*, 125–26

Uinta Mountains: geology and geography of Colorado, 6; and weather patterns, 3

Una Vida (Pueblo II town), 101

Uncompahgre Ute, 151

Upland Riparian zone, 10

Uplands Grasslands and Meadows zone, 10

Upper Republican complex, 73, 74–77

Upper Sonoran Agricultural complex, 89, 90

Utah: and Black Rock period, 114; and Dirty Devil phase, 116–17; and Great Basin culture area, 111; and Great Salt Lake Fremont, 124; and San Rafael Fremont, 126; and Uinta Fremont, 125; and Wendover phase, 113

Utes and Ute language, 84, 128, 150–52

V

Valley complex, and Early Ceramic period of Central High Plains, 66–67

Van West, Carla R., 108

Vegetation. *See* Plants

Ventilator shafts, and Antelope Creek complex of Middle Ceramic period, 79

Vermejo complex, 70–71

Vierra, Bradley J., 88

Villages: and Basketmaker II period, 92; and Basketmaker III period, 93–94; and Dismal River sites, 84; and Middle Ceramic period, 74, 76; and Pueblo I period, 95–97, 99–100; and Pueblo II period, 101; and Pueblo III period, 106. *See also* Hamlets; Towns

Vision quests, and sacred shrine sites in Mountain region, 146

W

Wallace site, 100

Warrior societies, Cheyenne and Arapaho, 157, 158

Wasatch Mountain region, and Fremont period, 120

Wedel, Waldo R., 70

Weeminache Ute, 151

Weissner, Polly, 104

Wendland, Wayne, 17

Wendover phase (Utah), 113

West Elk Mountains, geology of, 5

Western Colorado, and paleoenvironmental reconstructions, 17–22

Western complexes, of Plano period, *42*, *44*, 46–54

Western Stemmed tradition, of point types, 47–48

Wet Mountains, geology of, 5

Wheat, Joe Ben, 51

White Mountains, and Numic sites, 132

White River Plateau, geology of, 5

Whiterocks phase, of Uinta Fremont, 125–26

Wills, W. H., 90, 91

Wilmsen, Edwin, 36, 37–39

Wilshusen, Richard H., 99

Winds, climate and prevailing patterns of, 7

Winter sites: and Archaic period in southwestern Colorado, 88–89, 91; and stone circles, 77–78. *See also* Base camps; Seasonal rounds

Woodland cultures, and Post-Archaic era on Central High Plains, 63

Wormington, H. M., 44

Wyoming: and Mountain tradition, 137; and Plano period, 41, 52–54

Wyoming Basin, 6

Y

Yampa Ute, 151

Yellow Jacket ruin, 106

Yucca House site, 100

Z

Zimbabwe, and ethnoarchaeological research on bone flakes, 28